Sex,
Lies, and
Headlocks

Sex, Lies, and Headlocks

THE REAL STORY OF VINCE McMAHON AND WORLD WRESTLING ENTERTAINMENT

SHAUN ASSAEL and **MIKE MOONEYHAM**

 THREE RIVERS PRESS
NEW YORK

For Mom & Dad
        —SA

To Ruth, for her love; Dusty and Mikey, two fine sons;
my sister, Vicky; Dad; and the memory of Mom

                                                    —MM

Published by Three Rivers Press, New York, New York.
Member of the Crown Publishing Group, a division of Random House, Inc.

www.crownpublishing.com

THREE RIVERS PRESS and the Tugboat design are registered trademarks of
Random House, Inc.

Originally published in slightly different form in hardcover by Crown
Publishers, a division of Random House, in 2002.

Printed in the United States of America

Design by Susan Maksuta

Library of Congress Cataloging-in-Publication Data
Assael, Shaun.
    Sex, lies, and headlocks : the real story of Vince McMahon and World
Wrestling Entertainment / Shaun Assael and Mike Mooneyham.— 1st. ed.
    1. McMahon, Vince.   2. Wrestlers—United States—Biography.   3. World
Wrestling Federation—History.   I. Mooneyham, Mike.   II. Title.
GV1196.M43 A88 2002
796.812'092—dc21
    [B]   2002024708

ISBN 1-4000-5143-6

First Paperback Edition

In the ring, wrestlers remain gods because they are, for a few moments, the key which opens Nature, the pure gesture which separates Good from Evil, and unveils the form of a Justice which is at last intelligible.

—French literary critic Roland Barthes (1915–1980)

I have a tendency to take the business personally because it's my life and it's the life of my daughter and my son and has been the life of my family. So when people say, aw, come on, it's just business, I don't subscribe to that. It's personal. It's damned personal.

—Vince McMahon, owner of the World Wrestling Federation

INTRODUCTION
KANSAS CITY: MAY 23, 1999

As Owen Hart arrived at the Kemper Arena in Kansas City, he felt queasy about what his paycheck required of him. Most of the wrestlers, or the *Boys*, employed by the World Wrestling Federation were willing to do anything that Vince McMahon, its dimple-chinned owner, asked. But Owen had recently begged off of performing a seduction scene with a former Miss Texas named Debra Marshall. The WWF had just come through the May sweeps having notched the four highest-rated shows in all of cable television. And Hart knew that the children in his son's private school in Calgary—like those in schools across America—watched its show on Monday nights. He didn't want to confuse his son, who was just seven, or his three-year-old daughter, by flirting with another woman before 6 million viewers.

Unfortunately, his request for an alternative yielded something that was only slightly more appealing. McMahon had ordered him to resurrect the Blue Blazer, a silly superhero that Owen had used when he was starting out in the mid-eighties, when the business was still about cartoon costumes and simple morality plays. It required him to wear a full-face mask with dollops of silver and red, a blue leotard with a red spider on it, and a feathered shoulder cape, all of which he found extremely embarrassing. But he assumed that was the point. McMahon wanted to use him to needle all the moralists and handwringers who were accusing the WWF of peddling pornography and violence to kids. The more self-consciously pious the Blazer looked and acted, the better he served that purpose.

Because this was one of twelve pay-per-views that the WWF staged a year in addition to its regular cable TV shows, McMahon also wanted a little something extra from the Blazer tonight. Owen and his wife, Martha, had discussed it before he left for Kansas City, while they were walking through the five-thousand-square-foot home they were building in Calgary's pristine and woodsy Elbow Valley. Owen liked to quip that he was probably the cheapest man in wrestling, though he rarely joked when he sidled up to the younger Boys and implored them to be smart with their money, to save it for when their star eventually faded. He could have done without all those nights sleeping in cheap motels, eating bad buffet food. But at least he knew where it had gone—into this lakefront spread. Too many wrestlers his age had woken up with no clue. (And no house.)

As he looked at his wife, however, he could see she was worried about what the job required this week. Vince's writers wanted the Blazer to descend on a steel cable from the arena's rafters, looking clumsy and comical on the way down. Martha was concerned because her husband was afraid of heights; the whole thing just seemed absurdly risky to her. But Owen said that he'd made one stink already this month. He wasn't going to land deeper in Vince's doghouse by making another one so soon.

If there was any consolation, it was that the evening would end with him winning the Intercontinental belt, a mid-card honor that assured he'd be kept in the limelight. The writers had arranged that he'd get it from Charles Wright, a popular three-hundred-pound ex-Vegas bouncer whose character, a pimp called the Godfather, was escorted to the ring by faux hookers in a ho train. Once he made it into the ring he'd be fine, Owen told his wife.

But as the thirty-four-year-old walked past the guard station at the Kemper Arena, he had to admit he still felt uneasy. After making his way backstage, he grabbed a bite to eat at the preshow buffet and decided to use his spare time to climb up to the catwalk and look over the rigging. It featured a harness with a release mechanism similar to the kind used on a parachute; once he'd gotten all the way down, all he had to do was pull a lever and it would release him. It sounded simple, but neither three successful trial runs nor the backstage food had completely settled his stomach by show time.

The pay-per-view was called *Over the Edge,* and in order to boost the number of buys that night, McMahon used a tried-and-true gimmick:

On Sunday nights, the USA network broadcast another of his cable shows, which was called *Heat*. On the one airing tonight, he created a cliff-hanger ending that viewers had to pay to see resolved. He'd personally climbed into the ring to face a brawler with a tattooed forehead and in the process supposedly had his ankle shattered. As the show ended at 8 P.M., viewers saw the fifty-three-year-old writhing in pain, offering the lure of three more hours of similar action for just $29.95.

For the two hundred and fifty thousand viewers who bought *Over the Edge*, the next image they saw was of a hooded devil worshiper with white eyes, bathed in pink smoke and intoning, "Tonight, darkness will seize the land and destroy all you hold dear." This was the Undertaker, promising that later in the evening he would meet the company's biggest star, Steve Austin, and "devour your soul."

Owen was already on the catwalk by the time that part of the show went to air. Wearing coveralls to mask his costume, he'd made his way unnoticed through the crowd, reaching a ladder that took him to a juncture where three stagehands were waiting to help him get ready for the stunt. Before he'd arrived, he'd taped a video clip of his own, declaring, "The Blue Blazer is back because the WWF needs the Blue Blazer." Now, as he watched it flicker on two huge video screens in the arena, he breathed evenly and thought about how he was going to make the twenty thousand fans watching it laugh after he'd dropped down and released the harness.

Ringside announcer Jim Ross was in the arena viewing Hart's pretaped segment on his monitor when Owen started his descent, as was his partner, the acerbic colorman, Jerry Lawler. It was Lawler who first heard the words "Look out!" and glanced up to see Hart hurtling eighty feet down the rigging. Fans who saw the same thing thought they were seeing a mannequin falling headfirst off one of the padded buckles that connects the ring ropes, flipping over and collapsing in a heap in the corner of the ring.

Lawler elbowed Ross and mouthed the frightened words "He fell," then leaped from his seat and raced to the ring. When he found Hart lying on his back with his left arm extended in the air, Lawler's first reaction was relief: He thought the wrestler was signaling that he was still alive. But then the announcer looked more closely.

Hart's eyes were open, but they were lifeless. A gash had been torn in his arm, but there was little blood, a sign that his heart had stopped beating. As Hart's body changed in color from purple to blue to gray, Lawler cradled the dying wrestler's head in his arms, waiting for the paramedics to arrive.

A backstage producer feverishly screamed for someone to call the ambulance—the one that had been used in the night's earlier stunt with McMahon—to get it to turn around and head back to the arena. A child in the front row, assuming it was all part of the act, gleefully pointed at Hart's body, waving the Styrofoam middle finger he'd bought earlier. In the broadcast truck, the show's director screamed to cut back to the continuation of Hart's taped interview. And in that instant, the Blue Blazer reappeared before tens of thousands of television viewers, mugging for the camera and proclaiming that "the Godfather is everything that is wrong with the WWF. But the Blue Blazer will triumph over the evildoers."

Lawler got a sick feeling as he heard the chant "Owen, Owen" from fans who assumed the men in the EMT uniforms rushing into the ring were actors. "It doesn't look good at all," he said as he returned to the announcing table. As if the point needed embellishing, a fan behind him pointed to the ceiling and made a cutthroat gesture across his neck for the camera. Realizing that it was his job to fill the time, a shaken Ross told viewers, "This is not part of the entertainment tonight. This is as *real* as it can be."

In the seven minutes that the ring lay still and silent, McMahon called his crew together, forced to make the most difficult decision of his career. What should he do? Cancel the show? Christ, he was afraid he'd have a riot. No, he told his staff, they'd keep filming while Owen got aid. If anyone couldn't go on, he'd understand. Jeff Jarrett, Owen's tag-team partner, didn't have time to reply. As the stretcher carrying his old friend passed by, stagehands corralled him and Marshall, the former Miss Texas, to keep the show going. He rushed through a few unconvincing boasts, then made his way to the ring to meet a porn star character with slicked muscles named Val Venis and his butch-looking paramour, a muscular six-foot-two, 230-pound woman named Nicole Bass. Quickly getting down to business, Jarrett and Venis threw one another across the ring while Marshall jumped on Bass's back, wiggling provocatively for the camera. As soon as the act was done, Jarrett slid past a bloodstain on the mat and out of the ring, flagging down a cop to drive him the four miles to the Truman Medical Center.

The rest of the show continued the confused blur between fact and fiction. As Hart was being sped to the hospital, the ambulance that carried him was appearing to television viewers in the time-delayed skit involving McMahon's broken ankle. An even more disquieting match followed it in which one wrestler sealed his rival in a casket and smashed it with a sledgehammer. Backstage, the Boys waited for word on Owen's condition. Shortly after 8:30 P.M. central time, the word reached them. He'd been pronounced dead.

Should McMahon have stopped the show then? That was a question he'd get grilled about in the morning, when the front page of the *New York Post* screamed, "Death in the Ring: Thousands Watch TV Wrestler's Tragic Plunge." For now, he just knew he had to find a phone to reach Martha Hart.

By the time he got through, Martha had already heard from the Truman emergency room. She sat frozen when she hung up the phone, looking at the wedding ring she'd slipped on ten years earlier. She took a few long breaths before summoning the nerve to call Owen's parents.

Eighty-four-year-old Stu Hart was sitting down to dinner with his wife Helen when she called. A friend who was watching the pay-per-view from a sports bar had already told them that there had been an accident. Martha began the call with the words "This is the worst thing I'm ever going to have to say."

Stu and Helen raised eight boys who'd gone into wrestling and four girls who'd married wrestlers. How had the business come to this? They asked themselves that question over and over that night, as did many of the other people who remembered when wrestling belonged to a much simpler time.

ONE

ON JULY 14, 1948, the six men who controlled most of the wrestling in the Midwest met in a small room at the President Hotel in Waterloo, Iowa. None trusted the other more than was absolutely necessary, but they'd agreed to come here to discuss the kind of thing that can bind even the most suspicious rivals—money.

Arrayed around the room were P. L. "Pinky" George, a former bantamweight fighter who ran all the shows out of Des Moines; Al Haft, who liked to book big names in Columbus but couldn't keep them for long because he was notoriously cheap; Orville Brown, a 250-pound brawler from Kansas City; Max Clayton, a genial Omaha businessman who paid only $25 for a main event but made up for it by buying his favorite wrestlers straight whiskey and steaks; and Tony Stecher, who ran the Minneapolis territory while managing his brother Joe, a three-time world champion who could dent a sack of grain with his thighs. Finally, there was the man who'd called them together, a forty-two-year-old ex-sportswriter named Sam Muchnick.

Through most of the Roaring Twenties, Muchnick covered the Cardinals for the *St. Louis Times*, becoming close friends with the slugger Rogers Hornsby and weaving his way into a luminous world of late-night parties where he rubbed shoulders with Babe Ruth, Mae West, and even Al Capone. In 1932, when the *Times* was folded into the *St. Louis Star*, he lost his job, said good-bye to the news business, and went to work for the local wrestling baron in town, a Greek named Anthony Pakiotis whom everyone knew as Tom Packs.

Wrestling was at least as popular as baseball in St. Louis, and that was due to the biggest star on Packs's roster, a rock-jawed wrestler named Lou Thesz. Born Aloysius Martin Thesz to a Hungarian family that settled in a rural Michigan village called Bonat, the wrestler made his name driving a Model A Ford to as many gigs as he could reach with a tank of fifteen-cent-a-gallon gas. By the early 1930s, he'd played enough athletic clubs to develop a sizable following among émigré Europeans who'd landed in the Midwest looking for work. In his job for Packs, Sam Muchnick became an advance man for Thesz, hawking his matches from train platforms and saloons in tiny towns.

From the time Thesz became champion in 1937, the sportswriter and the wrestler were frequent traveling companions. Then in March of 1942, Muchnick began to feud with Packs and left to form his own touring company across town. He managed to mount just three shows before he was called into service for World War II, and when he returned the landscape in St. Louis had changed. An investor group fronted by Thesz had bought out Packs, assuming they could take control of the town without too much trouble. That was why Muchnick was in Waterloo, Iowa.

As he scanned the faces of the bosses, he knew he wasn't the only one who was having troubles. They all had problems keeping talent and avoiding bidding wars. Perhaps they should consider formalizing their ties. Surely they could see the money that could be made if they agreed to share their headliners, unite around a single champion, fix the wage scales, and blacklist any wrestler who refused to toe the line. Of course, what he was suggesting sounded an awful lot like a violation of the Sherman Antitrust Act of 1890, but they all had friends in high places and wouldn't be afraid to use them if the need arose.

No sooner had Muchnick left the President Hotel with their collective okay than his fortunes turned. Through the early part of 1949, he presided over a string of sold-out houses. As more promoters began to join the ranks of the Waterloo cartel, which they'd dubbed the National Wrestling Alliance, Thesz could see that he'd been outflanked. Unable to compete for long with the larger group, he broached to Muchnick the idea of merging their two outfits. Muchnick, who still harbored some doubt about the long-term prospects of the NWA and was eager to avoid a protracted battle with Thesz, quickly agreed. There was just one condition: He wanted Thesz to lose a title match to Orville Brown of Kansas City, whom the bosses had selected to wear their cartel's belt. In the interests of unifying the various factions, Thesz agreed.

As it happened, Brown never made it to their showdown. In early November 1949, he and his business partner, Bobby Bruns, were seriously injured when their car collided head-on with an eighteen-wheeler. (Brown and Bruns had wrestled each other in Des Moines earlier in the night. When the news broke that two "blood enemies" had been traveling together in the same car, it created an instant scandal in the press.) Days later, the cartel held their second convention in St. Louis and voted Thesz in as their new champion.

Thesz was no fool. He knew that one of the best ways to keep from being cheated was to make friends with the athletic commissioners in the towns he played, since they were the only ones who would give him straight answers about the number of tickets that had been sold. Thanks to those relationships, he frequently got 10 percent of the take for each show he worked. (An average wrestler was lucky to get a paycheck, let alone a percentage.) He could have made more, but he insisted on reserving another 3 percent for one of his idols, Ed Lewis.

In the 1920s, every child fan of wrestling aspired to be Ed "Strangler" Lewis, a five-foot-ten mountain with a twenty-two-inch neck whose drawing power was so immense that he demanded and received $125,000 guarantees to perform. The insouciant Lewis cut a wide figure in the social and sports pages, drinking late into the night with friends like Jack Dempsey and then waking up the next afternoon ready to wrestle for four hours at a stretch. Thesz was still making his way up the ladder in 1936 when Lewis happened by the Business Men's Gym in St. Louis and offered to mix it up with him for fun. Lewis may have been twice as old as Thesz, but he was also twice as fast and dropped him in their first clench. The Hungarian amateur was humiliated, but Lewis provided instant balm, kindly encouraging him to persevere and even calling his father to say it was his considered opinion that the boy would go far. The call quelled any doubts that Thesz's father, a shoemaker, had about his son's choice of career.

By the time Lewis was in his fifties, the star had become a tragic fig-ure. He was nearly broke, prone to staph infections from all the time he'd spent on dirty mats, and suffered from an eye disease that was causing him to go blind. Remembering the champ's kindness, Thesz made it his personal mission to keep Lewis alive and well when he took over the NWA title. He took Lewis away from a job working as a greeter at a Los Angeles athletic club and hired him as advance man with the 3 percent take. The arrangement infuriated the bosses but Thesz held it inviolate, arguing that Lewis's celebrity and connections helped them in any town they worked, especially in Washington, where he frequently lunched with J. Edgar Hoover.

During the 1950s, the spread of television made Thesz a wealthy man while increasing the powers of the NWA. Celebrity-hungry execu-tives looking for low-cost programming loved pro wrestling; it was easy to understand and inexpensive to produce, requiring only an announcer and a camera focused on a twenty-by-twenty ring. Between 1948 and 1955, each of the three major television networks broadcast wrestling programs at one time or another, with the longest-running one aired by the DuMont Television Network from the Marigold Arena in Chicago.

Those shows hastened the emergence of the wrestler as performer. The greatest *heel heat* (negative crowd response) was generated by wrestlers portraying stereotypical roles of America's enemies—whether it be Nazi Germany, Japan, the Soviet Union, or later on, Iran or Iraq. A pair of goose-stepping, swastika-sporting Nazis were more likely to hail from Berlin, Wisconsin, than Berlin, Germany. One of the early Nazi heels, Fritz Von Erich, was actually a Texan named Jack Adkisson who had shared the field with Doak Walker at SMU. "Russian" villain Boris Malenko was a Jew from New Jersey named Larry Simon. In some cases, the ethnic terrors were in charge of promoting their own terri-tories. The Sheik of Araby, who used a prayer rug to pray to Allah before each match, was Ed Farhat, a Detroit native who ran things in Michigan.

The first man to break out of this genre was George Raymond Wagner, the son of a house painter from Seward, Nebraska, who perfected the role of the imperious narcissist by dubbing himself Gorgeous George. Forever trailed by a perfume-pumping valet, the villainous George preened around the ring dressed in a lace and fur-trimmed robe, biting ears and gouging eyes and lustily insulting the fans who helped turn him into one of the first icons of television's golden age. Those were the days of wrestling board games, pulp posters, and cereal prizes, and Wagner was on all of them.

But by the late fifties, the networks had overexposed big-time wrestling and started dropping it from their lineups. The novelty of television wrestling faded, as did George. Shortly before he retired in 1962, the alcohol-ravaged showman opened Gorgeous George's Ringside Bar in Van Nuys, California, only to sell it off to pay for his hospitalization for liver damage a year later. He died after suffering a heart attack on Christmas Eve in 1963, hours after bumming drinks from the very bartender he'd hired. He was forty-eight years old. The wrestlers he'd once worked with passed around a hat to help bury him in an orchid-colored casket, beside which his last girlfriend, a stripper, collapsed crying.

The men who buried him were members of a closed society that had its own set of rules, even their own way of speaking. Their language hailed from turn-of-the-century carnivals, where house brawlers would take on challengers, also known as *marks*, from the crowd. When the best of them wrestled one another, they couldn't afford to go at each other for real, lest they get hurt. So they rigged their matches, deciding who'd win beforehand. Since more than a few were already on the lam from the law, conning the public came naturally. They even developed a secret language that allowed them to guard their secret—a pig-Latin dialect called carny. Whenever an outsider was in their midst, they'd quiet each other by saying *kayfabe*. In time, *kayfabe* became a metaphor for the wall of silence that wrestlers built around their business.

The business that employed them took place behind closed doors, in the locker rooms of smoke-filled auditoriums, in the offices of regional promoters, and at the conventions where the power brokers met to choose their world champion. Straight shooters like Thesz called those annual gatherings "meetings of a pack of thieves" for a reason. Most were hustlers who had ice water for blood, and allegiances could shift in the blink of an eye. As for real blood, it was commonplace to use it in this new world for ratings. *Blading,* or cutting one's self with the tip of a razor blade, not only roiled a rabid audience but allowed less-talented performers to connect with the fans. Those who *got color* (intentionally cut themselves) would get more *green* from their promoters.

Getting green also meant putting up with an endless calendar of one-night stands, making six bucks and spending four while spilling blood on canvasses in dingy union halls, some as far away as western Canada. "Those roads took a lot of people's lives," recalled Wayne Coleman, who wrestled as Superstar Billy Graham. "The oil would cover the ice and you couldn't see anything but black. It was legitimately sixty degrees below zero. Between Calgary and Edmonton and Saskatchewan, you had to stop at these horrible, horrible pit stops for food. It was like living on the edge of the earth."

On those trips to the middle of nowhere, wrestlers would dream about playing Sunday afternoons at the Chase Hotel in St. Louis, where Muchnick taped three installments of his flagship show, *Wrestling at the Chase.* It was held in the elegant Khorassan Room, in which linen-covered tables were arrayed around the ring and couples arrived in their Sunday best to hear a young sportscaster named Joe Garagiola emcee the show.

Muchnick demanded that his wrestlers behave like gentlemen outside the ring, down to wearing coats and ties on airplanes. He also enforced a widely accepted prohibition against *heels* (villains) and *babyfaces* (heroes) traveling together to maintain the facade, though occasionally a good guy would get caught socializing with an enemy. (He probably never knew that his heels and babyfaces would walk over to the corner of Eighth and Olive streets after a show and party together at the lounge of the Senator Hotel. They figured that since Sam would never be caught entering the joint, neither would they.)

In many cases, the Boys wouldn't even let their own families in on their secrets about rigged matches and role-playing. Most opponents of the long-haired, earring-wearing ruffian Mario Galento hated working with him because they feared his wife would be at ringside, toting a gun in her purse just in case things got out of hand—which they often did. The promoters who worked with Galento finally had to ask him to *smarten up* his wife by telling her the business was a *work*, or a con. She wouldn't speak to him for three days after he told her the truth.

The threat of being shot by a family member was rare. But the prospect of being attacked by an irate spectator wasn't. Women would jump from their seats to stick hat pins into the wrestlers they believed were villains, and their dates might throw rocks or even bottles. One evening in South Carolina, a seventy-eight-year-old fanatic with a hawk-bill knife stabbed one of the great heels, Al Rogowski. Though he received a hundred stitches across thirteen inches of his chest, he refused to be admitted to a hospital and drove back home, returning to the ring a day later.

In the 1960s, wrestling moved from its old home on broadcast television to the local scene. Independent stations and network affiliates paid nominally for wrestling, if at all; they held their noses and put it on as cheap late-night filler. But promoters quickly realized that even if they gave their shows away for free, they could still make a handsome profit. They used their shows as infomercials, acquainting fans with their stars first, then selling tickets to the local arena shows where the real money was to be made.

One of the savviest exploiters of the arrangement was Vincent James McMahon, who controlled much of professional wrestling's activities in the Northeast from his office in Washington, D.C. McMahon understood that a pro wrestling match, properly executed, was like a beautiful dance that told a story. But to adapt to the cultural confines of television, he wanted to tell that story more intimately and quickly. Like most promoters, he'd pledged loyalty to the National Wrestling Alliance for the first dozen years of its existence. But by the early sixties, he was joining a growing minority that believed the pendulum had swung back to favoring regional champs. The East Coast crowd that bought his tickets loved colorful pulp performers like the blond-haired villain Dr. Jerry Graham and an Olympic-style weight lifter from Pittsburgh named Bruno Sammartino. McMahon's personal favorite was an ex–police officer from New Jersey who traded in his name (Herman "Dutch" Rohde) and uniform for bleached-blond hair and the stage name Buddy Rogers.

Also known as the Nature Boy, Rogers played a central role in the founding of the NWA. On the July day in 1948 when the Midwest bosses met in Waterloo to form their cartel, Al Haft had agreed to loan Rogers to Muchnick, and it was Rogers who accounted for Muchnick's first sold-out show. But even the soft-spoken Muchnick had trouble putting up with Rogers, who started believing the world of make-believe in which he lived was real and refused to lose matches or take orders about whom he should wrestle. Over time, Rogers drifted away from St. Louis and toward the brighter lights of New York, where control of his bookings passed to the company run by McMahon. By late 1962, Rogers was the champion of the NWA, but McMahon was making noises about yanking him out of the group to start a break-away faction. Seeing that he was on the wrong end of a power play, Muchnick decided to make a preemptive move and strip Rogers of his title. In a curious realignment of old adversaries, Muchnick called on forty-seven-year-old Lou Thesz to defeat the Nature Boy in the ring.

Thesz was happy to come out of retirement for the job, if only because he thought McMahon was poisoning the business with a new breed of acrobatic heavyweights. Asked about another one of them, Argentina Rocca, he remarked, "Blessing him in the jockstrap was the Lord's way of compensating for not giving him any brains."[1] The trick to making the match was getting Rogers to show up. Fortunately the NWA's bylaws required champs to post bonds for just such contingencies. Muchnick was straight with Rogers: If he didn't lose to Thesz in Toronto on January 24, 1963, he could count on having his personal $25,000 bond donated to charity.

Rogers lost the world title that evening and, just like Muchnick predicted, was pulled from the NWA by McMahon shortly afterward. Severing the relationship finally and completely, McMahon formed the World Wide Wrestling Federation in May 1963 with Rogers as its standard-bearer. (To explain how he suddenly showed up with the belt, a story was concocted about Rogers winning a phantom tournament in, of all places, Rio de Janeiro.)

Astoundingly, Rogers only wore the belt for two weeks, after which the word went out that he'd suffered a heart attack and could no longer perform.[2] On May 17, 1963, he walked into the ring at Madison Square Garden for forty-eight seconds—long enough to submit to a few halfhearted moves and a bear hug from Bruno Sammartino.

Sammartino would hold the WWWF title for eight years. And by the end of the 1970s (when the company's name was changed to the simpler World Wrestling Federation), he'd helped McMahon turn it into one of only two legitimate rivals to the NWA.

. . .

---

1. Thesz also hated McMahon's aging partner, the old vaudevillian promoter Toots Mondt. "You could give Toots a million dollars, then come back a week later and he'd be broke," Thesz says. "He'd go through wrestlers' envelopes in the office and take out fives, tens, and twenties, saying, Ah, that's too much for this guy or that one. You couldn't trust him with a dog's dinner. The whole operation was being controlled by a thief."

2. An old friend of Rogers named Tim Woods insists the story was a fabrication, designed to give the tired star a sympathetic way to exit the stage after helping launch the WWWF.

THE NWA'S other rival was the American Wrestling Association, which was run by a Minnesotan by the name of Verne Gagne.

Though he was fifty-eight in December of 1983, Gagne could still look in the mirror and see the body of one of the most decorated college athletes of the 1940s—a University of Minnesota letterman in football who went to the 1948 Olympics as a star wrestler. In the 1950s, he found his way onto the DuMont Network's wrestling show and with the looks of a young Rock Hudson became a sensation. By February 1957, his main event match at New York's Madison Square Garden was as big as the Ziegfeld Follies. It nearly caused a riot on Seventh Avenue among the five thousand fans who'd been turned away and waited in the frigid cold for a glimpse of him.

In 1960, Gagne used his celebrity to acquire the Minneapolis Boxing and Wrestling Club and headline weekly matches there under the banner of the American Wrestling Association (AWA). In a pioneering move, he filmed each match and mailed the reels to any television station that wanted to air them. Gagne wasn't paid for the tapes; instead, he tailored each one for a specific market with custom ads hawking the shows he planned to hold there months in advance. Twenty years after he'd filmed his first match, Gagne had headlined enough bouts and sold enough tickets to move into an eight-thousand-square-foot building in downtown Minneapolis with a state-of-the-art television studio that tailored reels for the 128 stations he supplied.

In mid-December 1983, the reel he'd just sent out included a commercial featuring Terry Bollea, who was better known to his audience as Hulk Hogan, telling fans to buy tickets to a tour he was going to headline in a few weeks.

Gagne first became aware of Bollea in the mid-seventies, after he'd been discovered playing guitar in a Tampa nightclub and given the stage name Sterling Golden. Bollea was a six-foot-five, gentle giant of a man with doe eyes, a beach-bum tan, twenty-two-inch arms, and a comic book cleft chin. The first person to give him a job was Gagne's good friend and the man who controlled all of Florida's wrestling,

Eddie Graham. Upon seeing Bollea for the first time, Graham took two steps back and said under his breath, "Jesus Christ, he's huge."

In Florida, Bollea wrestled in high school gyms and tiny VFW halls for twenty bucks a match under the name Terry "the Hulk" Boulder. He was so green that he had to learn how to bounce off the steel cable ropes. Sometimes he'd get tangled in them; sometimes he'd fall right through them to the arena floor below. But with each night he spent on the road, he got a chance to study the older wrestlers and watch how they told tales with their bodies. When a veteran showman got hit, he didn't just fall down. He'd flail his limbs like his heart had received a fifty-volt shock, selling his suffering so that when he finally rose the fans believed he was a man filled with fury and not just a guy who took pratfalls three hundred nights a year.

Bollea learned enough moves in Florida to move to Memphis, a city so rabid about wrestling that on Saturday mornings, seven of ten televisions were tuned to the NBC affiliate that aired an hour of matches. He stayed on as a minor character there for six months, then received an invitation from Vincent James McMahon to work for the WWWF. McMahon bought Bollea his first thousand-dollar sequined cape and a pair of boots with lifts in them so he could lie about his height and call him the Incredible Hulk. For Bollea, it was the next step in his schooling. He learned how to grab a rival's ankles and yank them up so that his opponent got twisted into a backward crescent—a move known as the *Boston crab*. He watched how his elders locked their legs around him and flipped him like a fish (the *flying head scissors*). He saw that each move had variants, like dialects of a language. As far as storytelling goes, it was like learning adjectives.

But in the summer of 1981, Bollea was beginning to get stale in New York so he moved once again, this time to Minneapolis and a trial run with Gagne's AWA. He also began using the ring name Hulk Hogan.

Wrestlers come in two stripes: *talkers* and *workers*. Workers are the ring technicians who keep the action fast-paced and believable. The opposite of a good worker is a *stiff*—someone who needs to be helped, or carried, by a better-trained, better-conditioned worker. When Gagne first laid eyes on Hogan, he could see he was still a stiff. His reactions were a half-second late and his fists or elbows often missed their target, forcing his ring partners to work twice as hard as usual to sustain the illusion that they were wrestling. Gagne doubted that he could make Hogan a better worker. But he was sure he could make him a better talker. Like an acting coach, he started drilling Hogan in *cutting promos* (delivering his lines), teaching him to be more animated. "How come you never show off those muscles?" he chided one day. After that, Hogan started flexing and preening.

What put him over the top was a small cameo he'd snared in the movie *Rocky III*. Though Hogan got the part while working in New York, the film debuted in May 1982, while he was working for Gagne, and made him an even bigger star for the AWA. Gagne spliced a clip of the cameo into his TV show every time Hogan wrestled. As audiences started responding, Hogan refined his act, racing into the ring, striking a cartoon pose and cupping his ear, waiting for the crowds to roar at him. When they did, he'd point into the dark as if he'd heard each clap and saw the face of each one of the clappers. In 1982, Hogan helped Gagne sell out every arena show that he staged, from St. Louis to San Francisco.

But, to Hogan's increasing dismay, Gagne made sure that the AWA heavyweight title eluded him. Because Gagne had worn the belt for the better part of twenty years, he believed it should go to a rock-solid athlete cut from the same cloth as he was, not a showy ex–rock musician. That was why he kept it on an aging former University of Oklahoma football player named Nick Bockwinkel. By early 1983, however, it had become evident to Gagne that the fans who were fueling the sellouts were tired of seeing Hogan lose to a man twenty years his senior. So he ordered a series of *screw-job* finishes—matches with a bait-and-switch result. The fans would see Hogan pin Bockwinkel and win the title, then find out the next week that the denouement had been reversed on some technicality. Gagne may have thought the solution was crafty, but he ordered so many screw-job finishes over the next year that his ticket buyers began to expect that they'd never get to see Hogan win the title. In April 1983, they nearly rioted at a heavily hyped Super Sunday show in St. Paul when he beat Bockwinkel in the main event, only to have the call reversed. After several more months, Hogan began to believe he wouldn't get the strap, either.

On December 15, 1983, Gagne was opening his mail when he came across a telegram from Hogan. As he read its one line, he was sure it had to be a joke. "I'm not coming back" is what it said.

Gagne sank back in his chair and let out a long, slow whistle. Then he looked at the return address and started to feel better. It was from Florida. Gagne knew for a fact that Bollea was appearing in Japan, making some spare change as Hulk Hogan. Someone, he decided, was pulling his leg.

Just to make sure, Gagne called Hogan's hotel room in Tokyo. No answer. Then he dialed his friend Eddie Graham in Florida. The telegram was probably one of Graham's famous pranks. When he heard Graham's answering machine, he chuckled and said, "Great prank, Eddie."

As Gagne studied the telegram some more, he knew it couldn't possibly be real. How could Hogan leave? In the last week alone, he'd cleared $17,000. But then Graham called back to say he had nothing to do with the telegram. Another week went by with Hogan ducking Gagne's calls. Then a second wire came from the same Florida address with the same four words: "I'm not coming back."

This time, a pit opened in Gagne's stomach as he thought back to a conversation he had months earlier with the son of Vincent McMahon. The third-generation promoter, who everyone simply called Vinnie, had recently bought out his father and wanted to know if Gagne was having similar retirement thoughts. If so, Vinnie wanted Gagne to know he'd be eager to buy the AWA. Gagne didn't know much about Vinnie but respected his father enough to invite the younger man to Minneapolis to hear what he had to say. When they met, Gagne observed that young Vinnie McMahon was a lot slicker than his father.

He kept his hair in a pompadour and wore custom-tailored, neon-colored suits. What transfixed Gagne most, though, were his eyes. Their irises looked like the nubs of hollow-point bullets.

The first meeting broke up cordially, and when Vinnie called back six weeks later to ask for another, Gagne assumed he'd take their talks to the next level. To his irritation, when Vinnie flew back out to Minneapolis, he asked a number of questions about how the AWA was run and about its stake in an ownership group that had invested in Muchnick's St. Louis territory. But he never named a price. It was, Gagne decided, all a colossal waste of his time. After a long day, he drove his guest back to the airport and wondered aloud if they would soon start to negotiate in earnest.

As Gagne would remember it, Vinnie was halfway to the departure gate when he turned around, cupped his hands over his mouth, and yelled, "Verne, I don't negotiate."

Only later would the promoter learn what he meant. Without Gagne's knowledge, Vinnie had opened a back channel to the owner of KPLR, the station that aired Muchnick's seminal St. Louis show, *Wrestling at the Chase*. Vinnie insisted that if his company, WWF, was allowed to take over the time slot, he would produce a better show for St. Louis while kicking back more money to the station. The owner was intrigued and impressed with the young man as they ate steaks in the Tenderloin Room at the Chase Hotel. At the end of their dinner, Vinnie announced he had to leave because he had a meeting early the next morning. "I'm going to sign Hulk Hogan," he said. "I'm going to take over the world."

Not only would the young McMahon take Hogan away from Gagne, he'd lure away another three dozen of his stars, tearing the heart out of the AWA. The telegram was just the start. It was the first strike by the man with bullets in his eyes.

TWO

IN THE MID-1940S, the armed forces condemned tens of thousands of acres in North Carolina to build bases that would help gird the U.S. war effort. In just a few years, Fort Bragg was built for the army, with the Pope Air Force Base attached so the soldiers had a way to fly in and out. Ninety-five miles away, the Marine Corps put Camp Lejeune on forty-five thousand acres and placed the Cherry Point Air Station in a tiny town nearby called Havelock. At the time, it was so small that the U.S. Census Bureau listed its population at just over a hundred people.

That census included the family of Leo Lupton, an electrician with a son and daughter of his own and two other sons by his wife, Vicki's, first marriage. No one in town knew about the boys' biological father or what he did for a living. No one asked.

The boys lived in a manner far different from the way their absent father had grown up. Vincent James McMahon was raised in Far Rockaway, Queens, a stable, middle-class New York City neighborhood that was about as distant as his father, Jess, could get from the Commonwealth Sporting Club on 135th Street in the Bronx, where he put on fights, and still get home in time for dinner.

In 1925, when Vincent was just ten, Jess received a prestigious invitation to come to work at Madison Square Garden for Tex Rickard, a legendary gambler who'd promoted all of Jack Dempsey's fights and at his height built a new Garden on Eighth Avenue and Fifty-ninth Street to replace the old one on Madison Square. Needing someone to help him find fighters, Rickard gave the matchmaking job to Jess, a graduate of Manhattan College who knew how to run a tidy nine-to-five office.

The pair worked together for three years, during which time young Vincent James got to explore the catacombs beneath the Garden. It was the golden age of sports, and the eleven-year-old boy had a box seat to it all—at least until a scandal led his father to be suspended by the state athletic commission. It involved a deal between two managers to cheat a fighter out of about $5,000 and a bogus set of contracts that were placed on file with the commission. Jess, who winked at the shady deal but appeared not to take an active part in it, took the fall.

In 1935, Jess helped his son set up a small office that booked fights and concerts in an arena in Hempstead, Long Island, and Vincent worked there until the United States entered World War II, in which he served in the Coast Guard. Though he never publicly discussed how he met Vicki, their brief marriage didn't survive the war. While Vicki was left in North Carolina, Vincent moved to Washington, where he opened a company called Capitol Wrestling and spent a few thousand dollars to wire for television a dingy theater on W and 14th Streets. At the time, the top wrestling show in the nation was *Live from the Marigold Theater* in Chicago, which aired Saturday nights on the DuMont Network. In 1956, when DuMont went down, Vincent's gamble paid off. Since *Live* no longer had a national outlet, he convinced the DuMont affiliate in Washington to carry his matches. Since its owners had a sister station in New York, WOR (Channel 9), he parlayed the arrangement into a lucrative two-city foothold.

With his father's New York connections, it was only natural that Vincent would also gain the exclusive contract to book wrestling shows at the Garden.

By then, Vincent's two boys were living in a mobile home seven miles out of Havelock, under the names of Rodney and Vinnie Kennedy Lupton. Because Havelock revolved around the Cherry Point Air Station, they, like many of the local boys, considered Marines aloof intruders, and the Marines in turn tended to view the town people warily. While families of military officers were allowed to use facilities on the base, such as the pool and athletic courts, locals like the Luptons had to watch with their noses pressed against the fence. The mutual suspicion was in large part fueled by race. The only African American people that several longtime residents could remember living in Havelock at that time were the local sanitation contractor and his family, and they lived far out in the woods. When black Marines started trickling in, the native kids would hang out at the local drive-in, The Jet, waiting for them in the hope of starting fights.

Douglas Franks, a native who stayed in Havelock after many of his contemporaries left, says: "If we thought there would even be a whiff of trouble, we'd dress for combat in blue jeans, cut-off shirts, and big boots."

Franks remembers Rodney as someone "who didn't have to work at his charisma. It came naturally." Vinnie, on the other hand, tried to earn his stripes hanging out at The Jet. "He tried to be one of the gang kids, but he never quite made it," says Franks. "He was a wannabe."

By Vinnie's accounts, the atmosphere in the trailer home he grew up in alternated between moments of normalcy—as when they all watched *The Jackie Gleason Show* together—and frightful violence. In an interview with *Playboy*, Vince alleged that his stepfather started beating him when he was six with a pipe wrench. "My stepfather [was] a man who enjoyed kicking people around," he remarked. "It's unfortunate he died before I could kill him."

McMahon described his mother as "a real performer, a female Elmer Gantry," saying that she was "very striking" and had "an excellent voice" when she sang in her church choir. However, he also said that he was long estranged from her and hinted that the reason was sexual abuse. "Was all the abuse physical, or was there sexual abuse, too?" *Playboy* asked him.

"That's not anything I'd like to embellish," he replied, "just because it's so weird."

In separate interviews, two of his longtime acquaintances remembered Vince describing his childhood as so troubled that he once even flirted with the idea of drowning himself by walking into the sea along the Carolina coast.

Vincent James rarely talked about the boys he'd left behind in North Carolina. He'd become a stylish man who liked his limousines and his running reservation at the New York steak house Jimmy Weston's, where he'd go after a show at the Garden. He'd invite a dozen or so friends there, and they'd eat and drink on his tab late into the night.

In Washington, he ran things from a neat and proper suite on the seventh floor of the majestic Franklin Park Hotel. He also remarried, to a sophisticated native of south Florida. The couple wouldn't have any children of their own, but his new wife, Juanita, insisted that her husband get to know the children he already had. So in 1957, Vinnie and his older brother got their first look at their father when he came to visit them in Havelock. One can only imagine the two boys, 12 and 14, dressed in their best clothes to meet the father they'd only vaguely heard about, standing in front of the six-foot-five man with a kind, jowly face and a pocket full of jangling change. "I immediately fell in love with him," Vince once told *New York* magazine.

But Vincent wasn't about to let his long-forgotten sons get too close to wrestling, or for that matter too close to him. At the very least, Vinnie was a handful, certainly more than a man in a second marriage and in his mid-forties needed. Still, Juanita softened him up enough that the boys started spending summers with them in Maryland.

Vinnie went from being a military brat to a son of the circus, a wide-eyed kid in a world of new possibilities. His favorite wrestler became Dr. Jerry Graham, who at three hundred pounds resembled nothing so much as an inflated Jerry Lee Lewis with peroxided hair and a bloodred Cadillac convertible that matched the color of his threads. Graham lived life large, lighting his cigars with hundred-dollar bills—just the kind of outsized figure who could forever alter a young boy's image of what constitutes normalcy. Vinnie was so impressed with Graham in the summer of 1958 that he asked his stepmother to bleach his hair in the kitchen of their summer home in Delaware. She obliged, though her husband was far from amused when he got home. He'd be damned, he said, if his son was following him into wrestling.

At fourteen, Vinnie found himself enrolled in the Fishburne Military Academy, a haven for the sons of the wealthy in the rolling green hills of the Shenandoah Valley. Fishburne's yearbook from 1963 contains a photo of a six-foot-two, 230-pound Vince in a football uniform, staring off the page toward a future that lay somewhere between the bleakness of what waited for him back in rural North Carolina and the world in Washington he now knew he wanted to enter. Not completely welcome in either, he decided to go to a college that was fifty-five miles away from a girl whom he'd started dating in Havelock.

Linda Edwards, whose mother worked in the same Cherry Point base building as Vinnie's mom, was thirteen when she started dating the sixteen-year-old tough. "I had no idea what a family was until I met Linda and saw how they lived," he remarked in an interview with the magazine *Cigar Aficionado*. "It was an Ozzie and Harriet life. There wasn't screaming and beating." Vinnie quickly became a fixture in the Edwards home, and as soon as Linda graduated from high school (with honors), he asked her to marry him. Most of the guests at the small church ceremony were friends of her parents from the base.

Two years after Vinnie entered East Carolina University, Linda joined him there and squeezed her college work into three years so the two could graduate together. On the eve of their graduation day, Linda discovered she was pregnant with their son Shane. It was 1969, and wrestling would have to wait for Vinnie while he lived in Washington, D.C., and worked as a traveling salesman. Six months later, a ring announcer who worked for his father set the next phase of his life in motion. Because Vincent's wrestling shows were now airing across the East Coast, the unionized announcer wanted to be paid a national rate. Vincent grumbled about having to pay it (the employee was threatening to make trouble with the union), until he learned that union scale didn't apply to family. So he fired the ring man, and when Vinnie asked, "Who are you going to replace him with?" his father answered, "You."

Overnight, Vinnie went from doing part-time work setting up rings to appearing on television in neon suits that swallowed his rail-thin frame. The wrestlers laughed at the kid who was trying so hard to sound like Howard Cosell. But once the matches began, even his father had to admit that the boy had a surprising flair for making the make-believe seem real.

In 1971, the show was being seen in thirty cities in fourteen states and had outgrown its confines at the National Arena in Washington. Needing to find a larger space, the elder McMahon decided to tape his shows at a thousand-seat theater in Hamburg, Pennsylvania, and at a slightly larger pavilion nearby on a fairgrounds complex in Allentown, Pennsylvania. Because the shows taped only once every three weeks, Vinnie had ample time to try other things. At first, he tried his hand at booking oldies' shows with acts like Jerry Lee Lewis and Dottie West. But then one day his father got a call from a private investigator, looking for the Vince McMahon who'd run up a trail of bad debts. As the story goes, Vincent listened carefully, then realized the investigator was talking about his son. That was when he decided it was better to keep the kid close rather than let him run down the family's name.

In 1973, when an opening for a promoter arose in Maine, Vincent installed his son in the territory, telling him that if he wasn't able to make a living up there, he didn't want to hear any more talk about wrestling again. (There is some dispute over how the opening arose. In his *Playboy* interview, Vince insisted that his father fired the longtime promoter there for stealing. Others remember that the promoter had simply died.) On weekends, Vinnie would leave the West Hartford, Connecticut, trailer park where he'd temporarily moved his family and drive a beat-up blue Buick to Maine to make fifty or a hundred bucks a show. As Joe Perkins, a close aide to the senior McMahon, once remarked, "Vincent made it quite clear to me that his son had to pay his own bills and I was not to look to Capitol Wrestling if he fell behind."

Old-time wrestlers like Walter "Killer" Kowalski raised their eyebrows when Vinnie begged them to try new things, like taking their brawls out of the ring and into the parking lots of the new theaters and union halls that he was expanding into. Vincent took note of his son's growing aptitude, but he wasn't quick to talk about it or even acknowledge his son to others. "I talked to Senior every day for years in the seventies and I couldn't tell you a single thing Vinnie did for the company back then," says James Barnett, who controlled Georgia. "He never talked about Vinnie, which makes me think he didn't want anyone to know which ideas were his and which ones weren't."

ONE PERSON who began to see Vinnie as a figure apart from his father was a Brooklyn-born graduate of Harvard Law School named Bob Arum. Arum had been a federal prosecutor and a friend of Robert Kennedy's before he decided to leave the law and start promoting fights. He made his first match in 1966 between Muhammad Ali and a rough-and-tumble Canadian named George Chuvalo. By the time Vinnie walked into the promoter's Park Avenue office in Manhattan in 1974, Ali was an international icon and Arum had promoted a dozen of his bouts.

The reasons for Vinnie's visit made Arum chuckle. He'd been watching television at home one day when he heard Evel Knievel say in an interview that he dreamed of jumping over the Grand Canyon. Through some creative phone work, Vinnie managed to get Knievel on the phone and convinced him to meet in Las Vegas. Vinnie maxed out his credit card to make the flight, and in a brief session over drinks persuaded Knievel that they could make a killing if they broadcast the jump live by closed circuit. The McMahons had relationships with 130 theaters and arenas across the East Coast and knew promoters around the country who could fill hundreds more. Vinnie told Evel he could make millions.

When he returned to New York, Vinnie's father thought the idea was crazy. But it was just crazy enough to intrigue Arum, who had good connections at ABC, the network that aired Evel's other jumps on *Wide World of Sports*. Arum put together a deal in which the jump—whose location was changed to the Snake River Canyon in Idaho—would be seen live via closed circuit and rebroadcast for free on ABC a week later.

On the morning of September 8, every nut who wasn't stalking Elvis or waiting for an alien abduction was in Twin Falls, Idaho. Frank Gifford and the Hells Angels were there, along with a gaggle of blondes giving away free blow jobs. The only one who wasn't in a partying mood was Knievel, who'd convinced himself that he wouldn't make it off the 108-foot ramp in the bottle-shaped craft known as the Sky-Cycle X-2. The moment the rocket's thrusters started firing, a petrified Knievel threw the switch that deployed its chute. As a result, the sky-cycle barely cleared the ramp before falling 413 harmless feet to the canyon below.

Not only was the jump a bust, only a fraction of the theaters that showed it were full. "The problem," says Arum, "is that we did too good a job of selling it. Parents were scared to let kids see their big hero die." With sales only a fraction of what they had hoped, Knievel's promised $6 million payday shrank to $250,000—roughly the amount that Vinnie and Linda lost when they couldn't recoup the deposits they'd put down on the theaters.

Still, the experience convinced Arum that the McMahon kid had spark. That is why he called Vinnie again in early 1976, when Antonio Inoki, then the biggest wrestling star and promoter in Japan, offered $3 million if Ali would fly to Tokyo for a wrestling/boxing match with Inoki in which he'd lose. Arum, who was in the midst of arranging a third fight between Ali and Ken Norton, was intrigued by the idea. But he was out of his league when it came to wrestling. Vinnie's solution was to stage matches between boxers and wrestlers at six stadiums around the United States as a prelude to the closed-circuit showing of the main event. Arum liked that fine. Now all that was left was convincing Ali to bite.

As Arum would recall the story, Vinnie flew with him in the spring of 1976 to Chicago to meet Ali in a gym on the South Side. Ali loved wrestling. In fact, he'd patterned his preening and posturing after Gorgeous George, who made frequent stops in Louisville when Ali, then known as Cassius Clay, was growing up. But he blanched at taking a dive. The champ, surrounded by his Muslim retinue, listened skeptically as McMahon laid out his plan. For the first several rounds, Ali would pound the lumbering, six-foot-one, 220-pound Inoki, looking every bit like the champion that he was. But in the fifth round, Inoki would come out with a razor in his mouth and secretly use it to cut open his forehead. When Ali saw that he was gushing blood, he'd beg the referee to stop the fight. At this point, Ali started smiling, seeing the possibilities. McMahon went on, suggesting that while Ali's back was turned Inoki would give him a *enzuijiri*—his trademark kick to the back of the head. Japanese fans would be able to keep their champ, while Ali would return to America insisting that he'd been screwed.

"Okay," said Ali. "I'll do it."

Unfortunately, Vinnie failed to mention his plan to the advance men who were waiting for Ali when his flight landed in Tokyo. When he asked them when rehearsals were going to start, he was met with blank stares. No one knew what he was talking about.

"It was a mess," says Arum. "Ali thought he was being set up. Everyone was threatening to break everyone else's legs. Vinnie wouldn't come to Japan. I had to stay right beside Ali the whole time."

Eventually, a plan was worked out to assuage the champ. The two would fight for real, in what is known as a shoot match. But to favor Ali, certain conditions had to be met, among them that Inoki would have to keep both hands and a foot on the ground the whole time. Inoki was furious at being literally backed into a corner, but he agreed and the day of the match came prepared to make Ali pay. The Japanese legend may have spent the match like a spider on his back, but he kicked Ali so furiously that clots welled in Ali's legs. "By the eighth round Ali's legs were bleeding," Arum remembers. "Ali kept running after him, yelling, 'Get up, you little yellow mother-fucker, get up!'"

Ticket sales were only slightly better than for the Snake River fiasco. Once again, Vinnie's big payday failed to materialize.

In 1976 when Linda gave birth to their daughter Stephanie, and again in 1977, Vinnie had trouble paying his taxes, leading the Internal Revenue Service to eventually place a $43,000 lien on their home. Yet he knew that because his father was sixty-two, the subject of selling the WWF would have to come up sooner or later. He just needed to be in the right position when that happened. He found his way station in the spring of 1979 when he tried booking a show in a seven-thousand-seat arena in a coastal New England town called South Yarmouth.

Its owner, Ed Fruean, was a thickly built New Englander with a degree in electrical engineering and no appetite for show business. He'd built the Cape Cod Coliseum years before, leased it, and watched the prior tenant go bankrupt. Having had to take the coliseum over again to keep it afloat, Fruean was caught in a bind. Rock acts were the only thing that made him money, but a needling group of motel owners were trying to ban those concerts because of the "element" they brought into the quiet town. Fruean wanted out. Would Vinnie be interested? In April 1979, the pair struck a deal that involved no money down. Instead, Vinnie would pay a monthly mortgage held by Fruean, using the cash flow produced by the coliseum to come up with the payment.

Over that summer, the McMahons moved into a two-story shingled home down the block from Fruean and brought a minor-league hockey franchise into the Cape Cod Coliseum. Shane and two-year-old Stephanie's young lives were colored by visits from members of the McMahon wrestling troupe. It was perfectly natural, for instance, for Andre the Giant to stop by if he was in the area. One day, he visited while Stephanie was playing on a trampoline in their yard. The three-year-old no doubt assumed that everyone had Giants visit them on balmy summer days, and Andre held out his hand as she climbed into it so he could lift her to his face and she could kiss his cheek.

Having never before had this kind of responsibility, Vinnie and Linda worked all hours to make the coliseum a success. They landed an NHL exhibition game, for instance, by promising the Boston Bruins a $50,000 ticket guarantee; they made the gamble work by selling VIP tickets that came with extras like the meatballs Linda made in their kitchen. At the same time, they also learned to play what would later become a familiar brand of hardball. When a town selectman tried to limit the hours that they could sell liquor at the coliseum, Vinnie showed up at the next meeting with a cast of 170 supporters and a battery of lawyers. "We've had nearly constant harassment by a certain segment of the community," he said, staring down the selectman. "We've developed thick skins, but enough is enough." The board backed off.

Through the next couple of years, Vinnie ran the coliseum while taking time out every three weeks to tend to his announcing duties on his father's program, All-Star Wrestling. He shuttled from Cape Cod to Allentown, Pennsylvania, where the show was filmed at a small theater on the town fairgrounds. Their parents' schedule was taxing on the kids. As Stephanie would later remember, "My parents weren't around until later at night, so for the most part, Shane raised me. He not only toughened me up, but he kept me thoroughly entertained— most of the time doing impressions of our dad."

Older wrestlers like Bruno Sammartino still looked down on the boss's son, who drove a fancy car, dressed in flashy suits, and never seemed to get called to account for his numerous failures. But Vinnie was far closer to being able to take over the WWF than Sammartino or any of the other wrestlers who dismissed him realized. In Cape Cod, he was studying every act that came in, from the rock band Heart to the Harlem Globetrotters. He watched how they set their lighting rigs, wired their sound, placed their T-shirt stands. And, by Fruean's account, he'd learned how to break even. "I don't think he made any money, but he didn't stick anybody with any bills," says Fruean. "I held the mortgage, and there were never any questions."

BY 1983, when Vincent was sixty-seven, he began to talk about finally cashing out. He had moved to Fort Lauderdale several years earlier and enjoyed a peaceful life there. He and Juanita hosted well-attended parties and had full calendars, and though he only had to travel a few times a month for business—to the Garden once a month for a show and to Allentown every three weeks to supervise the taping of All-Star Wrestling—it was still growing tiresome. He called his son and asked Vinnie whether he wanted to make an offer.

In Cape Cod, Vinnie had assembled a kitchen cabinet, waiting for a moment like this to arrive. It included Linda, his closest confidant and adviser; a former New York Rangers right wing named Jim Troy, whom Vinnie had hired as the general manager of his minor-league team, the Cape Cod Buccaneers; and Joe Perkins, his father's syndication salesman. In the spring of 1983, Vinnie flew into Manhattan from the Cape with Troy in tow, carrying two huge briefcases full of contracts.

It was a cool and sunny New York morning, and as they walked into a suite at the Warwick Hotel they found Vincent and three other men. Vinnie's father was the public face of the WWF, but he didn't actually own it all alone. He gave pieces to three other men whose help he needed. They were Phil Zacko, his longtime treasurer and friend, and two of his star wrestlers: Gino Marella, a four-hundred-pound high school teacher who turned himself into Gorilla Monsoon, and Arnold Skaaland, known since his heyday in the 1950s as the Golden Boy.

After all the men got comfortable, Vinnie laid the contracts on the coffee table. As he started explaining the terms, he knew the offer was held together with rubber bands. His financing was a mix of loans he'd received from friendly New England banks (using his equity in the coliseum as collateral) and the cash flow he expected to produce with the WWF. Marella and Skaaland, he said, would get one and a half times the average wrestler's pay for every show he staged. (In other words, they'd receive $750 if the average wrestler was making $500.) Since the WWF was putting on three hundred shows a year, it was a considerable promise. Zacko would get regular monthly payments over two years, as would his father. There have been differing accounts of how much he offered his dad that afternoon—from $350,000 to as much as a $1 million. But Vincent thought it was a high-enough figure that he skeptically asked that a provision be inserted allowing him to nullify the sale if Vinnie missed a single one of the monthly payments. Vinnie agreed.

After all the documents were signed, Vinnie and Troy went down to the Warwick's bar and each ordered a Dewar's, neat. By nightfall, Troy recalled, "we were two of the drunkest men in New York."

NO ONE in the World Wrestling Federation's troupe of sixty wrestlers realized what Vinnie was up to when he suddenly decided to change champions in December 1983. Promoters have to be part casting agent, part scriptwriter, and part enforcer, deciding not merely who wins each match, but the manner of the win and the way it lays the foundation for the next match. The story arc is the bloodstream of the promotion, a current that leaves some talents mired at the bottom of the card and others carried to the top. Mixing and matching wrestlers is an art form in itself, since it has to factor in elements like personal chemistry, style, and fan appeal. Now that he'd taken over the company from his ailing father, he was ready to place his own stamp on it—and the first order of business was getting rid of its champion, Bob Backlund.

Vinnie had to admit that Backlund had served his purpose. Until his dad brought the native Minnesotan to New York years earlier, its wrestling scene was synonymous with ethnic champions such as Pedro Morales, Sammartino, and Killer Kowalski—men who shared the grainy UHF (ultrahigh frequency) universe with ice hockey, Roller Derby, and Charles Bronson movies. They were the pulp heroes of the immigrant labor class, actors without airs, and most couldn't have cared less if the world accorded them the respectability of porn stars. Backlund was a different wrestler in a different age, a collegiate medalist with a clean image built around a sensible six-foot-one, 191-pound frame.

However, Vinnie was tired of Backlund and ready to ride another shift in public sensibilities. He'd hired Hulk Hogan because he was everything Backlund wasn't. So as Vinnie waited to start filming the WWF's studio television show in Allentown, he motioned his champ to the ring. "Things are going to be changing, Bob," he started. "We need wrestlers who are bigger than life." Backlund winced, knowing what was coming next. "We have a guy coming in who's going to take us to the next level."

Vinnie knew he couldn't let Hogan take the belt directly from Backlund. Wrestling convention holds that babyfaces rarely battle one another. He needed a heel to stick in the middle of the transition—someone Backlund could lose to and Hogan could beat. Scanning his roster, he found his answer in an aging novelty act with curly toed genie sneakers: the Iron Sheik.

Wrestling has always fed off simple prejudices, and the papers were full of news about Iran sponsoring secret terrorist cells in the United States. It didn't matter that the Sheik, known to his friends as Khosrow Vasiri, helped coach the American wrestling team in the 1972 Summer Olympics or that he now lived in Atlanta. With anti-Iranian fervor at its height, he was the perfect choice to take the heavyweight belt off Backlund.

But when Backlund arrived at Madison Square Garden on December 24, 1983, he refused to lose to Vasiri. He'd held the company's heavyweight belt for six years; he had his pride. So a long backstage negotiation ensued. Finally, Vinnie agreed to let Backlund exit with an old boxing gimmick. He could pretend to wrestle hurt until his manager threw a white hand towel into the ring, signaling surrender.

The beauty of Backlund's surrender to the Iranian was that it required a swift corrective justice, something to reorder the moral universe that it had skewed. On January 23, 1984, Hulk Hogan was unveiled before a sellout crowd at the Garden to do just that. While the yellow taxis stacked up three thick outside Seventh Avenue as they always did on a big night, Hogan and Vasiri worked out their spots backstage, agreeing that the babyface would start the match by landing a double-fisted blow to Vasiri's head and follow it with an open-palm slap. Vasiri knew what was expected of him, and at showtime he paraded around the ring waving the Iranian flag and playing the foreign fool. Hogan's entry was simpler. He stalked up the runway in tight yellow trunks and a too small T-shirt that read "American Made."

Tradition holds that the heel calls the wrestling match, much like a lead dancer, in order to keep it in rhythm, and once Hogan locked Vasiri's head in the crack of his sweaty elbow the more experienced heel whispered their next move—a clothesline. Despite his improvements as a showman, Hogan was still stiff as a wrestler and the clothesline was one of the few moves he could pull off, or sell to the crowd. So as he threw Vasiri into the ropes and watched the heel sink into them, Hogan stuck out his left arm, knowing Vasiri would run into it when he bounced back. On cue, Vasiri did just that, falling hard to the mat.

Though exceptional workers could wrestle for as long as an hour, shifting momentum a dozen times, Vinnie didn't want to keep Hulk onstage anywhere near that long, in part because he didn't have the arsenal of moves to keep it interesting, in part because he wanted his new star to look dominating. All he wanted was a good five-minute match with just one twist at the end.

It began with Vasiri rolling himself along the ropes to avoid Hogan's lunge and Hogan falling woozily to the mat, as if blinded by cartoon stars. Next, Vasiri rolled him on his stomach and bent him into a Boston crab. Then, as he sat on Hogan's back, Vasiri slipped into a gimmick he'd performed for the better part of two decades, the *camel clutch*. Threading his hands under Hogan's armpits, he locked them around his chin, and, with his knee buried in Hogan's back, yanked up hard. Hogan strained, his face contorting as the Sheik sold a broad dinner-theater snarl. Then Hogan stirred...slowly...lifting himself to one knee...until he finally lurched up, sending Vasiri staggering back. Now for the big finish. Hogan flung himself off the ropes, catching Vasiri's neck with the point of his elbow. When Vasiri crumpled, Hogan fell on top of him, dropping his right leg over Vasiri's midsection. All that remained was for the referee to count to three as Vasiri lay pinned and declare Hogan the new heavyweight champion of the World Wrestling Federation.

Vasiri went to his Ramada hotel room on Forty-eighth Street and Ninth Avenue after the match, ate a quiet meal, and watched television alone. It was just another night for him.

But not for Hogan, or for thirty-eight-year-old Vinnie McMahon. This was their night, the night they moved the center of the wrestling world to Seventh Avenue in Manhattan.

THREE

IN 1984, THE YEAR in which Ronald Reagan was elected to his second term as president and Apple introduced its first Macintosh personal computer, 41 percent of America was wired for cable television—a huge jump from just a few years earlier. For the price of a basic subscription, a family could get ESPN, Lifetime, CNN, the Family Channel, and A&E. If they wanted to pay more, there was HBO. Still, most of what aired was bottom-rung network repeats or fringe sports. *TV Guide* didn't carry cable listings, and Nielsen was only starting to monitor the phenomenon.

One of the few cable stations with enough of an audience to command a Nielsen rating was the USA Network, a joint venture between Paramount, Universal, and Time-Life. USA was originally designed as a sports network and collected rights to major tennis tournaments, the NBA, the NHL, and the Masters. But when ESPN became a major player in televised sports, USA's penny-pinching backers changed gears and turned it into a dumping ground for cheap programming like *Robert Klein Time,* a game show with Don Adams, and *Southwest Championship Wrestling* from San Antonio, Texas.

The president of USA was Kay Koplovitz, a smart and savvy businesswoman whose tastes were grounded in her Kansas upbringing. Koplovitz understood wrestling had a niche; still, the only female studio head in either New York or Hollywood preferred to keep a discreet distance from it. But when two *Southwest* wrestlers hurled pig shit at each other on an episode that aired in October 1983, distance became a luxury she could no longer afford.

It was a public relations disaster and McMahon turned it to his immediate advantage. While USA's switchboard was still lighting up, he instructed his aide, Jim Troy, to call USA and offer an alternative. By the end of that week, a deal was struck in which the WWF became USA's new supplier.

In 1984, the opportunity to reach 24 million homes with a single broadcast every week was extraordinary. (At the time, USA was available in 29 percent of the 83.8 million homes that were wired for cable.) The McMahons were powers on the East Coast, but there were NWA wrestling czars just as powerful operating in cities like Memphis, San Francisco, Tulsa, St. Louis, Atlanta, Los Angeles, Houston, and Dallas. And the men who ran them were just as creative and strong-willed. Vincent James McMahon had warm relations with most of the NWA's members because they respected his gentility and dignity, not to mention the way he loaned out the acts that he had under contract at fair prices.

His son was the opposite. Having had to wait half his life for the chance to break into his father's company, he was desperate and hungry and disgusted at the fat old territory czars who'd grown lazy in the absence of competition. As Vinnie saw it, the beauty of cable was that it could take the McMahons into every market where the NWA operated, bypassing the czars' control. The cable airwaves could be used like a fighter squadron, providing air support for the live arena wars he was prepared to wage on the ground.

In fact, Vinnie was so convinced the extinction of the NWA lay in cable that shortly after he inked his deal with Koplovitz in the fall of 1983, he booked an appointment with her biggest cable rival, Ted Turner, to ask him if the WWF could simultaneously take over the production chores on the top-rated TBS program, *Georgia Championship Wrestling*. Turner wasn't crazy about the idea, but he was always on the lookout for talent and agreed to hear the young McMahon's pitch. Vinnie and Linda spent fifteen minutes in Turner's Manhattan sales office boasting about their stars, their youthful demographics, and the family name. When they were done, Turner was polite but noncommittal. Linda thought they'd made headway. Vinnie was skeptical.

WHEN TED Turner walked into WJRJ in Atlanta for the first time in 1971, he wasn't sure what to make of it. The rickety station, which broadcast on a low-powered frequency known as UHF, was the kind of place where employees would hang out smoking dope, playing banjos, and forgetting to replace the film reels when they ran out. Turner wasn't thirty yet, but with his days as a hell-raising redneck at Brown University behind him (not to mention a first marriage), he was rich and prominent and culturally worlds away from the hippies who now found themselves on his payroll.

Ted wasn't interested in the station at first. He was interested in the shell that owned it. WJRJ was the only asset in a corporation that was traded on the New York Stock Exchange. At the time, Turner was president of the company he'd inherited from his father, Ed, a blunt, cantankerous man who'd gotten into billboards at a time when new highway construction made it a booming business. Ed may or may not have been a visionary, but he was strong-willed and sure of himself—at least until his crowning achievement, his acquisition of a Cincinnati billboard supplier many times his size. It was a classic leveraged buyout, but instead of gloating Ed became oddly depressed about the debt he'd amassed, perhaps remembering how his father, a dirt farmer, had lost all his land in the Great Depression. Ed and his son started having shouting matches over Ed's decision to sell off what he'd just acquired. On March 6, 1963, Ed killed himself with a shotgun blast to the head in the bathroom of the family's plantation home in Savannah.

Ted had never shown a hint of his father's ambition, and Ed had whipped him for it before he finally put his son in military school. Oddly, Ted came to like the routine of the military, if only because it gave him a refuge from his volatile life back home. He also learned that he was good at arguing, which won him a medal for oratory. At Brown, he continued to refine himself, becoming gifted in the collegiate arts of reading the classics, bedding women, and drinking hard. After his father's death, most of Ed's friends assumed that Ted would want to sell off large chunks of the company so he could take a sizable cash payout and spend his years indulging his passion for sailing.

Ted surprised everyone, first by wanting to run the whole show and then by doing it well. He turned Turner Advertising into a tightly run and profitable ship, aggressively buying new plants while adopting his father's strategy of never using his own dime. He routinely shocked advisers who worried about him overextending himself by saying that if it all fell apart, he'd just take his daddy's way out. It was as if debt was a demon he felt compelled to stare down. As Judy Nye, his first wife, told Robert and Gerald J. Goldberg in their book *Citizen Turner,* "The dream was just to build on the dream until you can't go any further."

That's why, after he'd reached the limits of what he could borrow and was hard up for cash to finance his expansion dreams, the acquisition of WJRJ seemed attractive. If Turner Advertising could list on the New York Stock Exchange, then Ted could raise as much capital as Wall Street was willing to gamble on him.

"I never watched any television in those days," he told the Goldbergs. "I had no idea what UHF stood for. I had never even watched the station because I couldn't get it on my set." WJRJ had lost nearly a million dollars the year before, but Turner ignored the pleas of his closest aides and leaped at the chance to take it over. As soon as the deal closed, he changed the call letters to WTCG, for Turner Communications Group.

The potential for growth was certainly there. In 1971, UHF increased its reach over the bustling Atlanta market by so much that it covered the entire inner city and was starting to make inroads on the southside suburbs. Initially, Turner was too highly leveraged to afford much except cheap reruns of such black-and-white sitcoms as *Leave It to Beaver, Gomer Pyle, Petticoat Junction, The Beverly Hillbillies,* and *The Andy Griffith Show.* His only means of improving the mix was to wait for another station in town to cancel a show. Then he'd swoop in to cherry-pick the discards. His best source was the limping ABC affiliate, WQXI, which had just been bought by a New York outfit that was intent on improving the quality of what Atlanta watched. When WQXI was ordered to run news instead of *Star Trek* at dinner hour, Turner immediately grabbed the reruns—and their decent ratings—for himself. But the big score was Ray Gunkel's wrestling show, *Georgia Championship Wrestling*.

Gunkel was a six-foot-four, movie-star handsome wrestler with a flair for scripting fast-paced matches that showed off stars like Mr. Wrestling II, a masked babyface who dressed from head to toe in white, except for black trim on his tights and mask to differentiate him from the original Mr. Wrestling. (Mr. Wrestling II gained a measure of political infamy when he posed for a photo with then-presidential candidate Jimmy Carter holding him in a headlock. The photo delighted Carter's mother, Miss Lillian, a devoted wrestling buff who regularly attended matches in Columbus, Georgia, and believed every toss was real.) Under Gunkel, *Georgia Championship Wrestling* became the highest-rated locally produced program in Atlanta. But in 1971, new owners took over the station and seemed not to care about wrestling. They moved the show from one time slot to another until loyal viewers had trouble finding it and fell out of the habit of watching. Gunkel's live shows at the Atlanta City Auditorium suffered, too.

Turner heard about Gunkel's troubles through the wrestler's wife, Ann. Ann was fair-skinned, with could-be-model good looks, and most of her friends assumed her closeness with Turner implied an ongoing affair. Whether that was the case or not, he made it clear that he'd be more than happy to help the couple by offering Gunkel a time slot at six o'clock on Saturday nights—the same slot the show had to be moved from at WQXI. A grateful Gunkel quickly agreed.

Soon after that, Gunkel booked himself to meet a 310-pound wrestler with a Fu Manchu mustache and curly eyebrows named Ox Baker at the Sports Arena in Savannah, Georgia. Baker was dangerous—he'd been involved in a tag-team match in Nebraska in which one of the opponents died from a ruptured pancreas—but Ray didn't seem overly concerned. In fact, he went for a hearty lunch that afternoon at Mama's, a restaurant that sat its patrons family style and kept filling

the table with heaping portions of fried chicken, pot roast, and pota-
toes. Ray had more than his share of Mama's cooking floating around
his stomach when he took to the mat with Ox.

At first he looked sluggish, but he managed to hold his own as the
two men hammered one another with forearm smacks that left them
with blood blisters. Ray was keeping up until Baker leveled an anvil of a
blow to Ray's chest called the *heart punch*. It sent him to the mat, but
Ray got up in a hurry, fighting back so hard that he broke Ox's wrist en
route to pinning him for the win.

Ray was pale by the time he got to the dressing room, so he took a
long, cold shower, hoping it would make him feel better. It didn't. He
was toweling himself dry when his body heaved. He fell to the floor,
jerked twice, and was gone. Doctors would later conclude that Ox's
blow damaged a valve in Ray's heart. As Baker remembers it, "I was in
the dressing room trying to soak my wrist when a policeman came in
with a sawed-off shotgun. He said, 'Better get your ass out of here. Ray
just dropped dead in the dressing room.'"

Gunkel had barely been lowered into the ground when a full-scale
war over his territory broke out. Though Ann always seemed more concerned with fine clothes than how one fine-tuned a clothesline move,
she decided she was going to run the company herself—something
that didn't sit well with Ray's partners. "They figured she'd be happy to
go home and continue collecting her percent," says Joe Hamilton, one-
half of the masked tag team known as the Assassins, who worked
with the Gunkels. "But Ann was a ballsy woman. She once told me, 'If I
want something from a man, I just go in his office, rip my bra off, and
come out yelling and hollering. I always get it.' So when Ray's partners
told her to go home, she said, 'Fuck you, I'm taking over.'"

To just about everyone's surprise, Ann booked the Atlanta City Auditorium for Tuesday evenings, rivaling her late husband's partners, who
put their shows on there on Friday nights. Then she lured away
wrestlers who were loyal to Ray, such as Hamilton and Thunderbolt
Patterson, and created a new show called *All South Wrestling* that
Turner agreed to air at the five o'clock hour—just before *Georgia*

Championship Wrestling. (Making matters even more uncomfortable, both shows were taped on Saturday morning in the same studio.) She also locked up the rights to perform in towns like Augusta and Savannah, where the live shows that she staged on Sunday and Monday nights became instant hits, bringing viewers to her Channel 17 show. By 1973, Ray's ex-partners were so worried that they turned to an erudite southerner named Jim Barnett to help blunt Ann's advances.

Barnett was an odd mix of high and low culture, a modestly built man whose passion for fine art, Mozart, and penthouse living would lead a fellow Georgian, Jimmy Carter, to appoint him to the National Council for the Arts. The timber of his voice was gravelly, and he lingered over vowels as he began thoughts, which usually started with the phrase, *"My booooy."* One of the original scriptwriters for the DuMont Network's *Live from the Marigold Theater* show, Barnett had been promoting wrestling in Australia but was homesick and only too happy to hear about his friends' troubles when they buttonholed him at the 1973 NWA convention. He'd known the Gunkels for twenty years, ever since DuMont folded and he'd moved to Atlanta to start filming matches for television there. In fact, he was the one who introduced Ray to Ann. Still, Barnett had no problem working the other side of the street. He quickly agreed to take over the running of *Georgia Championship Wrestling.*

Within a few months, he'd wrested Augusta and Savannah back out of Ann's control by cutting exclusive deals with the cities' arena managers and helped revitalize the TV show. As 1974 began, his new partners were delighted; Ann was on the ropes. But Barnett had to be careful about coming on too strong. As Al Rogowski, who wrestled under the name Ole Anderson, remembers it, "Ann was connected with the mob, or at least she was rumored to know guys in it. One day in '74, she had one of them fly into Atlanta. A lot of us saw him, but we weren't sure, you know? Was this guy for real, or was Ann just being Ann? When he flew back to Chicago we all figured it was bullshit. Then, a few months later, I see a photo in the paper. It's this guy, and he was found in the trunk of a car parked at O'Hare Airport with something like twenty-two bullet holes in him."

Instead of testing Ann's connections further, Barnett approached Turner and asked him to float the idea of accepting a buyout past Ann. To his relief, Turner returned with the news that Ann was willing to make a deal. In the spring of 1974, she accepted $200,000, giving Barnett's *Georgia Championship Wrestling* control of the now-united territory, a two-hour block of time on Channel 17 on Saturday night.

By then, Turner had started to follow the progress of an upstart cable station based in New York called Home Box Office, which wanted to use a single, stationary satellite moored high above the earth to blanket the country with movies. Turner was fascinated by the idea and asked his aides how much it would cost for him to get such a satellite. Their answer was a million dollars.

Turner was already in his second year of owning the broadcast rights to the Atlanta Braves baseball team, which had increased his audience for Channel 17 so much that it now covered a forty-mile radius, making it the largest UHF station in the country. He'd also managed to syndicate the games across Georgia, the Carolinas, Alabama, and Florida. But even after Hank Aaron hit his milestone 715th home run in 1974, the Braves were still a tepid franchise. In 1975, when they traded Aaron to Milwaukee, they were in last place in the National League West. Fearing that the team's management was going to drive away his viewers, Turner decided to buy the club himself. He figured that if he could use some of his canny marketing skills to make the team more successful, he could use the new satellite technology to beam their games from coast to coast. A million dollars would be a small price to pay for a satellite if it gave him a team with a true coast-to-coast following. So Turner paid it, and on December 17, 1976, WTCG went up on a satellite called *Satcom 1* while, down below, operators at Channel 17 answered their phones with the catchphrase "The superstation that serves the nation, good morning." Turner's Superstation had situation comedies, movies, and a sports lineup that featured the Braves and two hours of Saturday evening wrestling.

It was an arrangement that served everyone well over the next half-dozen years. With the exposure that the Superstation offered, Barnett was able to build a traveling circus that descended once a week on small, culturally starved Georgia towns like Carrolton, Griffin, Athens, and Columbus. Among his stars were Rogowski and Jack Brisco, a curly-haired babyface from Blackwell, Oklahoma, who looked like Joe Namath.

Rogowski and Brisco never liked one another. In fact, Brisco tells the story that one evening in Columbus, Georgia, he wasn't feeling well and asked Rogowski to go easy on him. "I told him don't fuck with me, I'm sick as a dog. Right away, he comes at me punching my guts, trying to make me puke. I swear, I wanted to kill him."

The men were even greater rivals out of the ring than in it. Jack and his brother Gerald owned 25 percent of the Georgia troupe, and Rogowski had just 10 percent. But Barnett relied on Rogowski enough to make him its president. Over time, the Briscos began to feel that by paying himself a handsome six-figure salary, Rogowski was cutting into their share of the partnership profits. So in late 1983, the brothers convinced Barnett to give them control of his shares—a coup that gave them majority control and the right to strip Rogowski of his title.

In the course of fifteen years as a shit kicker, Rogowski had built up a fairly thick skin. In the days before wrestlers took painkillers, he'd lost most of the tendons in his left hand from seven different stabbings and earned a scar on his chest from the time a seventy-eight-year-old fan attacked him in Greenville, South Carolina. (One fan distracted him with a chair while the other gutted him from his neck to his ribs with a hawk-bill knife, leaving him for dead outside his dressing room.)[1] He'd also been sued three dozen times and claimed he'd never once lost. So when he got wind that the Brisco brothers were planning to

---

1. Rogowski had competition as a tough man from his wrestling "brother," Gene Anderson, the only real Anderson of the group. Once in a match with Wahoo McDaniel, Gene got all of his front teeth knocked back. As Rogowski remembers it, "his mouth was swollen and bleeding all over the place. He asked me how it looked. It was gross. But he refused to stop. He kept on wrestling. He didn't want to stop anywhere that night, so we went back to the motel and went to bed. The next morning I went to his room to get his ass up and go to the dentist. His mouth was all covered with blood from sleeping that way. He had them all pulled and never said a word."

depose him with their newly won voting control, he confronted them in the bar of the Atlanta Ramada Inn after a show in January 1984.

"What the hell do you think you're doing, Jack?" he said bluntly. "You can't run a fucking thing."

The three started arguing. But as they got drunker, the Briscos softened their stance. As long as he agreed to start mailing them better profit-sharing checks every week, they agreed to let Rogowski keep running things. Rogowski had watched *The Godfather* the evening before and drunkenly decided he wanted to seal the pact "like those mob guys do."

What happened next is the subject of some dispute. Jack Brisco says Rogowski grabbed him and dragged him to the hotel bar's bathroom. Rogowski insists it happened after the brothers invited him to their hotel room—an invitation that he suspected was made so they could get him alone and jump him. Either way, this much is certain: Gerald Brisco had a short-bladed knife, which Rogowski took and used to slice open a healed scar on his forehead with an old-time blading move. The brothers were dumbstruck as he gushed blood and handed Jack Brisco the knife, expecting him to do the same.

"Fuck you, you dumb Polack," Jack replied. "I ain't cutting my head. I ain't gonna be no blood brother with a dumb fucking Polack."

NOT LONG after that, Vince was sitting in an office he'd rented in Greenwich when he got a call from Jack Brisco, who was checking up on the health of a mutual friend in Vince's employ. It was a few weeks after Vince had made his unavailing pitch to Turner and because he didn't think he'd sealed the deal, he needed another way to get on TBS. He knew Brisco was a stockholder in *Georgia Championship Wrestling* company, so he quickly asked, "Can you talk?"

Brisco was in a room full of other wrestlers at the time, but looking around he said, "Uh, kinda."

Vince got to the point quickly. "Would you and your brother consider selling your stock to me?"

When Brisco replied that he would if the price was right, all three agreed to meet the next day at LaGuardia Airport in Queens, New York. "I'll have a prepaid ticket waiting for you," McMahon said.

Early in the afternoon of the next day, the Briscos found McMahon waiting for them behind a cocktail table in the Ionosphere Lounge, alone. He was just as direct in person as he was on the phone. "Where does the stock lie?" he asked. "Who do you have on your side?"

Jack answered that he and Jerry were only too happy to sell out and were sure they could deliver the shares of Barnett and a fourth partner, comprising a total of 90 percent of the stock. The only person they couldn't deliver was Rogowski, who had 10 percent. Vince told them they should all reassemble as quickly as possible—like next week in Atlanta.

On April 9, 1984, the group that convened in a downtown Atlanta law office included the McMahons and their New York attorneys, and the Brisco brothers. Al Rogowski wasn't there. He was in Wisconsin, caring for his ill mother. One by one, the partners signed away their shares for a total of $900,000 and then walked to their office nearby to inform their employees. Rogowski's secretary was crying when she called him in Wisconsin. "Vince bought the company," she sobbed. "He *bought* it."

Rogowski rushed back the next morning, just in time to see Vince walk into the TBS studio with the four-hundred-pound Gorilla Monsoon at his side.

"Get the fuck out of here, Vince," Rogowski told him.

McMahon was the picture of reconciliation as he held out his hand. "Come work with me, Ole," he said, using Rogowski's stage name. "I'll make you more money than you'll ever think possible." Later, Rogowski would wish that for once in his life he'd just shut up.

Instead he replied, "Fuck you...*and your wife.*"

FOUR

SINCE HIS EARLY DAYS imitating Howard Cosell under his father's watchful eyes in Washington, Vinnie had developed an easy manner on television. On one level, his job was simply to feed his wrestlers straight lines and let them react, thereby setting up the plot and foreshadowing the action. But that's like saying all Johnny Carson had to do was talk. Vinnie had to sell their answers, and he did it better than anyone. The man who'd wanted to be a wrestler since he was twelve had an obvious affection for his muscle-bound performers, and it came through on the screen. He dug trenches in the studio so his six-foot-three frame wouldn't tower over his shorter entertainers, and he always played the straight man so as never to steal their laughs. Imitating his father's decorum, he dressed in suits with vests and 1920s-style collars, always keeping an ironed hankie in the breast pocket. With his deep voice, cleft chin, and wide, stocky frame, he almost looked like a comic book character himself—the twenties banker or the vaudeville emcee.

And there was a lot of this Vinnie on television. Every three weeks, the company filmed a day's worth of wrestling matches at an old agricultural hall at the fairgrounds in Allentown, Pennsylvania, creating three hour-long installments of *Championship Wrestling,* the flagship show that he sold in syndication. Then the troupe would pack up and drive to a small arena thirty miles away in Hamburg, where more matches were shot, creating a second syndicated show called *All-Star Wrestling.* For a third show for markets with an insatiable appetite, he'd take scraps from the Allentown and Hamburg sessions, reedit them with new voice-overs, and sell them as *Superstars of Wrestling.*

His fourth hour of weekly television was *All-American Wrestling* on USA, and because Nielsen had just begun monitoring cable viewership it became Kay Koplovitz's first measurable ratings hit, easily outdoing

Robert Klein and Don Adams. Knowing a good thing when she saw it, Koplovitz asked Vince if he wanted to fill an hour-long hole in her Tuesday lineup as well. He had no idea what to do with it until he was out to dinner one evening with a director named Nelson Sweglar, who suggested, "Why don't you do a talk show?"

Tuesday Night Titans (or *TNT*) Vince's fifth program, was a radical departure for the WWF and wrestling in general. From a shoestring set with a boxy black-and-white skyline behind the talk show desk, he interviewed a parade of wrestlers as if they all lived in some parallel universe where everyone walked around in colored trunks, Arab headdresses, pink leisure suits, tribal feathers, and army fatigues. For a sidekick, he chose a diminutive British wrestler named Lord Alfred Hayes, who dressed in tuxedos and spoke with *Masterpiece Theatre* diction. Because the wrestlers could never leave character, *TNT* became a running improv built around sight gags and skits. Once a week Vince would fly in from New York to a small studio in Baltimore that looked like a loading dock and spend the afternoon filming the two-hour show. At first, the executives from USA didn't quite know what to make of the grandfatherly wrestler Freddie Blassie, who coined the phrase "pencil-neck geek," dispensing advice to the lovelorn on a rose-colored set. When Vinnie read him a letter from a woman complaining that her husband wasn't paying her attention, Blassie groused, "Has the woman tried taking a bath, used underarm deodorant, shaved under the armpits? You goofy broad, that's what you gotta do!" In another skit, he hosted a wedding for Butcher Vachon and followed it with an all-heel reception at a local banquet hall. Vince put in an advance order for forty custard pies and when a food fight broke out at the party, his cameras caught the mortified owner feverishly scraping pie crust off the walls.

Vincent James McMahon never saw *Tuesday Night Titans*. In January 1984, he confided to Jim Barnett that there was blood in his urine. What his doctors found was that cancer had spread throughout his body. Four months later, on May 27, 1984, he died, with his sons and wife at his hospital bedside.

Recounting the moment to *Playboy* years later, Vince said: "My dad was old Irish…and for some reason I don't understand, they don't show affection…. He never told me he loved me…. That time in the hospital, I kissed him and said I loved him. He didn't like to be kissed, but I took advantage of him. Then I started to go. I hadn't quite gotten through the door when I heard him yell, *'I love you, Vinnie!'*"

It was to be a final sadness that the man who spent his whole life in wrestling would have so few of his colleagues there to say good-bye. As Barnett remembers, "There was a very small wrestling contingent because all of Vincent's friends from the business were mad at Vinnie."

To the promoters of the crumbling National Wrestling Alliance, *TNT* was a heresy, something that transformed their life's work into a joke. They feared it would turn the public against them by altering traditional, physical wrestling into television comedy. But if the old-timers hated the show, just about everyone else seemed to love it. To *Sports Illustrated*, it was "maybe the most provocative talk show on television." To USA, it was another hit. And to a burgeoning rock manager named David Wolff, it was just the thing he needed to get his girlfriend's new album noticed.

Wolff, the thirty-two-year-old son of a life insurance salesman, was a fast-talking rock hustler with a full beard, sunken cheeks, and downtown clothes who'd grown up in Connecticut watching wrestling shows like *Bedlam from Boston*. He hadn't thought about wrestling in years when his girlfriend, Cyndi Lauper, returned home to New York from a concert in San Juan raving about a passenger she'd met in first class. His name was "Captain" Lou Albano, and he went so far back in the business, she said, he could remember being on the *Jackie Gleason Show*.

Lauper was no stranger to show business herself. She grew up in Queens and, after dropping out of a fashion college, where she developed a taste for vampish corsets and rainbow hair, knocked around with a rockabilly band known as Blue Angel. She quit the band after meeting Wolff, and though radio executives didn't care for her Betty Boop accent (one consultant went so far as to tell Wolff that "she talks like a duck"), Epic Records offered her a seven-album deal. Figuring that her image would help carry the first single, "Girls Just Want to Have Fun," executives at the label committed to make a video for it. The scenes were already drawn out on storyboards and the casting done when Lauper returned from San Juan raving about Captain Lou. At the last minute, Wolff asked Epic to call the World Wrestling Federation and inquire if Albano was available to play Cyndi's father. At first, the grandfatherly grappler said he wasn't interested, but on the evening before filming, his wife convinced him to change his mind.

As an overbearing father trying to contain his flighty daughter, Albano was delightfully campy. Even better, having a wrestler in the video was just the kind of quirky thing that the executives at MTV loved. In the spring of 1984, "Girls Just Want to Have Fun" became one of the network's most played videos, and Lauper was designated (along with Duran Duran, Adam Ant, and the Stray Cats) one of the station's core artists.

Knowing a good thing when he saw it, Wolff racked his brain for ways to leverage that exposure until he had a vision that made him, as he'd later say, "see the future." And so it was that he took the forty-minute trip out of Manhattan to Greenwich, Connecticut, where he met the president of the WWF for the first time. Grabbing a seat on a leather couch, Wolff thanked McMahon for making Albano available for the "Girls" video. Then he hit him with the idea that, he said, "will make us a fucking fortune, Vince. I mean it. A fucking fortune."

The idea, Wolff explained, was to stage a feud between his girl-friend and Albano, whose role in the WWF was as a manager. Managers are assigned to new wrestlers or to ones that need help getting over with the crowd. They walk their charges to ringside, make threats on their behalf, and stand by the ring in case someone needs to be hit with a metal chair or a tennis racket in the heat of the moment. Besides the loud Hawaiian shirts that stretched against his three-hundred-pound frame, Albano was best known for a safety pin that he stuck through his pierced cheek. For reasons Wolff never quite figured out, Albano used the pin to dangle rubber bands off his cheek like earrings. Wolff knew his girlfriend was no wrestler, but, he told Vince, she'd be a perfect manager and therefore a perfect foil to play off against Albano at ringside. Wolff suggested they start small, with the two appearing on a WWF show together. Then they could build up to a main event at Madison Square Garden, where both stars would come out managing wrestlers who'd fight their grudge match for them.

Vinnie had the perfect candidates. One of his oldest sideshow acts was Lillian Ellison, a South Carolinian battle-ax with red hair and garish blue eye shadow who broke into the business in the late forties as a slave girl called Moolah and had trained most of the female wrestlers who'd come along since. The other was one of Ellison's protégées, an auburn-haired Texan named Wendi Richter. Wolff said that sounded fine, so long as Lauper got the young one and the young one won.

In late May, Wolff and Lauper drove in a rainstorm from Martha's Vineyard to Allentown, just in time to make the taping of the syndicated *All-Star Wrestling*. After studying clips of the show, Wolff decided to start the feud on one of *All-Star*'s funniest and most unpredictable segments, Piper's Pit, which starred the combustible, kilt-wearing heel known as Roddy Piper. It was ostensibly an interview segment, but Piper tended to be less interested in getting answers than in getting offended and throwing his guests out of their chairs.

As Wolff rushed, dripping wet, onto the set on the fairgrounds (in the farmer's pavilion, which he noted smelled faintly like livestock), he explained to the cast that he wanted to keep things simple. Albano would answer one of Piper's questions in a manner that was insulting to Lauper, and she'd slug him with her purse. When the cameras started rolling, Albano delivered in spades. "Tell them how you came off my reputation, Cyndi!" he screamed, waving an indignant finger at the woman he insisted he had made a star by virtue of his appearance on her "Girls" video. "Tell them how all women are nothing! They're slime!" Lauper, just getting over a cold, had little trouble looking irked. She threw over a table, jumped to her feet, and clocked Albano with her purse. The only thing that took him by surprise was the bottle of perfume in it. It left a small welt.

That episode of *All-Star Wrestling* aired in mid-June. By the end of the month, Wolff, along with Piper and Albano, was in MTV's offices with a tape, pestering the channel's director of programming, Les Garland, for attention.

Since its debut in 1981, MTV had gone from reaching 2.5 million homes to nearly 20 million in 1984. With two-thirds of its viewers under the age of twenty-five, the music channel was discovering it had a remarkable power to push video-friendly acts up the Billboard charts. Garland was the man most responsible for pushing those acts. A onetime San Francisco deejay, he'd worked for Atlantic Records in Los Angeles before signing on with MTV. An impeccable dresser with a distinguished mane of salt-and-pepper hair, he had an office that was as well appointed as his wardrobe—filled with smart art, fresh flowers, ashtrays that he kept compulsively clean, and a putting green he liked to use during meetings. In that office, he charged up his creative staff to think of the most outrageous promotions imaginable to get the channel noticed.

When Wolff told Garland about his idea to draw attention to Lauper by creating a feud with Albano and asked whether Garland would give it airtime, Garland's eyes brightened. He'd taken in a few recent matches at the Garden and had been favorably impressed by Vinnie, whom he'd briefly met backstage. And though MTV had never done a nonconcert event, Garland said, "Not only will I promote it, I'll carry Cyndi live."

Wolff was ecstatic and didn't want to waste any time. He raced over to Albano's Manhattan apartment with a handheld video camera he'd borrowed from MTV. After rearranging some furniture, he filmed Albano slobbering milk from his beard and bellowing, "Ms. Lauper, you're a liar! You're a cheat! You're a disgrace!" (*Sports Illustrated* would describe his looks as "a gross meringue of facial hair, rubber bands and morsels of food that makes him look like Jabba the Hut.") Then Wolff raced over to the Epic studio where Lauper was recording and filmed Cyndi's answer, which went something like this: "I challenge you, you fat windbag!"

As the dueling clips aired during the early summer of 1984, Wolff couldn't believe his good fortune. Not only was the *She's So Unusual* album turning into a genuine phenomenon, on its way to selling 6 million copies, the disparate worlds of rock music and wrestling were seamlessly coalescing around the Garden event, just as he'd imagined. If one thought about it, the marriage wasn't so strange after all. Lauper needed to put distance between herself and another MTV discovery, Madonna. But with her secondhand Soho threads, she was also cannily winking at the downtown hipster crowd. When that crowd—which traveled as a pack between art galleries and clubs and hot new restaurants—followed her into wrestling, it brought its own publicity machine. Suddenly, the *New York Post* was reporting that Andy Warhol was thinking of painting Hulk Hogan and that David Letterman was raving to his high-powered friends at NBC about *TNT*. The irony crowd had discovered wrestling.

On July 23, the show that Garland dubbed *The Brawl to Settle It All* aired to the highest rating MTV ever had. Teenagers were discovering wrestling, too.

EARLY IN the fall of 1984, Vinnie called together a dozen of his top aides in the boardroom of his cramped Greenwich offices on Holly Hill Lane to announce his latest idea. A North Carolina wrestling company had just staged a huge event in Greensboro and simulcast it to two dozen theaters across the Southeast. Vince wanted to do a show ten times as large and broadcast it nationally by closed-circuit TV.

His top aides were skeptical. After all, his two prior closed-circuit endeavors had been fiascoes. And the company's cash flow was tight. He was paying out a small fortune—up to $10,000 a week to some stations—to guarantee that *All-Star Wrestling* and its siblings had berths on broadcast television in major markets such as Chicago. On top of that, Hogan's novelty was starting to wear off. They were going to need a new star soon. Did Vinnie really want to tie up his energy, not to mention what little cash flow he had, in a single supershow

that would involve hundreds of theaters and the inevitable technolog-
ical hassles that came with closed-circuit broadcasts, not to mention
advertising and promotion?

Vinnie wasn't listening. To have a truly national promotion, he
needed a national event. But six weeks before the show, when they
hadn't sold enough tickets to cover the deposits on the two hundred
theaters they'd booked, it looked like his advisers were right. This thing
they were calling *Wrestlemania* was going to be the Snake River
Canyon all over again. So Vinnie rushed out to the New York public
relations firm of Bozell & Jacobs with a $90,000 check. "I have eight
weeks to put a million asses in the seats," he told publicist Frank
Holler. "Make it catch fire."

Holler could have sent out all the press releases in the world, but
they would have fallen on deaf ears had Garland not been so ecstatic
about the ratings that *Brawl* achieved. He wanted another event on
MTV. So McMahon and Wolff came up with the idea of an award ceremony at the end of a December show at Madison Square Garden, pur-
portedly to reward Lauper for her work on women's rights. (As her MTV
image grew, Lauper used the mock feud with Albano to position herself
as a rock feminist.) Instead of standing outside the ring, Lauper would
be in it, receiving a plaque with Wolff at her side, when Roddy Piper
would storm inside. Then, in a move that would set up a whole new
rivalry, Piper would attack Wolff by lifting him into an *airplane spin* (bal-
ancing him on his shoulders and twirling) and throwing him hard to
the mat. Besides being shown on MTV, the surprise finish would be
shown and reshown on all the WWF's broadcasts, breathlessly billed as
an attack on rock and roll. It would divide the WWF into pro- and
antirock camps, setting up an inevitable confrontation that would be
tailor-made for another MTV special. A third special was important. If
Vinnie could get it to air just before the troubled *Wrestlemania*, the
publicity might be enough to put those "million asses" in the seats.

Wolff didn't know anything about those concerns and didn't care.
He was too busy meeting with Piper every afternoon in a Manhattan
gym to get ready for the December show, learning how to land with-

out hurting himself (he had to fall flat on the back to disperse the impact evenly). But it wasn't until he was actually in the ring, watching Dick Clark give Lauper her award and waiting for Piper's stage cue, that he fully appreciated how much real pain was involved in fake wrestling. Lauper and Albano were in the midst of a storyline reconciliation, and to further their rapprochement, Wolff decided that Lauper should give Albano his own award—a souvenir gold record copy of *She's So Unusual*. Wolff had spent the better part of the day getting the record gimmicked so that when Piper ran into the ring and grabbed it he could easily break it over Albano's head. Piper played his part to perfection, using the record as a weapon to attack Albano when he tore into the ring to interrupt the ceremony. Then he threw aside Lauper and turned to Wolff. With his body tensed, Wolff stiffened so it would be easier for Piper to lift him and twirl. What neither man counted on was how real it looked—not just to the fans but to a New York City cop stationed at ringside. He raced into the ring, imagining a felony was near. Piper cursed at the intrusion because the ring was small enough as it was. Now the cop was crowding him and screwing up his throwing angle. Piper pivoted with Wolff still on his shoulders, looked for an empty space, and finally let go of him in an awkward way. Instead of landing flat on his back, Wolff landed hard on his ribs. "Jesus," Wolff thought. "I'm gonna need acupuncture for this." Then, all of a sudden, he began to think like a wrestler and told himself: *Sell the pain! Sell the pain!*

The night was a publicist's dream. The next day, MTV viewers saw on-air personality J. J. Jackson reporting on the "shocking occurrence at Madison Square Garden last night…that left Cyndi Lauper's manager under medical supervision." The episode was so serious, Jackson intoned, that "lawyers and investigators are still holding up release of the actual video." That set up what purported to be an investigative special in which veejay Mark Goodman brooded, "It's plain to see the rock and wrestling connection has reached an all-time low," before introducing the supposedly embargoed video by saying: "Now, for the first time on national television, the event that's shocked the world."

Through the winter, Wolff did his part in keeping the feud in the public eye. At a *Ms.* magazine benefit for Lauper, Wolff borrowed an MTV camera that was on hand for the event and stuck it in front of the face of one of the guests, Geraldine Ferraro, who had just run as the first female candidate for vice president on the Democratic ticket, and along with her running mate, Walter Mondale, had been defeated. "Geraldine, do me a favor," Wolff asked sweetly. "Just say, 'Piper, you're going down!'" To his utter amazement, she did.

"She had no idea who he was," Wolff remembers. "So when Vince started running the clip over and over, he got a call from her law office pleading with him, 'You got to take this off.' She was mortified."

McMahon had a devious streak of his own when it came to getting press. On December 28, he let the *20/20* reporter John Stossel into the Garden and arranged to let him interview several stars, including a thirty-six-year-old heel from Tennessee named David "Dr. D" Shults, whose temper once caused him to have to leave the country because he'd hit a fan during a match. Before he went out, McMahon told Shults to "blast" the reporter, which Shults assumed was a license to get physical. When Stossel opined that the sport was a fake, Shults replied, "You think it's a fake? I'll show you it's for real," and knocked him to his knees with a cupped hand to the right ear.[1]

The ensuing furor made McMahon's business so hot that the third MTV special, *The War to Settle the Score*, aired live *and* in prime time. To ensure crossover appeal, a new member was added to the cast: Mr. T, whose career had been launched by *Rocky III* and was at his mass-appeal height as the star of NBC's action show *The A-Team*. On February 18, 1985, *The War* replaced *The Brawl* as the highest rated show in MTV history.

By now, it was obvious that MTV had transformed Vinnie's business. In markets like St. Louis, the ratings for his syndicated show were

---

1. Stossel collected $425,000 in an out-of-court settlement with Titan Sports. Shults was later fired for attacking the actor Mr. T in an unscripted incident on a WWF show from L.A.

doubling. Inside MTV, that fed a perception that the network was giving more than it was getting. The perception was particularly acute with Garland's boss, Robert Pittman.

"A year after we made the first deal with Vince, it had occurred to Pittman that he made one mistake," says Garland. "He didn't ask for a piece of the action. He kept saying, 'Look at how big we made it! We put MTV's seal of approval on it. Why don't we have a cut?'" So Pittman asked McMahon to a conference room in the company's corporate office and told him the price of continued exposure would be a cut of his gross. McMahon's reply was short and to the point: "As good as you've been to us, we've been good to you. *And I'm not asking for a piece of MTV.*"

"That was pretty much the end of that relationship," Garland says.

Vinnie didn't lose any sleep over the break. He'd gotten what he wanted. Now it was time to save *Wrestlemania.*

On March 27, four days before the show, Bozell & Jacobs booked Hogan to do a talk show, *Hot Properties,* hosted by Richard Belzer on the cable network Lifetime. But through an oversight, no one from the agency went along to chaperon Hogan. "Belzer wanted to be put in a headlock, so Hogan gave him one," recalls Vince Robatiello, who worked at Bozell & Jacobs. "Then Belzer started goading him, saying it wasn't much of a headlock. So Hogan kept putting more pressure on him." When Hogan let go, Belzer fell to the floor unconscious and cut his head. Though the show went on with a replacement host, Belzer wasn't amused when he woke up at New York's Mount Sinai Hospital after being stitched up. "At that point," says Robatiello, "I don't think you could have gotten any more press than we were getting." The buzz convinced *Saturday Night Live* coproducer Dick Ebersol, who'd already been getting an earful about wrestling from his close friend David Letterman, to invite Hogan and Mr. T onto the late-night show on March 30. It was the pièce de résistance. On March 31, the night of *Wrestlemania,* tens of thousands of fans walked up to theaters to pay fifteen bucks to see what all the fuss was about.

If Vince didn't possess the most talent-laden cast ever assembled, it might have been the most eccentric, owing to the curious collection of guests he'd hired as window dressing for the main event. Billy Martin, the former New York Yankees manager who was between jobs, was hooked into the appearance through his agent. Unfortunately, he'd never watched wrestling, so he wandered around backstage slightly drunk and muttering, "Who's this Hulk guy again?" Liberace, on the other hand, understood what Vince wanted right away. The legendary showman, who was headlining Radio City Music Hall that week, arrived in a girdle-tight white satin shirt, trailed by four Rockettes covered in rose red gowns and feathers. As for Muhammad Ali, the third guest looked like he would rather have been taking a pounding from Joe Frazier. Ali had been part of Vince's stunts before, but even a fat payday didn't seem to make it any easier for him to watch Roddy Piper and Paul Orndorff, along with a bagpipe retinue, strut around the same ring where he'd once awed the world. If the champ was grateful for anything, it was that he was allowed to wear a modest blue shirt and a plain tuxedo. Everyone else looked like they'd been dressed by the costume department of *La Cage aux Folles*. Jesse Ventura, the long-time wrestler (and future governor of Minnesota) who'd given up the ring for the less arduous job of being an announcer, was dressed in a pink satin suit and had an even pinker bandanna wrapped around his head. As Mr. T entered the ring fighter-style with a hooded bathrobe, trailed by his tag-team partner Hogan, Ventura had the line of the night. He said, "*Wrestlemania* is making history." And he wasn't wrong. Enough fans watched the show for Vinnie to gross $4 million, a figure that no one in the wrestling world had thought was possible for one night.

DICK EBERSOL was at a crossroads when he asked Vince to his Trump Plaza penthouse apartment for a meeting.

He'd just finished a second tour at *Saturday Night Live*, the show he'd helped to create, during which he'd assembled a cast that included Eddie Murphy, Billy Crystal, Julia Louis-Dreyfus, and Martin Short. Now he was looking for something that would let him spend more time at home with his wife, the actress Susan St. James, and their newborn son.

Ebersol liked *Tuesday Night Titans* because he thought it shared many of the same elements as *SNL*—namely, the improv, the sight gags, and the running sketches. In fact, it was close enough to the material he'd been producing that he told Vince he'd like to try his hand at producing a network version of it.

Brandon Tartikoff, NBC's vice president for programming, trusted Ebersol, who was a wonder at big-production jobs. The two had gone to Yale together and were neighbors in a tony suburb of Connecticut. But when Ebersol first floated the idea, Tartikoff didn't consider it a slam dunk. Primarily, he worried that the audiences for *SNL* and wrestling were too different and that *SNL*'s audience wouldn't watch wrestling in the same 11:30 P.M. time slot. Because NBC guaranteed a minimum rating to advertisers for the time slot—regardless of what aired—he stood to lose millions in "make-goods" if the ratings tanked. But when Ebersol assured him that they could get Cyndi Lauper for at least one show, Tartikoff green-lighted a pilot.

As he started to hang around WWF shows, Ebersol became impressed with the efficiency of the WWF crew. Gorilla Monsoon ran everything like clockwork from backstage and wrestlers like George "the Animal" Steele (who made his tongue green by eating Chiclets) did their jobs dependably, without much fuss. (Ebersol wished he could say the same about the *SNL* cast.) The problem was that the production values hadn't changed much since the fifties. Vince's MTV shows didn't impress him and *Wrestlemania* struck him as downright primitive. He wanted this new show to be filmed in an arena so that audiences would get the same electric feeling he got when he took in matches at Madison Square Garden. There would also be no more showing up at an arena with a single truck carrying a ring and some lights. Ebersol wanted four cameras at ringside with boom mikes to catch the grunts and groans that usually went unheard. He wanted state-of-the-art lighting rigs. He wanted concert quality sound. As general manager Nelson Sweglar put it, "Dick wanted to show us what was possible through big-time production."

Predictably, the egos grew in proportion to the expense. The WWF television people felt underestimated and pushed aside by the NBC veterans and by Ebersol, who liked to have his cigarettes lit for him and travel places by helicopter. But Vince had come through too much to be consumed by anything as trivial as jealousy. He studied Ebersol and the way he put together the show like someone being properly fitted for a suit for the very first time.

The maiden episode of *The Saturday Night Main Event* was filmed at Long Island's Nassau Coliseum on May 10, 1985, a Friday night. Mr. T was there, reprising his role as Hogan's tag-team partner. So was Lauper, who was using the show to promote a new single. In fact, the whole WWF cast was there, from the Iron Sheik ("U.S.A., acht, phew") to Rowdy Roddy Piper. The show ended at midnight, after which Ebersol and a small crew took the twenty cameras worth of film to a studio on Thirty-second Street and Park Avenue for editing. Through the night, they reassembled the show shot by shot. Early the next morning, Vince walked into the editing studio with Linda to see the final result and was stunned. It was faster paced and slicker than anything that had ever worn the WWF label. He didn't know wrestling could look like that.

That Saturday night, so many homes had tuned in to NBC to see it that it outrated anything in the time slot since the glory days of John Belushi at *SNL*. When Tartikoff saw the numbers, he told Ebersol that he wanted five more shows for that year.

It was the start of a five-year run for the show and a period of excess that nearly destroyed the McMahon family.

FIVE

WHEN TED TURNER HEARD that Vince McMahon was buying the stock of Georgia Championship Wrestling in April 1984, and taking over production chores on the two-hour show that aired on his Superstation, he didn't consider it bad news. Turner had formed a favorable impression of the third-generation promoter when Vince first came to sell him on the idea of airing the WWF on TBS. The little wrestling company seemed to be well financed, and its young owner obviously knew how to get ratings. There was just one thing that worried Turner, and he invited Vince to CNN Center in Atlanta to address it. Turner occasionally watched McMahon's shows, and he wanted Vince's assurance that he wouldn't use TBS as a dumping ground for second-run material. He wanted original studio wrestling. Vince extended his hand and gave Turner his word. Then he walked out and proceeded to break it.

On June 14, 1984, a solitary, round-faced man in a bad toupee appeared in place of the regular Saturday night wrestling announcer on TBS, welcoming Atlantans to a new era. It was, he said, the day of Hulk Hogan and his cohorts, Sergeant Slaughter and Gorilla Monsoon. Then he cued up a tape, and the scene switched to an arena somewhere in the Northeast.

Where the hell had Wahoo McDaniel, Tony "Mr. USA" Atlas, and Ric Flair gone, Turner's viewers wanted to know? They were icons. And who were these replacements? WWF stars grated on a fan of the National Wrestling Alliance like Harvard politics grates on a Vanderbilt man. They were too theatrical, too personality driven, and they didn't mete out enough action. Hogan was the biggest offender. His steps were herky-jerky and his holds looked phony. After six months of watching him, Turner decided he needed to find a way to get out of his contract with Vince.

One of the few territories not entirely overrun by the WWF was headquartered in Tulsa, Oklahoma, and run by a forty-five-year-old ex-wrestler named "Cowboy" Bill Watts. Watts majored in finance at the University of Oklahoma and was a smart-enough moneyman to be able to wring profits out of an area that had a fraction of the big venues of the East Coast. But that's not why his wrestlers fell into line. Watts kept the barrel of a Revolutionary War cannon in the yard of his Tulsa mansion and a World War II arsenal in his basement to complement it. His employees also whispered that he'd built a bomb shelter beneath the house to protect against a Soviet invasion. If the man was willing to arm himself for a Russian invasion of Oklahoma, they concluded, he wasn't going to suffer their foolishness lightly.

Watts was a study in contradictions, a son of the segregationist South who was also the first promoter to create a black champion. His territory encompassed Arkansas, Louisiana, and parts of Texas and Mississippi, where, Watts reasoned, blacks wanted to see one of their own win. He found his star in Sylvester Ritter, a Houston Oilers draft pick who'd blown out his knee in training camp and was dumped off on the World Football League, where he spent an uneventful year before giving up on football altogether. Ritter was using his six-foot-three granite frame to wrestle in Calgary, Alberta, when Watts asked him to drive to Tulsa for an interview. When he laid eyes on the 260-pound prospect, all he could think of was a line from the hit song "Bad, Bad Leroy Brown": "Badder than old King Kong, meaner than a junk-yard dog." As he tells the story, he threw a dog collar around Ritter's neck, dubbed him Junkyard Dog, and within a year had him headlining the New Orleans Superdome before thirty thousand fans, a record for an indoor crowd to that point.

"I knew a black would draw blacks," he'd say years later. "But the real secret was not letting a white man save a black. I put JYD in situations that were fucking impossible and he always saved himself. And guess what? The whites loved him for it. Everyone loved him for it. He was a black man who was his own man."

JYD wasn't the only memorable character that Watts created. He popularized a Venice Beach weightlifter named Steve "Sting" Borden; a group of teen heartthrobs called the Rock & Roll Express and their doppelgängers, the Midnight Express; and a sweet-voiced announcer named Jim Ross. Every week, Watts would gather them in the cramped Irish McNeal Boy's Club in Shreveport and put on the slickest, bloodiest, and fastest-paced wrestling show in the country, which he called the *Mid-South Wrestling Hour*. In January 1985, Turner called Watts and said he wanted to buy the rights to air *Mid-South* and put it on Sunday afternoons.

The show became an instant revelation for Atlanta's viewers, largely because Watts was his own best salesman. He announced the action so urgently and convincingly that fans believed that *he* believed it was all real. "One of my favorite angles of his was when Ric Flair came to Shreveport to defend the NWA title," says Jim Cornette, the high-strung manager of Watts's Midnight Express. (He was literally high strung: He used a tennis racket to bash rivals.) "Flair was challenging Ted DiBiase, but the *work* was that Dick Murdoch thought he should have gotten the title shot. So Murdoch jumps DiBiase, runs his head into the post, and gives him a gusher. Well, Flair decides he's gonna face DiBiase anyway. The place goes nuts. Watts is there cautioning the fans, 'If there's anyone squeamish, please, for your sake, leave right now.' And, of course, not a soul moves because Watts has built it up like, goddamn, DiBiase is on a pilgrimage. So Flair gets in the ring, and right away he rips the bandage off and the guy starts gushing. And DiBiase is selling this like Rocky in the first movie. The crowd starts chanting, 'Ted! Ted!' Then Flair kicks his ass for a while. But just as he's about to put him into a submission hold, Watts calls an ambulance and they cart DiBiase out. In one hour, Watts had convinced the people that Murdoch was mad at DiBiase for getting the title shot; that Flair was a chickenshit for even fighting a wounded DiBiase; and that DiBiase was the gutsiest guy who ever lived. It was beautiful, I mean *beautiful*."

Almost overnight, Watts's *Mid-South Wrestling Hour* became the highest-rated cable show on TBS and, by extension, on cable. In fact, its enormous popularity led Turner to approach Watts with the idea of him taking over the Saturday night slot then occupied by McMahon.

"Vince had a contract, but Ted said he'd sue to get out of it," Watts recalls. No sooner had they shaken hands on the deal than Watts went out and bought a half-million-dollar airplane, figuring that he'd be putting in a lot of miles shuttling between Tulsa and Atlanta.

He never got to use it.

AFTER EIGHT months of producing *Georgia Championship Wrestling* on TBS, Vince was getting sick of Atlanta in general and of Turner in particular. He had clear reasons for wanting to be on TBS; he could use the Saturday night show to brand his stars in the South and expand his national advertising base. At the USA Network, Kay Koplovitz allowed him to sell 60 percent of the commercial time on each show and pocket the proceeds (in exchange for her paying an unconventionally low licensing fee). Vince and Linda reasoned that if they could get the same deal at TBS, they'd be able to combine both shows with their syndicated programs and create a single-block buying opportunity for big-spending national advertisers. There was just one problem. Turner balked at giving up a penny of commercial revenue. In fact, he considered it to be the height of hubris that Vince would try to use two cable rivals, USA and TBS, to make side deals for himself.

Turner was already furious at McMahon, anyway. For eight months, he had flatly defied his promise to do a studio show and was using TBS as a dumping ground for previously taped bouts. Not surprisingly, ratings were nose-diving. In February 1983, *Georgia Championship Wrestling* had a 6.9 rating on Saturday night under Jim Barnett. Ten months after Vince took over, it was down to 5.3.

So a week after he'd started airing Watts's show on Sunday afternoons, Turner asked McMahon to a meeting in his Manhattan office to say he'd had enough. "I want you off my network," he said, "and if I have to sue you to do it, I will."

McMahon left the office fuming. Turning to Barnett, who'd come to work for the WWF after the Georgia takeover, he said, "I should have thrown Ted out that goddamned window. I invested a million dollars in Georgia. Now what do I do? It's no good without the TV."

Barnett had one idea. He knew Watts had the inside track to move from Sunday afternoons to Saturday night. He also knew that if Turner sued to get Vince off TBS and signed a successor deal with Watts, Vince would lose his million-dollar investment. In order to prevent that from happening, Barnett decided to call the only person he could think of who might be willing to buy Vince out of his jam before Turner ousted him.

THE CAROLINAS were known as a prestige territory in wrestling, and that was thanks to "Big Jim" Crockett, a jack-of-all-trades who staged Tommy Dorsey concerts and shows like *My Fair Lady* in the fifties while putting on wrestling matches and running restaurants with names like the Ringside. As the company bearing his name grew into one of Charlotte's largest, he added a minor-league baseball franchise to the portfolio and built a stadium in Charlotte called Crockett Park. His four kids—Frances, Jimmy, David, and Jackie—learned about life while driving to towns like Lumberton on weekends and helping to set up wrestling rings.

From an early age, Jimmy was embarrassed about that part of their lives. When friends would ask, he'd tell them that his father made the family money by promoting concerts, which was true to an extent, since Big Jim also arranged Saturday night dances for the city's blacks. But the old man was under no illusion about who or what he was. After he was offered the right to promote Harlem Globetrotters dates east of the Mississippi River, he turned it down because it would take too much time away from what paid the bills: wrestling.

Jimmy traveled with his dad the most and heard all of the stories he had to tell. Inevitably, they ended with such aphorisms as "Never promote what you like, son. Promote what the fans like." But when the old man died on April Fools' Day of 1973, the family's matriarch, Elizabeth, could see that Jimmy didn't want any part of it, so she handed the reins to her son-in-law, John Ringley, Frances's husband, who'd been Big Jim's right-hand man. Unfortunately, he didn't last long in the job. When he was caught having an affair with a former Miss Tennessee, the family gathered and voted to kick him out. At twenty-four, Jimmy was the only one in a position to take over.

Jimmy had no burning desire to become a public personality. While men like Watts and McMahon enjoyed calling their own matches, Jimmy considered it such a chore that he flipped younger brother David for the announcing duties and was happy to lose. Depending on how one saw him, he was either painfully shy or an aloof son of privilege. Either way, when his friends in the Charlotte GOP pushed him to run for the North Carolina Senate in 1974, he waged a reluctant country club campaign that left him sixth in a field of six. The round-faced southerner dropped politics after that and contented himself with controlling wrestling in cities like Norfolk, Richmond, Columbia, South Carolina, and Charlotte, which made him a regional power in the National Wrestling Alliance.

Like everyone else in the business, Jimmy Crockett was desperate to get on TBS and had been since the first time he'd met Turner in the mid-seventies. He'd made himself unforgettable by wearing a pair of white wool pants with cream and yellow checks, a blue shirt, and a yellow tie to that meeting, and while the station owner passed on doing business with Crockett that day, the outfit worked. The two maintained a casual friendship for years afterward, with Turner even inviting Crockett to a party he held on his yacht for the 1977 America's Cup time trials.

That's why Barnett decided Crockett was the only man who could bail McMahon out. He had the money, and Turner liked him.

Once he was approached, in March 1985, there was no hesitation in Crockett's reply. TBS meant national exposure and a chance to break into the hyper-lucrative arena of national ad sales. Madison Avenue advertising agencies wouldn't look at a tiny Charlotte promoter, but they would have to do business with one that had a top-rated TBS show that was capable of reaching 80 million homes.

It was a win-win situation for just about everyone. Vince got out of Georgia without losing a cent. Turner got McMahon out of his hair. And Jim Crockett Promotions, already the most successful southern wrestling company, became the second-biggest promotional outfit in the country.[1] The only odd man out in the sweepstakes was Bill Watts, who got dropped from TBS as soon as Crockett's deal was done.

Watts was sick about being outplayed. But what could he do? Unless he wanted to run up a white flag—something the combative Cowboy wasn't close to considering—his choice was clear: He had to go national, like Crockett and McMahon, to compete.

In early 1986, Watts quit the Irish McNeal Boy's Club in Shreveport and moved his operation to the six-thousand-seat Convention Center on the Tulsa fairgrounds to give the show a bigger, airier feel for television. Then he rechristened his Mid-South Wrestling company the Universal Wrestling Federation and sent his announcer, Jim Ross, on the road to sell it. Ross was a remarkable salesman. By late 1986, he got Watts into seventy major markets, up from a dozen the year before. But the size was deceiving. Most of the deals Ross struck were barter arrangements: The station got his show for free and most of the commercial revenue that came with it, while Watts got exposure to promote his arena shows.

The problem was that almost overnight, the UWF became the toughest driving territory around. Its wrestlers were driving up to forty-five hundred miles a week, and some were so tired that they had to take heavy doses of speed to get to the next gig. When the UWF branched as far west as Los Angeles, and as far east as Philadelphia, Watts had to start paying for his forty wrestlers to fly. Then he leased

---

1. In later years, Vince would claim that he told Crockett, "You'll choke on that million." But Crockett remembers that he wasn't at the Helmsley Palace in Manhattan when the ownership transfer was made. According to his memory of the transfer, just Linda showed up, and their meeting was cordial.

space in a gleaming office tower in Dallas, which he reasoned could serve as a way station between the coasts and present a better image. But week after week, he was paying the wearying price of being the third horse in a three-horse race. In better days, he could put on a shoestring show at the Arkansas fairgrounds and gross $70,000. Now he was playing unprofitable midlevel arenas like the nine-thousand-seat Olympic Auditorium in Los Angeles and taking a bath on it.

Maybe the Cowboy could have made it work with more time. But just as he was starting to expand, the oil-producing nations of OPEC caused an international glut by stepping up production. As a result, the economies of Oklahoma, Mississippi, Louisiana, and Texas got hammered. Not only were Watts's ticket buyers defaulting on their mortgages, but four bank failures in Oklahoma meant that the loan pool for risky new businesses was drier than a used Texas well. Watts was trapped. At the very moment he was having trouble selling tickets in Los Angeles, he'd lost his ability to sell out Oklahoma City and Tulsa. The regional wrestling empire that had made him $2 million in 1985 was hemorrhaging $50,000 a week. He had to take out a $20,000-a-month mortgage on his home just to stay afloat. As the Cowboy would say later, "When you're losing fifty grand a week out of your ass like that, you're either lying or you're dying if you claim it doesn't give you nightmares."

Before he lost it all, Watts picked up the phone to call Vince McMahon with an offer to sell out. But Vince already had more stations than he knew what to do with. Moreover, Watts's UWF looked like it wouldn't last through the summer. Why should Vince pay for something that he could get for free just by waiting?

On the way back to Dallas, Watts decided he had one more card to play. Vince may not have been interested, but Watts decided that Jimmy Crockett didn't have to know that. So once he got back to his office, Watts had Jim Ross call Crockett with a deception, saying that McMahon was close to buying the UWF. Watts followed up the call personally a week later.

"Vince is just about at the table, Jimmy," Watts purred. "If he buys us, he's gonna put you guys out of business."

Crockett had recently expanded into Florida, giving him a presence from Philadelphia to Miami. Watts was offering him arena contracts and local TV deals in the mid-South, the Midwest, and parts of the West Coast. And the more markets that he had for his show, the more he could promise advertisers a large single block of exposure. In March 1987, he flew to Tulsa to buy the UWF from an exhausted but relieved Cowboy Bill Watts.

"It was our downfall," Jimmy's younger brother David would say years later. "If we'd just sat back and let him go under, we could have had his TV contracts for free. Instead, we spent a million and inherited all of his past-due bills. And what the hell did we need with an office in Texas?"

FEWER THAN a million homes were wired for pay-per-view when the first *Wrestlemania* was produced in March 1985. By 1987, the figure was 10 million, and Jim Troy, McMahon's right-hand man, thought the time was ripe to test the new technology.

Troy realized it in 1986, after they'd drawn one hundred thousand pay-per-view buys to the second *Wrestlemania,* a three-city event broadcast from New York, Chicago, and Los Angeles. At the cable conventions he subsequently visited, cable operators were coming up to him to say that they had done unparalleled numbers. The technology was still primitive, and to enable it customers had to go to the office of their local provider and rent a cylindrical device that unscrambled the event's signal when inserted between the television and the cable jack. Still, cable operators who served as few as ten thousand customers were renting the devices to as many as 18 percent of their viewers. That *buy rate* "made them superheroes in their markets," Troy says. "It also created a buzz among the bigger cable providers."

In anticipation of the third *Wrestlemania,* Troy started bringing Hulk Hogan, Roddy Piper, and Macho Man Randy Savage to the conventions, creating even more of a stir. By early 1987, the *Saturday Night Main Event* was pulling in strong ratings on NBC, *All-American*

Wrestling was placing in the top fifteen of the new Nielsen cable ratings for USA, and the WWF's syndicated offerings were being seen on three hundred stations from coast to coast. Looking at the remarkable forces arrayed in their favor, Troy walked into Vince's office one day and said, "I don't want to scare you, but we're on track to do five times what we did last year."

Affiliates of the fledgling Fox television network were the biggest buyers of WWF's syndicated shows. The largest among them was in Detroit, home to the ninety-three-thousand-seat Pontiac Silverdome, where the pope had delivered Mass on his tour of the United States. Vince joked that since he was nearly as big as God, he should play the Silverdome, too.

To fill an arena of that size, he'd need the industry's two biggest draws as the main event, that much was clear. Hogan, the number one gate attraction in the business, was the obvious choice as the babyface. The choice of the heel was more problematic, because the only other man who Vince knew could guarantee a sellout was waiting to die in England.

Andre Roussimoff was the most traveled act that Vince's father had ever booked, a gentle giant from the French countryside who'd risen up to six-foot-three before reaching his teen years. His size lent him a precocious confidence, and he used it to leave home well before the other boys in his village, making his way to Paris, where he was discovered by a troupe of wrestlers. They took him to see Algeria, South Africa, Morocco, Tunisia, and most of western Europe, all before he'd reached his twenty-first birthday. Sadly, that was the midpoint of his life. The doctors who'd diagnosed Andre as suffering from gigantism had told him that he probably wouldn't reach the age of forty. Once he understood that he had to live twice as fast as other men, he indulged all of his appetites for alcohol and food, frequently driving with a trailer hitched to the back of his car that was filled with beer. World Wrestling Federation referee Tim White recalls having the unenviable task of helping to drag the six-foot-eleven wrestler (who was always advertised as being seven-foot-five) to his room after he drank a hundred of those bottles in a single sitting. During the late 1970s, he was the industry's biggest international box office attraction. Dubbed "Andre the Giant" by Vince McMahon Sr., he was sent to virtually every territory in the world until the wrestling war broke out in 1984 and McMahon refused to allow the Frenchman to work outside the realm of the WWF. Andre was beloved by his fellow wrestlers because of the money he earned them. As "Superstar" Billy Graham put it, "We drew great together, but if you couldn't draw well with Andre, you might as well get out of the business. He was always paid much more than the average Boys, but you couldn't get mad about that. Whenever we went to eat or drink, he'd never let me buy a thing."

By 1987, when he'd finally reached forty, Andre's drinking wasn't fun anymore. Instead, it masked the excruciating back pain that was the result of his sustained growth. He'd given up wrestling and was in England filming Rob Reiner's *The Princess Bride* when Vince called to beg him to come back to the States.

The Giant knew why the promoter was calling before he could even ask the question, and he told Vince to save his airfare. But McMahon wouldn't be that easily dissuaded, flying to England to make his case in person. As he'd later recall, "When I got over there Andre was in such a state of depression, I thought he really was looking for a place to die." Vince persisted in making Andre believe that he had one great performance left.

Before he left England, Andre would have to undergo back surgery so complex that the medical team was required to build customized surgical equipment just to operate. The most baffled member of the team was the anesthesiologist, who didn't want to administer so much to the five-hundred-pound patient that he'd kill him, or so little that Andre would wake up in the middle of the operation with his back laid open. Asked what he thought, Andre simply shrugged his shoulders and said that it usually took two liters of vodka to give him a warm feeling. Eventually, he came through the operation well enough to return to the United States so he could hear the one thing he hadn't yet heard in his fabled career: the sound of seventy-eight thousand people screaming his name.

Gerald Brisco, who was running a closed-circuit viewing of the show, remembers getting goose bumps when the first live feed from Detroit came over the screen at the Civic Center in Lakeland, Florida. He'd packed venues in towns like Atlanta, Charlotte, and Tampa in the seventies and eighties, but they weren't a tenth the size of the Silverdome. Aretha Franklin was singing "America the Beautiful." There were gimmicks like wrestling midgets, Alice Cooper, and Brutus Beefcake shaving Adrian Adonis's head bald after the four-hundred-pound Adonis lost his match. And there were serious wrestlers, such as Ricky Steamboat and Randy Savage, who turned in a match for the ages. But at the top of the ticket lay the pairing that caused traffic to snake for miles around the Silverdome.

Forced to wear a back brace beneath his long wrestling tights, and with numbness below his knees, Andre was a shell of his former self. That meant Hogan had to carry the match, or *sell it*, making it seem that Andre's plodding was part of a strategy and not just painful immobility. Hogan resurrected Andre's better days for ten nostalgic minutes, generously selling all of his chops and headbutts, after which he moved into his patented finisher, the *Superman* comeback—a familiar series of moves in which Hogan would throw his opponents into the ropes, put a boot to their faces as they repelled back into the ring, and then drop his leg across their upper torsos when they went in for the winning pinfall. Andre didn't think much of the finish, but as the two clenched, he whispered into Hogan's ear, "Slam me, boss." And at that, Hogan scooped up Andre's massive frame and ended the Giant's career by sending him to the mat.

In Pontaic, $1.6 million worth of tickets sold that day, but it was the pay-per-view sales that dropped jaws across the industry. According to the WWF's figures, more than half a million other fans parted with

$19.95 to watch the three-hour event, adding another $10 million to the bottom line.

Jim Troy was right. Pay-per-view was the future of the business.

AS JIM Crockett was the first to admit, he couldn't write a story to save his life. That's why he needed someone creative at his side. Someone like Virgil Runnels Jr.

Runnels was the son of an Arkansas plumber and a graduate of West Texas State, a pipeline for football players turned wrestlers. He began his career in Dallas in the late 1960s as half of a tag team called the Texas Outlaws, weighing 275 pounds of nearly pure fat and having dark, silent-movie actor circles around his eyes. But with bleached blond curls, sequined clothes, and a love of Western props like cowboy bells, he was just eccentric enough to catch on in the Lone Star State and become a staple of the pulp magazines.

Runnels, who wrestled as Dusty Rhodes, was a fast talker, and when he spun a story about a hardscrabble childhood in Austin "where I got my first paycheck at eight diggin' ditches," it delighted working fans. He said that he grew up in a "colored neighborhood" in Austin, and he spoke like it. His rapid-fire dialect was part Mississippi and part Mexico, but he called it Texas jive. Wrestlers grow stale repeating themselves, however, and in the mid-1970s Rhodes dropped the outlaw image to reinvent himself, using his real-life rags-to-riches story to create a character he called the American Dream. It was a canny move, cementing his role as the plodding workhorse foil for glamorous heels like the sequin-wearing Ric Flair. As Rhodes's lunch-bucket celebrity kept rising, he kept growing more eccentric, wrapping himself in mink coats that reached down to his spurs. His act reached its zenith in 1981, when his forehead was a puffy mass of scar tissue and the NWA's bosses briefly let him wear their heavyweight belt.

It was Rhodes's burgeoning reputation as a booker, however, that caught Crockett's eye. In Florida, where he'd gone to work in the seventies, Rhodes invented several memorable storylines, or *angles*, the last of which involved a feud with a Satan-worshiping wrestler named Kevin Sullivan. In their bloody final blowout in the fall of 1983, Sullivan entered Lakeland's Civic Center chanting, "The American Dream will die!" Rhodes was bitten, beaten, and ultimately pounded into the mat that night. But soon thereafter, he turned up in Charlotte, where he helped create the first of a new generation of multimatch supershows, which he named *Starrcade*.

This was still two years before the first *Wrestlemania*, and the maiden *Starrcade* drew fifteen thousand fans to the Greensboro Coliseum, while twice that number watched via closed-circuit in theaters in three states. Its 1984 successor was an even bigger affair, with stages in Greensboro and Atlanta equipped with closed-circuit screens so fans in one place could see the action happening in the other. By 1987, *Starrcade* was larger and more established than *Wrestlemania*, and its architect was considered the idea man who'd turned Crockett into the only promoter in the country with the wherewithal to mount a challenge to the WWF's hegemony.

McMahon and Crockett both grew up in their father's wrestling companies with dreams their daddies dared not have. But Crockett didn't have the burning ambition that it took to fuel those dreams. He took on McMahon for the same reason he'd run for the North Carolina state senate those many years earlier: because it was expected of him, and he was a man who'd always done what was expected.

So Crockett went to New York and hired consultants to vie for the same national ad accounts that the WWF was going after. He also decided, much as Bill Watts had, that it made sense to move the family's headquarters to Dallas. After all, he was recently remarried, and the cliquish social circles of Charlotte were making him feel claustrophobic. And so it was that in the summer of 1987, Jim Crockett picked up stakes and moved into the old Dallas office of the UWF.

If Crockett liked Dallas for the change it provided, Rhodes loved it for the money it let him spend. One could only be so flashy in Charlotte, but in Dallas the native Texan bought a red convertible Mercedes and a house in a pricey suburb where several of the NFL Cowboys lived. He also had Crockett sign the checks for lavish perks, like a ten-seat, state-of-the-Falcon jet that reached a top speed of seven hundred miles per hour. "We were living like Frank Sinatra," says Arn Anderson, a member of Dusty Rhodes's inner-circle. "Your wife would drop you off at the airport and two captains would be there to pick up your bags. Then you'd fly to the date in this private jet, and a limo would be waiting to take you to the show. When you were done, it took you to a four- or five-star hotel. I remember there was a little guy who worked for Jimmy, he must have weighed a buck-and-a-quarter, and one day he walked out of an outdoor show in Florence, South Carolina, with his coat so stuffed with money that he probably weighed three hundred pounds. We did $45,000 that night, all cash and carry. But did we need two planes? Did Ric Flair need to run up a $60,000 limousine bill one year? No."

With their expenses ballooning, the Crockett family needed an especially good showing from *Starrcade '87*, which shouldn't have been a problem with 10 million homes wired to get pay-per-view. To lend it a more cosmopolitan air, Jimmy decided to move the production to Chicago. Fans in Greensboro, who felt responsible for the successes of the prior four events, were stunned. To them, it was no different than Walter O'Malley moving the Dodgers out of Brooklyn. But Crockett was looking west, not back east. From where he sat in Dallas, there wasn't time to worry about bruised feelings in Greensboro. Two hundred cable systems had signed up to carry *Starrcade*. If he did anything remotely close to a buy rate of 10 percent at $19.95 a show, he could buy half of Greensboro with the eight-figure take he expected.

In retrospect, he would have been better off with a more developed sense of paranoia. Because Vince McMahon had no intention of letting Crockett crash a party he'd started. *Wrestlemania III* had turned into the mother of all pay-per-view events up to that point. On the heels of its success, Vince announced that he was going to air a new event called *Survivor Series* on Thanksgiving, the very same day as *Starrcade '87*. A cable company that wanted *Survivor Series*, not to mention future WWF events, had to promise it wouldn't air any other pay-per-view that day.

It was a bloodbath. Only five cable companies out of the original two hundred stayed loyal to the Crocketts. *Starrcade* wound up being bought by just fifteen thousand homes, leading the company to take in just $80,000 after expenses. Crockett might have weathered it if he had a strong base. But as he looked around, he realized that the twin revenue streams he'd hoped would carry him to the top—pay-per-view income and national advertising sales—were bone-dry. What he needed was a sales force akin to the one Vince had built. Instead, all he had was a few fast-talking consultants in New York and a bunch of grateful wrestlers driving Mercedes in Dallas.

As he turned to his bankers to make up for cash flow problems, resentments in the family began to flare. David, who'd grown up sharing the same room with his brother, had to choke back disgust every time he flew to Dallas and saw the suite of marble-floored offices bearing his father's name. Big Jim always told them never to flaunt their money before the public, which is why he ran things out of his house until his wife got a new white carpet. Only then did he move his office to a boarded-up convenience store. Marble floors? David was sure their father was turning in his grave.

Like many of the wrestlers, David also believed that Rhodes was running on fumes. For one thing, he'd all but given up on writing. The days of his half-hour classic matches were gone, replaced by bland, blink-and-you-miss it playlets. Rhodes argued that he didn't want to give away the best material free on television because he needed to save it for pay-per-view. Either way, the Saturday night show on TBS that McMahon had left with a 5.3 rating was doing a 2.9 in October 1987.

The ennui extended down to the arena shows, where Rhodes insisted on penciling himself in as Flair's challenger long after the fans stopped caring. Worse, he'd fallen in love with a transparent trick ending: Dusty would win their matches, only to have the referee disqualify him on a technicality after the bell tolled.[2] The scheme allowed Flair to retain the NWA belt but at a cost: his title was diminished while Rhodes, whose weight problem was becoming embarrassing, clung to the limelight.

At Christmas of 1987, Rhodes launched a last-gasp series of *Bunkhouse Stampede* events in which two dozen wrestlers started in a ring and got eliminated as each was thrown over the ropes, until one was finally left standing. Rhodes had wrestlers flinging garbage cans and tire irons while dressed in Stetsons and spurs, and after eight successful shows he decided to turn the whole thing into a pay-per-view. The main event was to be a cage match—literally, a match held inside a locked wire cage placed over the ring—among the prior eight *Bunkhouse* winners. Once again, he penciled himself in to win the main event.

The January 24, 1988, show might have done business in Atlanta or Dallas. Yet Crockett inexplicably decided to stage it at Long Island's Nassau Coliseum, a place that owed more to Billy Joel than Billy Jack. Making matters worse, McMahon once again counterprogrammed another show aimed to hobble Crockett. This time, he decided to attack via cable, creating a battle royal of his own and airing it free on USA. More than three million homes tuned in to see his show, called the *Royal Rumble*, a record up to that time for the network and the most homes ever tuned to a wrestling show.

Jim Cornette remembers sitting in the coliseum's locker room for the Crockett show and looking around at the long faces. "We wanted to be there like we wanted to have our mothers hooked up to a

---

2. Although not invented by Rhodes, he used it so often that it would become synonymous with his name and come to be called "the Dusty finish." There were variations on the theme, but a common Dusty finish would feature the babyface challenger scoring an apparent pinfall on the heel champion after the referee had been knocked out. In the meantime, a second referee would be summoned to the ring to count the apparent pinfall, awarding the title to the babyface and sending the fans into a frenzy, thinking they had seen a title change hands. Then the catch would come: the original referee, now "revived," would overrule the second referee's decision.

machine. The crowd was dead. They hated everything because they'd never seen it."

After it was over, several wrestlers climbed into a limousine to head to the Helmsley Palace hotel in Manhattan. Tully Blanchard, who was in a foul mood, was one of them.

"Dusty should just book himself against Dusty," he muttered.

At the hotel bar, Blanchard's mood got worse with every new drink that got poured. Finally, he and Crockett exchanged words.

"Dusty's a genius," Crockett insisted and walked away.

"This thing is going to hell and he can't see it," Blanchard said to no one in particular.

Through the late winter and spring, the hard travel and small audiences made it difficult for everyone to keep going. Rhodes and Flair started feuding, causing matches to be rewritten at the last minute because they wouldn't work together. In one instance, Crockett had to go to Flair's Charlotte home and beg him to work just to keep things afloat. Guaranteed half-million-dollar contracts with balloon payments needed to be paid.

Gasping for air, Crockett decided to take one last vindictive swipe at the WWF. In March 1988, he created a show called *Clash of the Champions* that he decided to air on TBS at the same time as McMahon's *Wrestlemania IV*. It turned out to be an exceptional show with two matches that earned *Wrestling Observer*'s best-of-the-year honors.[3] But it was a Pyrrhic victory. The morning after it aired, Crockett was called into the office of TBS's president, Jerry Hogan. He'd never been anything but kind to Crockett, but there was nothing kind or gentle in his voice now. The cable operators who'd abandoned Crockett's *Starrcade* the prior November were irate at what was viewed as a malevolent move designed to rob them of millions in pay-per-view revenue.

---

3. One was an all-out brawl pitting the Midnight Express against the Fantastics. The other was a star turn for Sting, in which he wrestled Flair to a draw after forty-five minutes.

"You will never, ever do anything like that again," Hogan said. "Understood?" The blood drained out of Crockett's face.

The dam burst the next month. His family's accountant, who also worked for the company, came to him in a panic. He'd spent a long weekend studying the books and had discovered they needed a million dollars quick. Crockett's word was still good with a few banks, so he went out and borrowed it. Two weeks later the accountant was back in Crockett's office, his face grimmer than before. It was worse than he'd first projected. They needed another million just to make it through the summer. Crockett let out a long slow whistle. Then and there he knew he'd lost. The only question was whether he could find anyone to bail him out.

In a curious twist, the same man who'd helped him buy Georgia Championship Wrestling so he could get on TBS three years earlier now worked for him. So he went to that man, Jim Barnett, and asked for advice.

Barnett had just come through a terrible personal ordeal. While he was working for McMahon in Connecticut, he quietly kept in back-channel contact with Crockett. It was a stupid thing to have done. Barnett knew he was duty bound to McMahon, who was obsessive about secrecy. But Barnett had a faith in his ability to play both ends against the middle. When Vince found out he was talking to the enemy, he called Barnett into his office, demanded his resignation, and ordered him out of the building. Barnett was one of Vince's father's best friends and was distraught at being so summarily cut loose. That night, he went home and overdosed on sleeping pills. The McMahons sent flowers to their old friend in the hospital, and Linda sat at his bedside. But they didn't invite him back. After he recovered, he picked up, moved to Dallas, and started working for the Crocketts in the fall of 1987. As the cash crisis loomed, he asked his new boss, "How would you feel about selling to Turner?"

The weary reply he heard was "I wouldn't mind that."

After months of negotiations, Jimmy gathered the family in their home back in Charlotte to discuss the inevitable. His mother and his sister Frances were there, as were David and their youngest brother, Jackie.

David pleaded the case for hanging on. He was incensed that his bullheaded brother squandered something that wasn't only his.

"Let's take the thing Chapter 11 and start all over again with the core of people we have," he pleaded.

But Jim Crockett was well past that. After having his grand dreams crushed, he couldn't see starting all over in a small town like Spartanburg, South Carolina, listening to Ric Flair complain that he wasn't going to work with Rhodes and trying to manipulate Dusty into letting someone else star in a script that he'd written for himself.

"If we don't sell," he told David finally, "our mother is going to be out of her pension and on the street."

On November 21, 1988, the children of Big Jim Crockett gathered in their lawyer's office to sign over their assets to Ted Turner for a package that included guaranteed jobs for the brothers and some cash. The brothers barely spoke to one another. They just glared.

After it was over, David went home and kissed his family. "Okay, I guess I'll work for crazy Ted now," he said.

A few days later, the phone rang in Vince McMahon's office in Connecticut.

"Guess what, Vince," Turner said when McMahon got on the line. "I'm in the rasslin' business."

SIX

THE CANARY YELLOW SUIT was something to behold. Vince liked to tell people that "you have to wear your promotion on your back." And tonight on a balmy May evening in 1989, he was doing just that at the premiere of the first movie he'd ever produced. Walking up to the screen of the State Theater, a second-rung movie house in Springdale, Connecticut, he thanked everyone for coming and told them that what they were about to watch was the realization of a dream for him, as well as a new beginning for the WWF.

Everyone in the audience knew they'd been invited to be cheerleaders for a boss who'd just sank $20 million into an action vehicle, *No Holds Barred*, for the company's biggest star, Hulk Hogan. And two hours later, when the lights came up, they gave the boss a standing ovation.

Ever since *Wrestlemania III*, the WWF had been on a roll. The company was doing nine live shows a week, had three hundred stations carrying its three syndicated programs, dropped jaws at the USA Network with an 8.2 rating for a *Royal Rumble* special, the highest in its history, and was having its licensed merchandise flying off toy store shelves. So much cash was flowing into the little private company—it generated in excess of $125 million—that it was becoming a struggle to spend it all.

He wildly outbid HBO and his old friend Bob Arum for the rights to promote Sugar Ray Leonard's fight against a journeyman named Donnie Leland. (The $9.5 million in guarantees to the fighters guaranteed that Vince lost money on the November 1988 bout.) He spent another fortune testing a WWF perfume he was sure women would love. (It never left the lab.) And he was pouring tens of millions more into a monument to himself—an eight-story Stamford office building off the interstate that would come to be known as Titan Tower.

But *No Holds Barred* was the most personal of the projects. Since Turner called him to announce "I'm in the rasslin' business," McMahon had become obsessed by the billionaire. Vince's last real setback was when he had to give up the Saturday night time slot that he held on TBS and watch Turner give it to Jimmy Crockett. In the four years since, he had vanquished the Crocketts, driving them out of the business. Now he was out to prove that he was in Turner's league.

In some ways, the men were strikingly similar. They were both willing to take companies they'd inherited and expand them to the brink of bankruptcy on mere intuition. Turner had done it with CNN, Vince with a very different gamble, *Wrestlemania*. The men also shared a history of womanizing. In the late eighties, the WWF was awash in cocaine. (According to one Titan Tower intimate, Vince liked to brag with apparent justification that "I can snort as much of that stuff as anyone can put in front of me and never get hooked.") And in the haze, the divide between work and play crumbled. Marriages broke up as bosses slept with their secretaries. "There were no boundaries, and little by little, since we all knew what Vince was doing, the barriers just wore away," says a onetime family friend.

Yet in one important area—knowing how to be rich—Turner had an insurmountable head start. He'd grown up with money and played like the ultrawealthy do. Between his runs for the America's Cup, the parade of young lovelies, and the quixotic creation of CNN in 1980, he'd become an American business icon. Still, if history had proven anything, it was that Vince was a fast learner. He moved Linda and their two children, Shane and Stephanie, into a gated community of mansions in old Greenwich that no one could get into without passing a guard tower. Their new home was a classic colonial with a sweeping spiral staircase, chandeliers, and art that included a portrait of a bronzed-colored Vince sitting on a Harley before gathering purple clouds.

"The whole thing was done by a decorator," says a family friend. "Not one single knickknack was theirs. Down the road, they'd feel entitled to their wealth. I remember Vince getting enraged when Linda had to stop and pump her own gas. But back then it was new to them. Vince and Linda were just amazed by the things they had in their own home. Vince liked to say, 'It wasn't that long ago that I was pumping my own septic tank.'"

Vince regularly had a Greenwich jeweler come into his office with cases of gifts and sat behind his desk picking out pieces worth hundreds of thousands of dollars. When the McMahons traveled to Paris for the first time in the spring of 1989 for Linda's birthday, she left with an elaborate new wardrobe. Then they bought a second home in Boca Raton, Florida—a spacious pink split-level on a channel with wall-to-wall windows, porticoes, and terraces—and surrounded themselves with toys like a fifty-five-foot cigarette boat.

All of this turned Linda Edwards of Havelock, North Carolina, into Mrs. Vincent K. McMahon of Greenwich, a title she fiercely cultivated. She asked friends to invite her to the polo matches at the tony Greenwich Country Club and filled her closet with Chanel suits. And she elevated her role as a lobbyist, appearing before the New Jersey legislature in late 1989, for instance, to make the once unthinkable admission that wrestling was fake so she could get the WWF exempted from a 10 percent tax on tickets that were sold to legitimate sporting events.

In many ways, her hopes of belonging to the Greenwich social scene were no different than Vince's ambition to belong to Turner's world. But, as was always the case with Vince, he approached things more personally. Nowhere was that more evident than in his decision to put $20 million of self-financing into *No Holds Barred*. Though he hired a Hollywood writer who'd done two screenplays for Clint Eastwood, Vince insisted on being intimately involved in the plot. What emerged was a story about a menacing Turner-like television executive who wanted to steal Hogan away from a promotion that was good and just. Unfortunately, moviegoers weren't as enamored with the idea. The *Washington Post* called it "charmless, stupid and badly made." Most other reviews weren't much better. The movie did an underwhelming $5.2 million in its first weekend and dropped like a stone after that. It was the first time that Vince paid Hogan a million dollars for anything, and after it was clear *No Holds Barred* didn't have a prayer of earning his investment back, he was incensed that Hogan insisted on receiving the full fee.

In the larger scheme of things, though, there wasn't time to slow down. McMahon had waited too long to get here. Friends saw his drive in the manic way he worked out in the gym, competing with stars like Randy Savage until his arms were monstrous. Sometimes during shows, he'd disappear into a side room with dumbbells and emerge with his face red and wet. Someone would inevitably tell him, "Vince, you look better than your wrestlers," and he'd smile proudly. If that behavior had been seen in anyone else, it might have looked like a midlife crisis. But the six-foot-three promoter was always obsessed with size. He even went so far as to hire an assistant whose primary job was to keep tabs on his high-protein diet and feed him huge quantities of tuna fish. (New employees who walked by the kitchen attached to his office were usually taken aback by the strong smell.)

Shortly after it became clear that he wasn't going Hollywood any-time soon, McMahon decided to turn that obsession into his next and most fateful gamble.

A POPULAR piece of reading material around Venice Beach, California, gyms in the early eighties was a fanzine called the *Underground Steroid Handbook*. It not only reviewed drugs like Deca-Durabolin, growth hormones, methyltestosterone, and Periactin, it advised its readers how to take them and which mixtures produced the most rapid muscle growth. In an introduction, its anonymous authors wrote:

> We haven't told you horror stories of steroid abuse because we really don't know any. We personally have not encountered ath-letes dying or becoming gravely ill from steroid usage. Sick people, we have, but not healthy athletes. And we don't live apart from civilization. We live in a part of the USA that has the highest

usage of steroids by athletes. We won't come out and say the steroids are not dangerous; we just feel the dangers have been misrepresented.

Part of that judgment came from wrestlers. Superstar Billy Graham, a former WWWF champ with twenty-two-inch arms poured straight out of a vial of Dianabol, was one of the most devoted spreaders of the steroid gospel. "You can feel your body stretch," he'd enthuse to anyone who asked him. "Just lay in bed and you'll feel yourself grow."

One of the people he spread the gospel to was Hogan, who still had a smooth face and a full head of hair when Graham bought him a drink at the Imperial Room in Tampa. According to an interview that Graham gave writer Mark Kriegel, Hogan "explained that he had done some wrestling out west but he wasn't getting over. He asked me about steroids, wanted to know what I took." Superstar told him about Dianabol, and about something called Winstrol, an injectable steroid that he chased down with Valium to smooth the harsh rush. "I freely gave him this advice," he told Kriegel. "There was no reason not to. It wasn't illegal."

Approximately ten years later, Superstar saw the results of that meeting. The men were sitting in the locker room of the Pontiac Silverdome, waiting for *Wrestlemania III* to start. As Superstar told the syndicated show *Inside Edition*, "We went off to a shower stall and [Hogan] pulled down his wrestling tights. I injected him with six hundred milligrams of testosterone in the right buttock. He had scar tissue on his butt from so many injections over the years, and it was hard to shove the needle in."

Hogan wasn't alone. In 1988, the Canadian sprinter Ben Johnson was stripped of his Olympic gold medal for failing a drug test in South Korea. *Sports Illustrated* devoted a dozen pages to a riveting first-person account by a University of South Carolina lineman named Tommy Chaikin, who talked about nearly shooting himself to death with a .357 Magnum as a result of the suicidal tendencies he'd developed from his college steroid addiction. Americans were reported to be pouring $100 million into the underground steroid economy. Some were serious athletes, but many were guys looking to get rid of their beer bellies and high school kids wanting to look cool by their muscle cars. Prior to the mid-eighties, no one had ever been prosecuted for dealing *roids,* as they were called, so it was seen as relatively safe. As a result, every town and city had a local guru who claimed he could put fifty pounds of muscle on just about anyone overnight. Steroids from labs in Mexico, Europe, and South America were as common as aspirin in certain "drug gyms."

The average male produces 2.5 to 10.0 milligrams of testosterone a day—enough to keep bone, muscle, skin, and hair growing. Load up the body with extra testosterone and the muscles grow before your eyes. But other things happen as well; namely, the body stops making the hormone when it senses a flood of it coming in from the outside. That leads to several side effects, including testicular atrophy, low sperm counts, and feminization. Longer term, steroids alter cholesterol counts (raising the bad, lowering the good) and pump up the blood pressure, causing hypertension, or what's commonly known as *roid rage.*

Or at least that is what doctors warned could happen. But those concerns were largely drowned out in the steroid frenzy, especially when every gym had at least one guy who'd been using for years and seemed perfectly healthy. As the chief medical officer of the U.S. Olympic Committee remarked to the *New York Times,* "Some people have no gain and are fine. Some may get some gain but they also get sick. And some just grow as they sit in front of you. It's like they pop a pill and just get bigger."

On the surface, William Dunn was one of the success stories. The strength and conditioning coach at the University of Virginia had been using steroids for ten years. But the truth was that in August 1987, he was a mess. His joints were causing him screaming pain, and the only way he could alleviate it was by popping painkillers. He ran from one doctor to the next until he was rotating among fourteen of them to keep up with his constant need for Valium and the powerful Tylenol 4.

The scam only fell apart when a pharmacist pegged Dunn for what he was—a nervous, four-hundred-pound druggie—and called the cops.

The night of his arrest, Dunn raged across his cell like a caged animal, his body literally short-circuiting. It wasn't until he'd detoxed enough to think clearly that he told cops he had something to offer: a dirty doctor he knew in Harrisburg, Pennsylvania. The cops in Chesapeake, Virginia, had more pressing concerns. They filed the information away.

In the meantime, the explosion of addicts like Dunn was convincing Congress that something needed to be done about what was clearly becoming an epidemic of abuse. In November 1988, the Omnibus Anti-Drug Abuse Act toughened penalties for steroid trafficking and increased the money available to drug task forces to prosecute the pushers. By the time Dunn came up for sentencing in February 1989, his dirt about the doctor who'd provided him with his drugs had become decidedly more interesting to Harrisburg's cops…and to the FBI.

DR. GEORGE Zahorian grew up in an Armenian household just outside New York City in the 1950s, when Argentina Rocca and the World Wide Wrestling Federation owned Saturday nights. Through his teen years and after he graduated with a degree in osteopathic medicine from a college in Philadelphia, Zahorian continued to take pleasure in wrestling. So when the opportunity presented itself to take a part-time job with the Pennsylvania Athletic Commission, the regulator of matches in the state, he leaped at it.

Since the McMahons filmed their syndicated TV shows at the fairgrounds in Allentown every third Thursday, Zahorian became the house doctor, taking the wrestlers' blood pressure and making himself available in the event a performer got hurt. He arrived at the tapings with his hair slicked back and wearing a bow tie, dressed in the hopes the camera might catch him applying bandages or first aid. Before long he was a fixture, dubbed "the good doctor" by the Boys.

How good a friend he was became clear when Dunn struck a deal with federal prosecutors to wear a concealed recorder during a visit to

Zahorian's medical office in the fall of 1989. As the sun started to dip on a bright mid-October afternoon, he found the forty-one-year-old doctor waiting for him.

"Man, you look good," Zahorian said, holding out his hand.

"Tryin' to stay healthy for an old man," Dunn replied.

Zahorian ushered him into a chair in his office and asked, "So, what do you think you'll need?"

Dunn launched into a $650 shopping list that included a hundred steroid pills, eighteen vials of injectables, and a couple of hundred painkillers.

"Syringes?" Zahorian asked at the end.

Realizing he was out of practice since he'd gone straight, Dunn quickly added, "Really, yeah, I need some syringes."

"Okay," said the doctor, "I'll throw them in for nothing." Then he added something that piqued the interest of the agents listening. "I'm giving you better prices than *the wrestlers* [emphasis added]. But I know you, okay? I make it worth your while."

On November 17, Zahorian took another $1,000 of Dunn's money for 53 vials of injectable steroids and 500 painkillers. On January 19, 1990, Zahorian agreed to send 90 more vials and 245 more painkillers to Dunn's South Carolina home by Federal Express, this time for $2,000. But that was all just a setup for the mother lode—an order Dunn told Zahorian he wanted to fill that would last him through a trip across Europe.

When Dunn walked into Zahorian's office to collect it in March 1990, he found Zahorian a more nervous man than he'd been before. Thanks to a tip that had been received by the McMahons from a closely guarded source, Zahorian now knew the feds were snooping around his affairs. In fact, the McMahons had told one of their top aides to call him from a pay phone so they wouldn't be recorded, and tell him to move all the records he kept on wrestlers out of his office fast.

"I'm not carrying as much as I used to," Zahorian told Dunn apologetically. "I don't see wrestlers anymore. I don't see anybody. I don't need it. I don't need the aggravation. I mean, they're watching the wrestlers very close. Very close."

Then he leaned into Dunn and said, "You just watch yourself, okay?"

As Dunn nodded, Zahorian filled his arms with a staggering supply of drugs: 60 Vicodins, 1,128 Halcions, 952 Xanax, 48 Limbitrols, 4 vials of testosterone, and 85 Darvocets. In all, Zahorian had sent Dunn off with $25,000 worth of steroids and painkillers—more than he could possibly use in a lifetime.

That was all the feds needed. As soon as Dunn walked into the parking lot, his FBI control agent, trailed by an investigator from the Food and Drug Administration, walked back inside with a search warrant.

Zahorian started shaking when he saw them, and asked the men to wait in the hall outside his office while he called his lawyer. But with the door half open, the men could hear the sounds of paper tearing. "Hey, stop that," the FBI agent said, rushing back in. When he unfurled Zahorian's hand, he found torn Federal Express receipts bearing the name of the WWF's tuxedoed announcer, Lord Alfred Hayes, and its star heel, Rowdy Roddy Piper.

IN THE summer of 1990, Vince stunned his aides with a decision to enter the business of competitive bodybuilding. It wasn't that the idea struck them as narcissistic. They knew Vince was using steroids. His frame, normally stocky, had widened considerably, and his neck and shoulders had ballooned. The boyish look that he'd kept throughout his thirties was giving way to a ruddier one. Age lines had started to creep across his forehead.

What troubled them was that two California brothers named Joe and Ben Weider controlled the business. Why would they want to pick that kind of a fight in a business they had no idea how to market?

The Weider brothers grew up in Montreal in the 1920s and 1930s, where their experiences with anti-Semitism caused them to transform themselves from ninety-pound weaklings into musclemen. They went on to create a multimillion dollar empire that controlled everything from the sport's top magazines to the International Federation of BodyBuilders, which hosts the Mr. Olympia contest, the Super Bowl of the sport.

After Arnold Schwarzenegger retired in 1979, a parade of southern Californians started posing in Weider events with odd-looking bodies built around superdeveloped, almost freakish, parts. One of the biggest names of the post-Arnold eighties was Tom Platz, a Venice Beach native who was famous for monster thirty-six-inch thighs. Platz made a small fortune promoting supplements, posing for magazines, and giving speeches as far away as Sweden. By 1986, the year he retired, he'd become one of the most recognizable faces in his business.

But the business was going through another sea change by then. Uneven, asymmetrically developed bodies like Platz's were being replaced by superbodies, in which every part was as proportionately big as the legs. Muscles rippled out of muscles, bulging through shrink-wrapped skin, all helped by a new generation of growth hormones that were undetectable because they were masked by the body's natural chemicals.

During the summer of 1990, Vince's presence at IFBB competitions created quite a stir, and Platz was among those who assumed he was up to something. When the promoter called Platz to ask if he'd be interested helping launch a new league, he leaped at the chance. By January 1991, Platz had assembled a list of thirteen of the most photogenic and personable bodybuilders he could find. Most had been making less than fifty grand a year competing in the Weiders' events. The McMahons offered them contracts worth at least five times that. After all thirteen signed, they turned themselves over to the image makers at the parent company that Vince and Linda created for the WWF, Titan Sports.

As Platz watched them turned into cartoon characters—like the Rock & Roll Wild Child, the Iron Warrior, and the Flying Dutchman—he quietly thought to himself, "Vince has to know what he's doing, doesn't he?"

Platz didn't want to hear the answer that Nelson Sweglar, Vince's television general manager, had come up with. As Sweglar staged rehearsals for the maiden event of the newly christened World Body-building Federation in June 1991 in Atlantic City, he decided Vince hadn't just misjudged this. Running through the musical numbers (yes, there were musical numbers), he decided that Vince was radically wrong. No one would ever watch bodybuilding the way they did wrestling, no matter how much of a spectacle he tried to turn it into. The average sports fan would think what Sweglar and most of the WWF's hierarchy thought: Watching thirteen oiled-up freaks on steroids posing for two hours was, well, creepy.

THEODORE SMITH III had been a federal prosecutor for just eight months when Bill Dunn's case file was dropped on his desk. A stout thirty-five-year-old with a gut that showed his love for Philly cheese steaks and the pinot noir that he made from the grapes he grew in his backyard, Smith had spent most of his career doing drug cases for the local district attorney's office in Harrisburg, Pennsylvania. When Congress started toughening the federal drug laws and more narcotics cases began flowing into the federal courts, U.S. attorney offices nationwide hired additional staff. Ted Smith was swept into his federal job with that tide. One of the new laws that he was charged with enforcing was the 1988 measure that criminalized the distribution of anabolic steroids. It also moved dozens of drugs—including Tylenol 4 and Valium—onto the Food and Drug Administration's list of controlled substances.

In October 1989, Smith finished listening to the tapes that Dunn had made during his drug buy in Zahorian's medical office and concluded it was one of the stronger hands he'd been dealt. As he'd say later, "It was an unremarkable case with the most remarkable characters I've ever seen." But Smith wasn't about to get cocky, especially when dealing with a doctor. So he waited for investigators from the FBI to slowly build a case.

One of the things the feds did was subpoena the complete records of Zahorian's Federal Express account, and in so doing discovered a regular pattern of shipments to Vince McMahon, Terry Bollea, Roddy Piper, and dozens of other wrestlers on Vince's payroll. Many of the packages were shipped to hotels in cities where the WWF was touring. A dozen more were brazenly sent directly to Titan Tower in Stamford. What was in those packages? Smith subpoenaed a parade of wrestlers, including Piper and Hogan, to answer that question before a federal grand jury. On March 27, 1990, the grand jurors had heard enough to indict Zahorian on fifteen counts of distributing controlled substances, the main one being steroids.

Fortunately for McMahon, the indictment of a pill-pushing doctor in Harrisburg was minor news, and the identities of patients he was accused of supplying were cloaked with John Doe references. The connection between Zahorian and the WWF went entirely unnoticed. It might have stayed that way had Zahorian's attorney not tipped reporters off to the fact that two of those John Does were Hogan and Piper. "The use of steroids isn't limited to these wrestlers," the attorney said on the eve of his client's June 1991 trial. "They're used throughout the WWF. Wrestlers either use them or they don't participate."

That quote, intended to show that Zahorian was simply helping famous athletes get through their taxing work, turned the unassuming little prosecution into a national story overnight. When Zahorian was first indicted, a wave of concern swept through Titan Tower. Vince took the supply of steroids and needles he kept in his office and threw them away. But there was nowhere near the panic that ensued when, on the eve of Zahorian's trial, USA Today ran a headline on its front page asking, "Hulk: Bulk from a Bottle?"

Vince told his lawyer, a bulldog ex–U.S. attorney named Jerry McDevitt, to get Hogan out of testifying. McDevitt appeared before a federal judge named William Caldwell and argued that Smith didn't need Hogan to make his case. He was only listed six times on the FedEx logs, McDevitt argued, far less than Piper. The collateral damage that would be done to the company by unnecessarily singling out Hogan would be immense. Caldwell bought the argument, and McDevitt rushed to his office to dictate a press release that was sent to any reporter who called. "Hulk Hogan did nothing illegal and is not charged with any illegality," it said. "He has no place in this trial, and will not appear there. Instead the focal point of the trial will now return to its proper place, the alleged illegal activities of a physician."

On Monday, June 24, the trial of Dr. George Zahorian began in a small Harrisburg courtroom overrun by reporters. Smith called just nine witnesses, among them Piper, who seemed to have stayed up late the night before because, much to Smith's aggravation, he had a hard time focusing. Fortunately, Smith only needed him on the stand for fifteen minutes, just long enough for this exchange:

"Did you have occasion to call Dr. Zahorian on March 23 of 1990 and ask him for anabolic steroids?"

"Yes," Piper replied. "I did."

"And what did you ask him for?"

"I asked him for some Winstrol, and I believe some Deca-Durabolin, and I'm not sure, maybe an anti-inflammatory, too."

"Did you receive the anabolic steroids you ordered from Dr. Zahorian in California?"

In a low voice, Piper answered. "Yes, sir."

After lunch, Smith rested, confident that it hadn't blown up in his face and his jury had been handed enough evidence to convict. Then, as he sat through a parade of character witnesses who took the stand for Zahorian, he prepared for the doctor to face the jury himself. If Smith had one worry, it was that physicians were skilled persuaders who jurors intuitively wanted to trust. If Zahorian did a good job portraying himself as a physician who felt compelled to help wrestlers in pain, that could hurt Smith's case.

"I knew these individuals," the bow-tied doctor began calmly. "I treated these individuals. I had carried out physicals and histories on them. They were taking minimal amounts of medication that was given to them in minimal doses. I knew it wasn't going to harm them. Over the ten years that I knew most of the individuals, not one was sick, not one developed anything that stopped them from wrestling."

Smith worried about the last point. It was the doctor's one reasonable claim. He prayed the jury would not get sidetracked on it. It was a legal blind alley.

The jurors got the case at 1:30 in the afternoon on June 25. Three hours later they told the judge they had a verdict. Smith felt a pit opening in his stomach. Quick verdicts were usually acquittals. Juries that were about to send someone to jail generally took longer, if only out of guilt.

So Smith let out a long breath when the foreman announced that the jury had found Zahorian guilty of the first count of illegally dispensing steroids, and then said guilty to eleven more.

The next day, every major newspaper in the country covered the conviction and the trial's damning disclosures about steroid use in the WWF. As he read the stories, McMahon winced. He was addicted all right, but not to steroids. He was addicted to pay-per-views. And he could imagine what Zahorian's allegations were going to do to his business.

Since 1985, the WWF had slowly been weaning itself off closed circuit and onto pay-per-view. The $350 it cost to get a satellite feed to a television cable provider was considerably cheaper than the $5,000 it cost to rent a closed-circuit theater, not to mention an arena. Because the profit margins were enormous—the WWF could charge $15 to $25 per airing and keep roughly half after paying off its cable partners—McMahon decided to produce a trinity of new pay-per-views to add to *Wrestlemania*: *Royal Rumble* would air in January, *Summer Slam* in August, and *Survivor Series* in November.

That decision would earn him the label of visionary in the still nascent world of alternative distribution. By quadrupling his pay-per-view product, he was creating an industry out of the shards of a few boxing matches and his annual *Wrestlemania* show. Before too long, Turner would follow suit, and the two companies would be running pay-per-views every month, bringing in hundreds of millions of dollars in revenue. The only thing McMahon's aides would lament was that he wasn't more ambitious. If he was, he could have bought out the cable operators that were providing the linkups and become the owner of the industry, instead of its most sought-after content provider.

However, that discussion was still far off. McMahon had other, more immediate things to worry about. Quarterly pay-per-views created a domino effect. Before, he could spend a whole year leading up to *Wrestlemania*. Now he needed to have story arcs that peaked every three months, driving his USA cable television viewers to reach into their pockets to see the climax on pay-per-view. It was a relatively simple strategy, but it required two things: well-thought-out story lines and the stars to sell them.

Unfortunately, just as McMahon was mapping all this out, the steroid allegations were peaking and Hogan was deciding to take a sabbatical from wrestling to explore an acting career.

Needing a new marquee face, Vince started pushing a newcomer, Jim Hellwig. In the era of Rambo, Hellwig wore jungle-combat face paint and tied tassels around his biceps. On stage, he used the name Ultimate Warrior, but behind his back the Boys called him Anabolic Warrior for all the steroids it took to gain him his superhuman frame.

On April 1, 1990, Vince got Hogan to help with an orderly transition by losing his heavyweight belt to Hellwig at *Wrestlemania VI*. More than sixty-four thousand fans turned up at the SkyDome in Toronto to see the two giants square off. Although Hellwig was a poor technical wrestler, Hogan gave him the kind of star send-off that made him look positively daunting. Writing in his *Wrestling Observer*, Dave Meltzer dubbed it Hogan's finest bout.

But over the rest of the year, Hellwig had difficulty stepping up his profile. His Rambo act wore thin, and he couldn't seem to connect with the crowds. Thus Vince decided it was time to restore Hogan to the top of his card for *Wrestlemania VII*. But this time, his instincts for what the public wanted had been blunted by the drug investigation. The man who'd produced such insouciant sketch comedy on *Tuesday*

Night Titans was in a darker mood. He ordered Hellwig to lose his title to the square-jawed Sergeant Slaughter, who was ordered to play an Iraqi sympathizer at the height of the Persian Gulf War, at the *Royal Rumble* in January 1991. (Their meeting came four days after the U.N. deadline for Iraq to withdraw from Kuwait.) Slaughter's turnabout act was supposed to give Hogan a pretext to take back the title at *Wrestlemania* as a superpatriot, much as he had against the Iron Sheik seven years before. But there was none of the earlier innocence of Hogan's debut in the WWF. Quite the opposite. Slaughter was getting death threats that caused him to fear for his life when McMahon asked him to burn an American flag in the ring. Slaughter refused, not that the stunt would have helped much. The story line was so poorly received that Vince had to move the pay-per-view event from the outdoor Los Angeles Coliseum, where he thought he could sell more than a hundred thousand tickets, to a nearby arena that was a fifth of the size.

Now that Hogan was being dragged through the mud, accused of being a steroid addict, Vince saw his company under the kind of attack from which it might not recover. If he wanted to save it, he'd need to go on a public relations offensive.

The opening salvo came with an op-ed piece in the sports section of the *New York Times* on Sunday, July 14, in which he announced that he was going to start testing his wrestlers for steroids. Three days after the media had a chance to mull that over, he walked briskly into the Terrace Room at the Plaza Hotel in Manhattan, dressed sharply in a gray suit and a green necktie. Wine-colored velvet curtains hung in the background, lit by eight-foot floor lamps that sprouted golden candelabras from a marble base. Marble archways framed the stage with a flowered carpet underfoot. Before twenty reporters, he contritely conceded that yes, he'd used steroids. But it was only once, he insisted, and in the late eighties. As Associated Press writer John Nelson observed, "This was a place for high society and tea parties. Not Haystack Calhouns.... But there was no doubt that Vince was making a serious effort to gain our trust."

McMahon would have preferred to leave things there, but Hogan insisted on making his own appearance later that night on a talk show hosted by the comic Arsenio Hall. Looking dewy-eyed at his host, Hogan also made a concession: He'd taken a synthetic hormone three times, but just to get over a shoulder injury. Incredulous that anyone might question his integrity, he took out a picture of himself as a twelve-year-old Little Leaguer. "I trained twenty years, two hours a day to look like I do, Arsenio," he said. "I am not a steroids abuser and I do not use steroids."

Ted Smith happened to be cooking shrimp at home when the show aired. Watching Hogan lie, he shook his head in complete disgust.

SEVEN

THE STEROID ALLEGATIONS CONSUMING the WWF in the summer of 1991 were ratings death. The company's Saturday night cable rating on USA declined by 16 percent, and, with Hulk Hogan in self-imposed exile, its house show attendance was down by a third. It was the perfect time for Turner's two-year-old investment in Georgia Championship Wrestling, which had been renamed World Championship Wrestling, to pay off. But as everyone from Turner on down in his organization had learned, wrestling wasn't like any other kind of programming they did.

For one thing, it fit uneasily in a corporate culture where the heads of CNN, the Headline News Network, TBS, and TNT already felt as if they had to fight for respect among the big three networks. Men like Tom Johnson, the former *Los Angeles Times* publisher who ran the Cable News Network, blanched at sharing an organizational chart with wrestlers. While McMahon drew most of the heat for running a company built on steroids, Turner's top executives only had to look in the commissary line to see men like Rick Rude, a surly shitkicker who took so many steroids that his heart would give out when he turned forty. Turner had just sunk $44 million into the 1990 Goodwill Games as part of a continuing quest to fashion himself into a global ambassador of athletic ideals. Those executives weren't about to have men slicing their heads open with razors and gushing blood on the Superstation. And, to some extent, Turner agreed with their caution. Wrestling was a source of ratings for him, not a crusade. That was why, soon after taking over the company in 1989, he had asked his vice president of syndication, Jack Petrik, to run it. On paper the appointment made sense. Petrik was a turnaround expert and knew the syndication world. But he was just four years away from retirement and had little interest investing much of his personal or budgetary capital in the little orphaned division. So he'd handed WCW to an old friend by the name of Jim Herd, who'd once run the St. Louis television station KPLR. Since KPLR carried Sam Muchnick's *Wrestling from the Chase*, Petrik assumed that Herd knew about wrestling. Herd assumed the same thing, projecting a well-mannered assurance when he met Turner for the first time. They'd barely sat down to lunch in October 1988 when Turner said, "Why don't we get some big broad and have her whip the hell out of all the guys."

"You can't do that," a slightly stunned Herd replied. "We need a legitimate look."

"You can't?" Turner replied, disappointed.

Herd ushered the show out of its cramped home in TBS's studios and into a warmer Shakespearean theater a few blocks away. He also paid for a more elaborate set complete with indoor pyrotechnics—the first time they were put to such use. But as the weeks passed, Herd came to realize that he had few allies at TBS beyond his old friend Petrik. When he asked Turner Sports to run promos for his pay-per-views, he was given a cold shoulder. When he requisitioned time on one of CNN's sets so he could film a mock wrestling news show, he got a call from a furious CNN executive who yelled, "You will not belittle our organization." Any request for cross-promotion was a war. The welcome mat was out, but the door was closed.

Herd decided that he needed a way of getting Turner's attention, not to mention a locker-room emissary who could keep the twenty wrestlers who hated him away from the twenty who didn't. For that he turned to Ric Flair.

Flair had rolled into Charlotte in 1974 after driving in from Minnesota and never looked back. He seemed to come fully formed, with a trademark war cry that once heard was unforgettable. It started deep inside of him, and by the time it rose through his lungs, his cry of "Whooooo!" sounded like the whiskey-drenched scream of a hillbilly who'd shot himself in the foot. Playing every small town from Atlanta to Miami, Flair picked up nicknames like Nature Boy, Slick Ric, and Space Mountain (as in: "Space Mountain may be the oldest ride in the park but it still has the longest line, *whooooo!*").

When Jimmy Crockett started gaining power in the NWA and demanded that his position be recognized by having a world champion drawn from Charlotte, the NWA's bosses agreed to vote in Flair. A hard-line believer in kayfabe, he didn't acknowledge to anyone, not even his to kids, that what he did was fake. He figured that there was nothing fake about the blood blisters he left the ring with every night, the gashed foreheads that streaked his blond hair red, or the cartilage that rattled around his knees.

But despite the years he'd invested in the NWA, Flair was ambivalent about remaining in Atlanta. The star makers in Stamford had helped get Hulk Hogan a line of lunch boxes, a cartoon on CBS, and a movie. What had the NWA given Flair? A reputation as the all-time greatest wrestler among an increasingly irrelevant audience of little old ladies and lunch-bucket true believers. Herd's internal research told him everything he needed to know about where the business was going. The new war was being waged over eight- to ten-year-old boys. The question was whether a forty-year-old man from another era could adapt.

Surprisingly, Flair and Herd started off the year of 1989 with promise. Flair talked up one of his oldest friends, the veteran Ricky Steamboat, and Herd flew to Charlotte to sign him. Steamboat was what bookers called a *cherry*, a handsome, wholesome babyface with wide-set eyes and chiseled muscles. He was a student of the craft, too, an artist who studied boxing matches so he could imitate what it looked like to stagger back after being hit, with air whooshing from the lungs and the eye squinting from being poked. As the two men came to know one another in the seventies, their plays became increasingly intricate, jockeying between sadism and surrender.

When Herd reunited them it was as if no time had passed at all. They started with a match in Chicago that included twenty-four two-counts over twenty minutes and reached a crescendo when Steamboat climbed to the top rope and flew off, twisting his body in midair so that he took out Flair *and the referee* when he landed. They went at it so hard a few weeks later in New Orleans that by the end of the fifty-five-minute match, Steamboat feigned being unable even to stand over the laid-out Flair, letting his legs give out beneath him.

Once Herd saw that Flair and Steamboat had reached their absolute peaks, he added a new character—a forty-five-year-old Texas brawler named Terry Funk. Where Steamboat was pretty and athletic, Funk, who'd held the world title fifteen years earlier, looked like a ferret, with a body covered by scars from barbed-wire slashes and one too many chicken-wire matches. Knowing his job was to get down and dirty, Funk waited until Flair had pinned Steamboat to reclaim the title in Nashville in May 1989, then rushed into the ring, grabbed Flair by his trunks, and drilled him headfirst with a *piledriver* into a table at ringside. Chaos ensued as Flair was carted off to a local hospital. Over the next few weeks, fans saw brilliantly taped spots of Flair in his recovery bed, threatening every manner of revenge. Herd was so excited about Flair's return in July that he went to the Maryland Athletic Commission to ask for a waiver of an AIDS-inspired law that banned excessive bleeding from sporting events. He got what he wanted, and so did the 150,000 fans who bought Flair's return match on pay-per-view. After the men spent a half hour pummeling each other from pillar to post, Flair limped to victory covered in blood.

Herd was on a roll and started experimenting with ways to make the violence seem more real. In a famous bout that would come to be known as the "I Quit" match, he gave the referee a cordless microphone, and when Funk gave Flair one of his piledrivers, the sound of Flair's head crashing to the mat reverberated into the cheap seats. The two went on to whip each other like dogs until finally, as Funk slid through the ropes, across a table, and to the cold concrete floor, he screamed, "I quit." The match was seen in 3.3 million homes, tying a record for the most-watched match in cable.

Unfortunately, not everyone at CNN Center shared Herd's euphoria about the ratings. At TBS, an executive who allowed the word "damn" to go out over the air could expect to find a reprimand in his or her personnel file. When Funk pretended to asphyxiate Flair with a bag in another of their struggles, Herd found a memo on his desk the next morning telling him to come to the fourteenth floor posthaste. "You can't goddamn choke people with plastic bags," Turner yelled as soon as Herd walked in. "We have kids watching."

But by then, Funk was also starting to run his course. And because the WWF was in the midst of a muscular offensive—in effect daring the WCW to match it bicep for bicep—Herd decided Flair should lose to Lex Luger (Larry Pfohl), the biggest body in his arsenal. Unfortunately, Flair had a clause in his contract giving him final say over how he dropped his title belt. Insisting that it was beneath him to lose to Luger, Flair demanded that Herd either scrap the idea or release Flair from his contract, freeing him to sign with the WWF.

Herd was furious. After an aide got into a screaming match with Flair, he asked how it had ended. Told that the two men had settled their differences, he groused, "God damn it, none of my prayers are ever answered. I was hoping that son of a bitch would get his lights punched out." Still, Herd couldn't fathom explaining to Turner how he'd let his favorite wrestler fall into McMahon's hands. So he folded, agreeing to let Flair drop the belt to Steve "Sting" Borden, a budding superstar from California.

If the misadventure taught Herd anything, it was that you needed more than just a couple of big names to avoid being held hostage by your talent. But creating wrestlers was a more subtle science than it first appeared. Herd gathered focus groups. He commissioned surveys. He even tried creating a few acts of his own. (One day he stunned his booking committee by saying, "Let's get a tag team with humps. We'll call them the Hunchbacks. It'll be great because they'll never get pinned!") After the July 1990 match that moved the title from Flair to Sting, Borden was finally paired with what looked to be a promising creation—a masked ghost from his past who appeared from the rafters in puffs of fire and smoke to taunt him. Inexplicably, a different actor played the masked Scorpion at each taping. (At house shows it was worse; the mask was handed to any available body without regard to talent.) A bogus cliff-hanger promising an unmasking didn't help: Sting ripped off Scorpion's black mask to reveal a red one while the "real" Scorpion cackled over a loudspeaker from the wings. By the time of *Starrcade* in December, there was so little life left to the angle that Flair was hastily inserted to end it. But even that surprise ending was a bust. There was no mistaking that the long flowing blond hair beneath the mask belonged to Flair. A month later at the Meadowlands in New Jersey, the Scorpion angle was history and Flair was given the belt back for a seventh time after pinning Sting.

Frustrated beyond measure, Herd did something he would sorely regret. He picked up the phone and called Dusty Rhodes.

Rhodes failed to make the transition into TBS with the other Crockett alumni (he was fired), and he blamed Flair for it. The men had barely spoken since the last days of the Crockett empire, when Rhodes kept Flair on an embarrassing losing streak with the notorious *Dusty finish*. In the interim, Rhodes went to work for Vince McMahon and allowed himself to be cast as a buffoon. When he wasn't being portrayed as a plumber with his head in toilets, he was sent into the ring wearing unflattering polka-dot suits, often with a chunky fifty-five-year-old African American valet named Sapphire beside him. It wasn't just a matter of Vince indulging his passion for humiliating ex-NWA belt holders whenever he could. It was, Rhodes's friends decided, the worst case they'd ever seen of someone willing to mortgage the last bits of his pride to stay in the limelight.

But the call from Herd proved there would always be a hapless executive who could be conned. So Rhodes arrived in Atlanta early in 1991 with a bevy of his own acolytes to run things. He quickly holed himself up in an office down the hall from Herd and, like a writer possessed, started throwing off ideas. He sent three wrestlers out into the West for location shoots where they met odd and often funny characters. He dressed a six-foot-ten, 305-pound former Tennessee basketball center named Kevin Nash as Oz and introduced him into the ring with midgets as Munchkins and a monkey that couldn't control its bladder.

Most of all, Rhodes decided he wanted a whole lot less of Ric Flair. First he told Flair that he wanted him to cut his hair and change his act, turning from a heel into a babyface. When Flair resisted, Rhodes paired him with a clumsy, seven-foot-five Argentinean named El Gigante. And finally, when Flair was starting negotiations to extend his contract, Rhodes told him he needed to think about cutting back. How much? Flair asked suspiciously. In half, came the answer.

Flair balked and once again threatened to decamp to the WWF. This time, Rhodes told Herd, "Let him go. We'll be stronger without him." Herd was getting uncomfortable with the power Rhodes was amassing, but he agreed they had no choice. Calling Flair's attorney, he said there would be no more negotiations. He was free to leave.

It never occurred to Herd to ask Flair to return the WCW title belt first.[1]

When Flair turned up on the USA Network the following October wearing the WCW belt in a WWF ring, Herd got a sinking feeling. He knew Turner would hear about it first thing in the morning, if not sooner. He also knew he had a contract of his own that was due to expire in two months. The next morning, Herd took the CNN Center elevator up to the fourteenth floor and marched into Jack Petrik's suite.

"Jack, this has gone too far," he started, summing up his view that Flair's defection was part of a larger pattern of costly power plays and misjudgments by Rhodes. "Dusty is out of control. It's either him or me."

---

1. Through the politics of the business, Flair ended up keeping the original NWA belt, for which he had posted a $25,000 deposit with the secretary-treasurer of the NWA, like other champions had done in the past. However, when Crockett sold the remnants of the NWA to Ted Turner, the money that Flair had put up—wherever it resided on the accounting ledger—was considered part of the sale. From day one, Flair had insisted he was owed the money with interest, since it was traditionally returned when the champion lost the belt. But since he never received the money, he kept the belt.

Looking at his old friend's face, Herd knew that the decision had already been made. He'd lost $19 million in three years.

"Okay," he said finally. "I guess it's me."

BILL WATTS walked into CNN Center seven months later, in May 1992, dressed in blue jeans, cowboy boots, and his Stetson. Looking up the atrium that rose all the way up to Turner's office, he thought, "Wonder what it would be like to take a piss off there."

Watts was invited to Atlanta by the new man Turner had selected to run World Championship Wrestling, Bill Shaw. A young-looking fifty-three-year-old, Shaw had worked his way up the ladder of the human resources department and now oversaw all of Turner's buildings, including the Omni Coliseum, where wrestling shows were held. His office was precisely 143 feet away from Turner's, and that was exactly the kind of fact that a man who specialized in running operations would know.

Shaw may not have been steeped in wrestling, but he knew the name Bill Watts. The Cowboy was still a giant in the business and probably the best television producer for wrestling around. If anything, that reputation had been burnished by the five years he'd spent in exile in Tulsa since selling his ill-fated Universal Wrestling Federation.

In someone's attic lay old black-and-white photographs of the Cowboy when he had a cleft chin, Charles Atlas muscles, and a corn-fed smile. But that wasn't the man who was sitting before Shaw—the man who'd spent the past five years peddling insurance and marketing vitamins. This one had a wide patch of baldness running down the middle of his head, glasses that magnified his narrow eyes, and a desk-job belly.

Those looks, however, were deceiving. Watts was a soldier stuck in peaceful society and had the hungry look that Shaw had seen before. It was the desperate look men get in their fifties when they worry they're no longer in control of their own destiny.

Shaw was prepared for Watts to be an atypical Turnerite. He rode his motorcycle to work, flouted the starched-shirt-and-tie dress code, and farted in the middle of his sentences, just to show that he could. There were also things Shaw wouldn't anticipate, such as the fact that Watts would call women cunts, smoke a joint or two on his balcony, and take the occasional piss into the parking lot. But Shaw was on a mission to turn a sick company around. The typical WCW arena event attracted fewer than twenty-five hundred fans and grossed just $25,000—roughly a third of WWF shows. He'd promised the TBS board of directors that WCW wouldn't "lose over a million eight again this year," and he was serious. He needed a bastard to get things in order. And Cowboy was the biggest bastard around.

Watts reported for work in early June and, before his first television taping, gathered his wrestlers at the Center Stage Theater to tell them how things would be changing. Real wrestling was reactive, he told them. It was thinking on your feet, throwing in surprises, being spontaneous. It wasn't memorizing the same damned dozen moves night after night until the whole thing looked choreographed. This New York style was a fad. If they just stayed with him, they'd all win in the long run. Then he began describing what he called his Ten Commandments. The first thing to go was going to be mats outside the ring. Not only did they make the show look fake, they encouraged guys to throw each other through the ropes and waste time. There would be no low blows or lewd hand gestures, no guests in the dressing rooms, and no fraternization among heels and babyfaces in public. Acrobatic leaps off the top of the ring rope were out, too. He wanted his boys to stay inside the ropes. He wanted them hungry. They found out how literally he meant it when they showed up at the next taping on Saturday afternoon to find that the usual preshow buffet had been scrapped in favor of boxed airline lunches.

If surveys guided the brass at TBS, faith and vanity guided the Cowboy. If he was going to reinvent WCW, he needed young wrestlers whom he could mold, teach, and bloody up for cheap. He needed men who could help him remake WCW in his image. In other words, he needed his son, Erik Watts.

The quarterback from the University of Louisville had earned his bachelor's degree in three years and was halfway to an M.B.A. when he decided to take a summer off and enroll in the WCW's suburban Atlanta training gym, the Power Plant. He still had nine days to go in its thirty-day program when the call came from the front office, telling him he was being sent on a Tennessee swing through Knoxville, Nashville, and Bristol for the weekend. He'd barely unpacked after coming home when the front office called again, this time with a contract to appear on television.

Wrestling locker rooms are full of second- and third-generation grapplers, and no one begrudged Cowboy's kid a shot at the big time. But the Boys were understandably resentful when Erik showed up at the Center Stage Theater with one weekend's worth of experience. They were being asked to bust their asses to help make the neophyte into a star while the cost-cutting ax hung over their own careers. Some were better natured about it than others. A five-year veteran of the business from Dallas named Steve Williams may have groused, "Goddamn, you're not ready for me." But once he saw himself penciled in against the boss's son, the man better known as Steve Austin muttered, "As long as I have to fling your sorry ass around all night, we might as well get it right."

Rick Rude wasn't that patient. The surly Minnesotan was as big a star as the industry had in the mid-eighties; he was among the first to chisel his chest and sculpt his arms with steroids. Part thug, part gigolo, he once entered the ring with the face of Jake Roberts's wife painted on the crotch of his spandex pants. But Rude fell into the trap of believing his own act. By the early 1990s, he was taking so many steroids that he was as miserable out of the ring as he acted inside it.

In New Orleans one night, Rude was sitting in the corner of the locker room, dressed in a silk shirt and slacks, his trademark cigarette dangling from his lower lip. "I'm sick and tired of hearing all this bull-shit about amateur wrestling," he grumbled to no one in particular. Then he mentioned that the evening before, a friend who'd once been a champion amateur wrestler couldn't tip him when they sparred. "No man can turn me over," Rude boasted.

Out of nowhere, the following words welled up in Erik's throat: "Well, your friend must not have been very good." As soon as he said them, he instantly regretted that he had. The locker room was filled with men who wanted to kick the shit out of him in the best of cir-cumstances. Now he noticed them slowly gathering around, backing him toward Rude.

The young Watts tried backpedaling as fast as he could, but Rude would have none of it. He tossed off his expensive leather loafers, got on his hands and knees, and challenged the rookie to turn him over. Erik wanted to be anywhere else at that moment, but he also realized that he'd do himself far more damage by retreating. So he rolled his arm under Rude's belly, counted to four, and flipped him completely. Rude rose, his face crimson, and insisted that he wasn't ready. Watts did it again with the same result. This time Rude placed his shoes back on, brushed himself off, and left the room. To hear the young Watts tell it, Rude was so mad that night that he picked a fight with a fan and broke his jaw. Of course, it's entirely plausible that one had nothing to do with the other. Rude carried around enough rage that he could break jaws when he was in a good mood. But when he got back to Atlanta, he had a screaming match with the Cowboy, insisting he wasn't going to be a baby-sitter anymore. He even packed a revolver in his boot for the meeting, mindful that Erik's father carried a loaded pistol in his briefcase. Watts didn't need to fire his gun. He fired Rude instead. He wasn't about to be bullied by any has-been steroid hag.

With each new week, another star followed the same path. Scott Steiner quit after Watts ran out of patience with his costly fetish for hurting newcomers by dropping them on their heads from the top rope. Paul E. Dangerously (the stage name of Paul Heyman), leader of the Dangerous Alliance, was fired for expense fraud. (He strenuously denied the charge.) Arn Anderson, a veteran heel, was axed because he was told he looked too old. By fall, Cowboy Bill had cut the company's payroll by 25 percent, and he was just getting warmed up. Paranoia was starting to creep in everywhere—which, of course, was just the way he wanted it. He was going to burn the village to save it.

He might have, too, if it was truly his village to burn. But the regular phone calls from Shaw reminded him otherwise. Without Rude or Steiner, Lex Luger or Sid Vicious, the average Saturday night rating had fallen to 2.04 from its 2.53 mark of a year earlier. Pay-per-view buy rates were down by 40 percent. Watts was sure that if he could just get to Turner—just get past Shaw's office and bridge a few of those 143 feet—he could make Ted understand that they were on the right track.

But every time he tried to get close, he found a door locked, an aide shunting Turner in another direction, or Shaw standing in the way. And on February 9, 1993, a fax came into Henry Aaron's office at CNN Center that made sure he never would.

Aaron was already in a horrible mood when his secretary handed the fax to him. He was stewing about an interview in which Cincinnati Reds owner Marge Schott called two of her ex-players "million dollar niggers." After Schott's comments made national news, Aaron argued loud and hard that baseball needed to take a clear stand. He wanted Schott banned from the sport and baseball to make a clear commitment to its minority players. Toward that end, he lobbied for himself to be named to the vacant commissioner's post. So it stunned Aaron when a panel of owners recommended a slap on the wrist for Schott: a one-year suspension and $25,000 fine. Aaron saw it as an insult to himself and to all black players. The sting of that insult was only ten days old when he started to read the fax sent to him by a sportswriter working on a story about Bill Watts.

A year before Watts came to TBS, he allowed an extensive interview to be published in a weekly wrestling newsletter called *Pro Wrestling Torch*. Few who knew Watts believed he was a racist. At worst, he affected a kind of frontier libertarianism that allowed him to bluster on about free will. Except this time, he blustered too much, lapsing into a phobic stream of consciousness.

"If you own a business why shouldn't you be able to discriminate?" he asked rhetorically. "I mean, why should I have to hire a fucking fag if I don't like fags?" On the subject of African Americans he hardly sounded more enlightened: "If I don't want to sell fried chicken to blacks, I shouldn't have to. It's my restaurant."

It's hard to believe the interview was not read before Watts was hired, though Shaw insists he never saw it. Watts insists it had been vetted and excused. But maybe he just assumed that since there always seemed to be someone around to defend him as an eccentric genius. Unfortunately for the Cowboy, there was no one left to apologize for him when Aaron finished reading the interview.

Since Aaron reported to Shaw, he walked the interview over to Shaw's office. He did not ask that Watts be fired. He simply asked that Shaw look into the matter. That's when Shaw called Watts and asked him to stop up and see him.

"I don't deny what I said," Watts said calmly, "but anyone who thinks I'm a bigot is an idiot." Then, seeing Shaw's cool expression, Watts realized he'd never get closer to Ted Turner than he was right now. "You know what, Bill?" he said. "I'm done with this damned business. You take it from here."

EIGHT

A MONTH BEFORE BILL Watts left Atlanta, an assistant U.S. attorney from New York drove down Interstate 95 to meet his federal colleague, Ted Smith, in Pennsylvania.

After Smith had won the conviction of George Zahorian, he'd thought long and hard about whether he had enough evidence to mount a case against Vince McMahon. And he'd decided against it. First, there was the venue issue: Nothing happened in the middle district of Pennsylvania, centered in Harrisburg, to tie McMahon to a crime. But just as important, the whole thing had become a circus that he felt no need to join. Superstar Billy Graham, for one, had given him fits by telling reporters that Smith had begged Graham to wear a concealed body recorder wire in an FBI probe of mob links to wrestling. To quell the bogus rumor, Smith's boss took the rare step of authoring a letter to Vince's attorney in which he denied being "aware of any connection between McMahon and the Mafia."

But if Smith's interest in McMahon was on the wane, the colleague who drove to see him on the morning of January 4, 1993, was another story. Sean O'Shea, the head of the Business and Securities Fraud section of the U.S. attorney's office in Brooklyn, believed McMahon was guilty of a lot more than bad taste. And he'd been calling wrestlers into a grand jury back home to prove it.

O'Shea, who was in his mid-thirties, worked for one of the leading U.S. attorney's offices in the country, one that had distinguished itself by disassembling the mob hierarchy in New York through the convictions of John Gotti and the bosses of the Bonanno and Colombo crime families. It was also known for fearlessly attacking public corruption—winning, for instance, a fraud conviction against the speaker of the New York State Assembly. By having a grand jury investigate McMahon, O'Shea was putting him in some fairly select criminal company.

Smith opened his records to the prosecutor, showing him an accordion file thick with notes he'd accumulated. But as Smith recalled it, the conversation was one-sided. O'Shea was circumspect about the work he and his grand jury were doing. Of course, Smith had his guesses. It wasn't hard to guess, considering all that had transpired with the World Wrestling Federation in the prior year.

HOMOSEXUALITY AND wrestling have been bedfellows since Gorgeous George, trailed by his perfume-pumping valet, played on his audiences' homophobia in the 1940s. Jim Barnett, one of the most influential promoters of the last fifty years, was rumored to have had a torrid affair with Rock Hudson when he was living in Louisville in the 1950s. But to be gay in wrestling was also to be wary of being too open about it. For every Gorgeous George there were thirty Cowboy Bills, men who considered homosexuality as good a reason as any to start a fight. That created a strange, often paradoxical assignment for gay men in wrestling. They understood, even nurtured, the homoeroticism of the business. But they also had to watch audiences jeer and humiliate the effeminate characters sent into the ring. By the early nineties, those jeers had become more open than ever. When a tag team called the Bushwhackers met a prissy pair called the Beverly Brothers, adolescent boys in the audience shouted "faggot" until their throats were hoarse.

One of the men who had a key role in writing those scripts was Pat Patterson, who wrestled in the 1960s under the name Pretty Pat. The Montreal native was a staple of the McMahon family's Greenwich-Boca social axis and a constant presence at Vince's side. Patterson, who was openly gay, went to work each day with the expectation that his private life would be treated as just that: something private. But in February 1992, he watched it made public in the most humiliating possible way. A twenty-nine-year-old announcer named Murray Hodgson filed a lawsuit that claimed he'd been fired after spurning one of Patterson's advances. Those who'd spent time around Vince's right-hand man regarded the charge as implausible, and the suit received little notice until an investigative reporter from San Diego who was working on a story about drugs in wrestling got wind of it. In pursuing the rumors, reporter Jeff Savage learned that another WWF employee, this one a ring boy, claimed to have been fired for spurning the advances of one of Patterson's aides.

Ring boys are mostly fans who show up at arenas on the day of the show looking for work. In the WWF, one of the men who supervised them was a road agent and a friend of Patterson's, Terry Garvin. Like Patterson, with whom he worked in the WWF front office, Garvin was a gay ex-wrestler from Quebec. But unlike Patterson, Garvin wasn't discreet about his lifestyle. He used his job to arrange trysts for himself and saw no reason to be particularly secretive about it. Nelson Sweglar, then the company's operations manager, remembers walking into a bus and seeing Garvin, whom he found likable, "hard at it" with a ring boy.

"Everyone knew what was going on, but it would have taken someone within the brotherhood to have moved on it. And none of the people who knew about it moved on it," Sweglar says. "The general corporate culture was that there were these two worlds, the professional world of those of us who worked on the TV product, and the wrestling gang. And Vince always identified with the wrestlers. Many of them were unmarried without family, and they picked up sex here and there. After ten years of incredible success, a lot of the guys felt like they could get away with just about anything. Its people kept its own secrets. And the corporate culture said you had to be really careful about crossing that line."

But Savage was about to expose one of the most lurid of them all. Garvin's assistant had an address book with the names of kids around the country that he'd call on when the WWF hit their town. They were usually kids from broken homes whose parents would be only too glad to send them off to do a day's work. One of them was a slightly built New Yorker named Tom Cole. Garvin had taken enough of an interest in the boy to offer him a full-time job.

Cole had barely started work as a warehouse clerk when Garvin asked the nineteen-year-old to join him on a quick ride to his suburban

Connecticut home. As the teen remembered it, he was surprised the house was empty when they got there, with no sign of Garvin's wife and two kids. Garvin sat Cole down in the living room and started going over the dates of upcoming shows, asking him if he wanted to go to this place or that. Then, rising, he turned on his television and pretended to be casual about the fact that an adult movie was flickering across the screen.

"Has your girlfriend sucked your dick like that?" Cole remembered him asking. "Let me suck your dick like that."

"Look, man. I don't want any part of this," Cole said, rising to his feet. "I want to go now."

But it was snowing heavily outside, and Garvin replied, "I don't know if I can take you." So Cole made a makeshift bed in the van parked in the driveway. The next morning he was dropped off at the warehouse, only to learn he'd been fired.

The outlines of Cole's allegations appeared at the bottom of a lengthy story that carried Savage's byline in the March 11, 1992, edition of the *San Diego News Tribune*. Two days later, Vince was on CNN's *Larry King Live*, rebutting it.

"Are you thinking they're all jumping on top of you now for some reason?" King asked. "This is all coming together? I mean, why you? Why now?"

"I have no idea. I have no idea. I mean..."

Before he could finish, King switched to a guest on the phone—a former WWF wrestler named Barry Orton who claimed that Garvin also accosted him in Texas in 1978, when he was just nineteen.

"Barry," King asked, "why didn't we know about this sooner? Fourteen years ago when you were accosted, why didn't you come forward?"

Just then a third guest, Bruno Sammartino, interrupted King and Orton. "Larry, tell him who the man was," he said. Then, realizing he'd addressed the wrong man, he hastily added, "I mean, not Larry—I beg your pardon, Barry."

"You're a little confused, aren't you, Bruno," McMahon jumped in, a trace of a smile playing around the edge of his lips. It was the kind of deflection he did masterfully, and as the night wore on he kept doing it, making his accusers look bumbling and unsure. Yet he also knew that he couldn't have too many more nights like this one. Tom Cole needed to be muzzled.

The next Monday, Orton and McMahon met face to face, this time for an appearance on the most-watched talk show in America, *Donahue*. As he sipped warm coffee in the green room, Orton felt something fishy was going on. He and Cole spoke regularly, but he hadn't heard from him all weekend. Backstage, Orton turned to another invited guest, the *Wrestling Observer*'s Dave Meltzer, and said, "Something's not right. Vince is up to something." He was dead-on. Unbeknownst to either man, Cole's brother had hired a lawyer to strike a settlement with the WWF. The deal gave Cole a new job at the WWF and $150,000 in back pay, two thirds of which went to his lawyer. In the fold once again, Cole agreed to accompany Linda McMahon to the taping and sit with her in the fifth row of the audience as the show unfolded. After the taping ended, Lee Cole accompanied his brother down to the stage. As reporter Jeff Savage would recount in an article in *Penthouse*, Lee told the producer, "This show was bullshit. There's only one guy here who cares and it's that guy."

Savage followed Cole's pointing finger to Vince McMahon.[1]

IN THE daytime talk show world, one of the people who wasn't going to be outdone when it came to reporting scandals was Geraldo Rivera. He had the ability and the manpower to leap on a story he loved. And he loved this story. What he especially loved was that his team had found the most sensational allegation yet: that McMahon was being accused of rape.

The accuser was Rita Chatterton, who'd worked for the WWF in the early years, when Vince was first taking over the company and *Tuesday*

---

1. Any good feelings didn't last long. Within a year, Cole found himself released from the WWF once again. When he went to collect unemployment, he says the WWF fought the request, with Linda personally attending the seventh and final hearing in which he finally received benefits.

Night Titans was still the rage. She called herself Rita Marie then and was a struggling bookkeeper with one daughter and a dead-end job at Frito-Lay. Vince turned her into one of his cheesecake girls, giving her a layout in the WWF's pulp magazine and a job as his first female referee. Did the two also have an affair? There are harder things to believe. Around that time, he was known to be carrying on several extramarital relationships. But Chatterton didn't allege that when she met with Geraldo's aides. What she alleged was that Vince hoisted her on top of him in the back of his limo and sexually abused her.

Taken in conjunction with the other allegations, it was a devastating charge. So devastating that the Geraldo team hurriedly stitched it into a feature for their syndicated show, *Now It Can Be Told*. The show also featured Murray Hodgson; a ring ref who was coming forward to allege that Garvin offered him $500 for sex; and Sammartino and Orton, both of whom repeated their charges that Vince knew and turned a blind eye.

Being accused of letting subordinates run the WWF as a personal sex shop was one thing. After Garvin and Patterson both resigned under pressure, Vince could claim that he didn't know what was going on under his roof but had acted swiftly once the details emerged. This Chatterton thing, however, was pure evil. Though the criminal statute of limitations had passed and he couldn't be charged, picketers had started to gather in front of the office, accusing him of peddling porn. Worse, Geraldo's people were planted by the entrance, sticking microphones under the noses of McMahon's employees and asking for comments.

In calls to the chief counsel for Geraldo's syndicator, Tribune Broadcasting, and a subsequent suit that alleged intentional infliction of emotional distress, the McMahons insisted that Chatterton was using them as part of a $5 million shakedown operation. (They claimed to have proof that Chatterton had been put up to the story by David Shults, the ex-wrestler who'd gained infamy by punching ABC reporter John Stossel.) Rivera was unpersuaded. On April 3, 1992, viewers of *Now It Can Be Told* heard Chatterton say, "He made me have oral sex. And he started to get really excited and I pulled away and he got really angry and said that's worth a half million dollars a year. And when I said no, he said I better satisfy him and he pulled off my pants and he pulled me on top of him and he satisfied himself through intercourse."

IF HAVING Geraldo and a grand jury on his back wasn't enough, Vince also had to deal with the fact that the World Bodybuilding Federation wasn't turning out at all like he'd planned. A Saturday morning show on USA called *Body Stars* was supposed to make its lifters into TV-friendly fitness gurus. (Vince even tapped Matt Lauer to film a pilot but dropped him after deciding his abs weren't up to snuff.) So was the hiring of Lou Ferrigno, who gained a measure of fame starring in the hit 1970s series *The Incredible Hulk*. But *Body Stars* only taped once a month, and the lifters had little else to do. So they stayed home, taking copious amounts of drugs to stay in shape while Vince was running around telling America his company was drug free.

As they were building to their muscular peaks for the second WBF pay-per-view in June 1992, Vince called them together at the Airport Hilton in Los Angeles. Looking over their inflated physiques, he realized what was evident to everyone in that room—that they'd be dead giveaways to anyone looking to finger him for running a steroid outfit.

Vince was businesslike and brief: With the feds sniffing around, he couldn't afford to have them juicing. That's why he'd brought along someone he wanted to introduce—a chemist from Canada named Mauro DiPasquale.

DiPasquale needed no introduction. All the lifters knew him. They called him the Steroid Hunter. In fact, it was DiPasquale who nailed Jim "Ultimate Warrior" Hellwig for using steroids the prior September. He began gently, saying he didn't want to persecute anyone. He was there to help wean them off their chemical dependencies. Just the same, there would be random drug tests. If the genetic evidence from their urine samples was altered in a way that showed they were juicing, they'd be out. "This is bullshit," Ferrigno hollered, according to one of the men there.

Like his colleagues, Ferrigno seemed to see the move in terms of dollars and cents. If the lifters wanted to stay huge in time for the second event, they had to move on to human growth hormones, which unlike steroids were undetectable because they mimicked the body's naturally produced hormones. It wouldn't be a contest to see who could lift the most or condition themselves the best. It would be a race to see who could get the best drugs and use them the most wisely. Ferrigno walked out and quit rather than get into that kind of race. But the others who weren't as famous didn't have anywhere else to go. The Weiders had blacklisted them, and there were no other events to compete in.

"We all had our connections on the streets," said one of the lifters. "If you were smart, you could get around the test. The ones who could afford it just moved to human growth hormones taken from human cadavers, which was the latest thing. I wasn't worried. It was my knowledge against Vince's. But some of the guys just fell apart."

Vince tried putting them on a supplement that he'd started selling—one developed by Fred Hatfield, an expert nutritionist who went by the nickname Dr. Squat. When Nelson Sweglar, the television general manager, was tempted to try one of the supplements, he asked Hatfield what was in it. "Ground antler of lactating deer," Hatfield said nonchalantly. Sweglar passed, as did most of the lifters.

Without steroids, their bodies started to go into shock. Some couldn't leave their homes and grew depressed looking at themselves shrinking day by day. "These guys measured everything they put in their mouth to the gram. They were unlicensed chemists," says Jon Flora, an amateur lifter who was the marketing director for the league. "At the elite level of any sport, the amounts of drugs athletes take are unhealthy. But at the elite level of bodybuilding, it's almost suicidal. When they had their tool taken away, they were lost."

They grew tiny, bloated, and sullen. One experimented with a high-fat diet and simply got fat. Determined not to admit he'd made a mistake, Vince put another million into the television production, creating lavishly filmed introductions for each of his WBF *Body Stars*. But by then the whole thing was unsalvageable. All the show biz in Vegas still couldn't turn it around. The second WBF event at the Long Beach Convention Center on June 13, 1992, aired to such a dismal reception that a Massachusetts cable company with seventy thousand wired homes reported just twenty buys.

On the flight back to Connecticut, Sweglar ran some numbers through his head. He decided that if they had paid each of the thirteen thousand people who'd bought the show $10,000 each and had never started the WBF, Vince would still be ahead of the game.

By January 4, 1993, the day New York prosecutor Sean O'Shea had his meeting with Ted Smith, Vince had finally pulled the plug on the WBF.

But neither that nor Vince's protestations that the WWF was drug-free could persuade O'Shea that he was on the wrong course. In fact, he was more sure of his cause than ever. He'd come to see McMahon as more than just devious or even depraved. He'd come to see him as a steroid-pushing egomaniac who was peddling junk TV and lies to kids. Yet Vince kept expanding his hegemony. In fact, his newest show aired at 9 P.M. on the Monday after O'Shea returned from Harrisburg. It was a live show that was filmed twenty minutes by subway from the U.S. attorney's office in Brooklyn, in a theater across from Madison Square Garden called Manhattan Center. *Monday Night Raw* was an edgier show than Vince had ever done before, filled with the energy of New York City. Taking a cue from David Letterman's early days, he opened the hour-long broadcast with live remotes from the street, where his wrestlers bounded off moving taxicabs and crowds of commuters cheered them on.

Raw was a ratings hit almost from the start, placing in the top fifteen of cable shows nationally. But O'Shea felt it was a fraud. His thinking was reflected in a memo from early 1993, written by an FBI agent who was working with him. In the memo, the agent wrote that O'Shea "is not sure where the case is leading.... He advises at the present time it is primarily focused on steroid abuse and sexual exploitation of children within the professional wrestling industry.

However, through grand jury testimony, he is attempting to determine the extent of a fraud being perpetrated on the general viewing public through misrepresentations made by professional wrestling figures. A determination should be made within the next few months as to the direction the case will take." A later memo from the same agent shows that O'Shea was specifically interested in showing "fraud on the legitimate major suppliers of toys, vitamins, and NBC, who were unaware that the majority of talent at the WWF were steroid abusers."

The paradox was that O'Shea was trying to save people who didn't want to be saved. Despite all the setbacks and negative publicity, there were still few shows in television that reached kids as well as the WWF did. And the scandals did nothing to turn away advertisers such as Hasbro, Nintendo, Sega, Nestlé, Gap, or Slim Jim, which poured a combined $20 million worth of revenue into the WWF's bottom line. As a senior vice president at Grey Advertising told *Media Week* in March 1993, "I haven't heard anybody talking about [the sex and steroid accusations]. Once people decide to go into wrestling, they're not going to be bothered by this stuff."

Nor was it just corporate America that was willing to lend McMahon cover. Connecticut's Republican governor, Lowell P. Weicker Jr., helped Vince wash the stains of the Chatterton story off his hands with an appointment to the International Special Olympics committee. (Weicker would be named a director of the renamed World Wrestling Federation Enterprises after it went public in 1999, earning an estimated $25,000 a year with options on twenty-five thousand shares of stock.)

But the Brooklyn prosecutor remained single-minded. Through the spring and summer of 1993, wrestlers were being called before his grand jury nearly every day, and employees at Titan Tower were asked to comply with subpoenas for nearly everything in their desks. Agents from the IRS were camped out full-time in the finance department as well, fishing for any evidence that the cash-rich company might be involved in money laundering.

Vince, for the most part, never let his guard down, never let his employees see him as anything but supremely confident. But in truth, he was positive he was going to jail. When a friend told him that federal agents could listen to conversations through glass using state-of-the-art microphones, he started shooing aides away from his panoramic office windows and talking to them in the middle of the room. "They're going to nail me for something," he whispered to one of them, looking around at ghosts. "It's just a matter of what." He auditioned a series of people as stand-ins for him while he was away and began setting up lines of authority so he could run the company from prison.

Paranoia was in the air and in two high-profile lawsuits as well. In the first, McMahon accused Shults, Chatterton, and Geraldo of conspiring to shake him down through the airing of the controversial *Now It Can Be Told* episode. Then he filed a defamation suit against the *New York Post* and his fiercest critic there, columnist Phil Mushnick. Vince prided himself on being able to seduce the reporters who buzzed around him, either by giving them jobs or by convincing them he was just a harmless circus master. But Mushnick was another kind of reporter, an outsider who was willing to take Vince seriously. In the winter and spring of 1992, Mushnick started writing a series of blistering columns. In one, he warned his readers that

> never will you encounter a human more cold-blooded, more devoid of honor and propriety than Vince McMahon, America's foremost TV babysitter. In your wildest, most twisted dreams, you won't meet up with a the likes of McMahon, a miscreant so practiced in the art of deception, the half-truth and the bald-faced lie as to make the Artful Dodger appear clumsy.

Only the prosecutors know what discussions they had behind closed doors through September and October. But it stands to reason that they spent a fair amount of time and energy searching for a justification to bring a case that didn't really belong to them. They were New Yorkers. Yet they were targeting a Connecticut company and using as a star witness a doctor whose crimes occurred in Pennsylvania. A WWF case, if one existed, would have been better suited to Pennsylvania or Connecticut. But Ted Smith already decided the evidence didn't exist to try it in his district. And Connecticut prosecutors were clearly going to tread lightly where a friend of the governor was concerned. Nonetheless, late in the fall of 1993, Sean O'Shea decided to stake his own claim to Vince McMahon.

On November 19, Vince strode into the glass-and-steel federal court-house in Uniondale, Long Island, to see what his accuser had come up with after nineteen months of intensive looking. The indictment contained three counts that accused McMahon of conspiring with Zahorian to distribute steroids to his wrestlers, in violation of the new Food and Drug Administration laws that criminalized distribution. The key count—the one that established jurisdiction for O'Shea—involved a packet of steroids that Vince was purported to have had delivered to Hulk Hogan for a show at the Nassau Coliseum on October 24, 1989.

Curiously, no one in the U.S. attorney's office had bothered to check the date. Hogan wasn't at the coliseum that night, and neither was the WWF.

The government would have other problems with its case before the trial was over in July 1994. But no one in Titan Tower knew that. And they weren't about to underestimate the fight they had ahead of them to keep their boss out of jail.

It wasn't so much the legal costs as the time that Vince was spend-ing away from the office with his lawyers. Without the WWF's chief visionary, scripts began to wander. The *Survivor Series* and *Royal Rumble* in November 1993 and January 1994 had the second- and third-lowest buy rates in the company's six-year history of doing regular pay-per-views. At the same time, the company was hemorrhaging affiliates. One internal analysis showed a hundred stations had stopped buying WWF programs over the prior year, more than half of them Fox stations that needed to make room for new shows like *The X-Files*. As a result, huge holes started forming in its national patchwork, causing some advertisers who'd been promised national coverage to decline to renew their deals. There were also a lot of worried people at the USA Network. If not for *Raw,* they might have given up on wrestling altogether. As it was, Kay Koplovitz warily agreed to renew their deal for only one year.

Vince refused to show the strain in front of the Boys. "I remember when he was under indictment and they were saying they were going to close him down," says Kevin Nash, who'd appeared as the characters Master Blaster Steel, Vinnie Vegas, and Oz in WCW before joining the WWF. "I never saw his spirits flag. I never saw him drop his chin. And I spent a lot of hours with that man." But with bad news everywhere, Vince's advisers suggested something that would have seemed unimaginable six months before—selling to Turner. Bill Shaw at TBS had been making quiet inquiries, wanting to know if Vince was open to a sale in which Turner would buy the WWF and put it on TBS, using it to replace the existing WCW product. The deal was win-win, they argued. Vince could claim victory under the guise of eliminating the WCW. Meanwhile, Turner could crow that he'd bought the competition. But the look on Vince's face when his advisers suggested the idea showed that they'd misjudged their boss. As one put it, "It was a look that said he'd rather sell pencils on the street."

SEAN O'SHEA built his case around five people: Zahorian; Pat Patterson; Hulk Hogan; Vince's personal secretary, Emily Feinberg; and Anita Scales, who reviewed the company's contracts and reported to Linda McMahon.

In general, the assistant U.S. attorney was accusing McMahon of a conspiracy with Zahorian to keep the WWF awash in illegal steroids. Specifically, he was going to show that those steroids were delivered to his biggest star, Hogan, on two dates in 1989—April 13 and October 24.

O'Shea ramped up his case on Thursday, July 7, 1994, by calling the disgraced Dr. Zahorian. Having spent three years in prison, the ex-osteopath was gaunter than he'd been the last time he was in open court, and his eyes were harder. Over two days of testimony, he repeated much of what he'd said at his 1991 trial, recalling how he'd set up shop in the locker rooms of the farmer's pavilion in Allentown, handing out steroids in brown paper bags to the Boys who'd lined up before him. There were new details, too, specifically that Vince's secretary called him at least five times to place orders for her boss and Hogan. Yet under cross-examination, Zahorian portrayed McMahon as a distant figure. They'd spoken a half dozen times at most, he said. The first time was in early 1988, when Vince summoned him to ask if he was supplying the Boys with steroids. He told the boss that he was, but only because they'd be forced to turn to the black market if they couldn't get their juice from him. The next time he said they spoke was a few months later, when Vince asked for his own dose. It was hardly a description of two men working in lockstep.

When Zahorian's testimony concluded after the weekend, O'Shea turned to Rick Rude. Having been forced out of WCW by Bill Watts, Rude knew that there would be nowhere for him to go if Titan Sports went under. So he looked as bored as he could as O'Shea directed him to a night in June 1989 in Madison, Wisconsin, when Rude was still a headliner in the WWF. Rude said Vince approached him, concerned that the star was losing his chiseled looks. Rude replied that he'd stopped taking steroids because he and his wife wanted a child. Did Vince then tell you you should *go on the gas*? O'Shea asked. "Not in those words," Rude answered. "He may have said when you're down or sore you have to push yourself."[2]

Another wrestler, Kevin Wacholz, followed Rude to testify about the same evening, and his memory was decidedly more clear. Yes, Vince had specifically said, "I suggest you go on the gas." And it wasn't the first time. In January 1992, Vince had also used those words to tell the three-hundred-pounder that he should bulk up as well. When he tried to politely sidestep the issue, Wacholz testified that McMahon replied, "Well, life's not fair. The ball's in your court."

As the testimony dragged into its third day, O'Shea called a witness he knew would be tricky. Pat Patterson was central to the prosecu-

---

2. This quote was part of an exhaustive chronicle of the trial published by Dave Meltzer in the August 1, 1994, edition of the *Wrestling Observer*.

tion's conspiracy theory. He was the hatchet man who cut Zahorian loose on orders from Linda, having been told to instruct the doctor to destroy all his records of steroid shipments to wrestlers. He was also a died-in-the-wool loyalist, a man who owed his livelihood and lifestyle to the McMahon family. So O'Shea went at him hard.

"You saw wrestlers lined up to get steroids, didn't you?" No, Patterson insisted, they were lining up to get their blood pressure taken. "You knew what he was doing was wrong?" No, Patterson said, he didn't. "So you never heard about steroids?" No, he never even talked about it. O'Shea was sure the jury would see through Patterson's performance. But just in case, he produced a 1989 memo from Linda McMahon to Patterson in which she warned that the Justice Department might be onto Zahorian and that they should cut their links with him fast. Patterson was nervous, and McMahon tried to calm him with his eyes. Glancing at the memo, Patterson said he'd never seen it before, nor had he ever spoken with Linda about it. He also denied something that O'Shea said he testified to before the grand jury: that he asked Zahorian to call him back from a pay phone because he was afraid of being overhead by the feds. When asked whose idea it was to warn Zahorian, Patterson fell on his sword. "It was my idea," he said.

By Tuesday morning, the fifth day of testimony, O'Shea needed a strong—not to mention friendly—witness, and he got one in Anita Scales. Scales was a no-nonsense clerical expert, taciturn and jaded. As she sat in the witness box, she explained that a change in Pennsylvania law in July 1988 meant that Athletic Commission doctors were no longer required to be at ringside during wrestling matches. Once the law changed, Scales told Zahorian he was no longer needed because she was finding someone else. But the doctor called several times, begging to be kept on. "The Boys need their candies," he pleaded.

"Well," she recalled answering him, "the Boys can get their damn candies somewhere else."

Nonetheless, Zahorian showed up at the WWF studio in Pennsylvania for the taping in late August on his own, ignoring the fact that a new doctor had been hired, and continued to lobby to keep his job.

A month later, Scales became so disgusted that she went straight to Linda, fuming. "I've heard bad things, and I don't want him there," she warned. But Linda waved her away and told her to follow the wishes of Patterson, who wanted Zahorian retained. So, she said, she returned to her office to mail the osteopath a letter informing him that he could work at the December tapings, too.

Not long after that letter was sent, Scales was summoned back to Linda's suite. Between the two visits, Scales was told that Linda had received a call from an unnamed source in Washington, D.C., who'd told her that Zahorian was too hot to be in Eastern Pennsylvania. At that point, Scales said she was ordered to write a new letter, this time retracting the invitation to Zahorian that she'd just reluctantly made.

As Scales finished her story, O'Shea stepped back, hoping the jury would see this as the smoking gun. But there was another, more equivocal interpretation. By having Scales withdraw the offer to let Zahorian work in Pennsylvania, the WWF's lawyers could argue that he never really worked for the World Wrestling Federation. He'd only been to the matches as a legal appointee of the Pennsylvania Athletic Commission.

With two days of testimony left, O'Shea turned from the conspiracy to the distribution charges, calling his star witness, Emily Feinberg.

Feinberg had been hired as a secretary to one of Vince's aides when, on a lark, she modeled for *Playboy* and was chosen to be one of its playmates. Not long after that, Vince asked her to be his personal gate-keeper, the figure at the desk in the anteroom of his office. In the haze of the late eighties—when the WWF was still a tiny company awash in money, drugs, and interoffice intrigues—Feinberg became close to her boss, perhaps too close. Now she was paying the price for being seduced by the wrestling world on trial.

As she entered wearing a demure skirt and suit jacket, Vince couldn't look up. And for good reason. These two people, who'd once gone on boat trips and vacationed with their families, were now locked on opposite sides of an impossible divide. The future husband of one of Vince's lawyers had even approached her, posing as a producer for a tabloid television talk show who was willing to pay big bucks for her story. (The government would later argue that approach came perilously close to obstruction of justice by attempting to set Feinberg up so that the defense could claim she was trying to profit by selling her story.) In the end, she didn't fall for the offer. But she also didn't do the damage that O'Shea was hoping for.

She started her testimony by recalling the summer of 1987, when she first began to work at the company. She recalled that roid rage was a frequently discussed topic in Titan Tower, especially when the bills arrived from hotels that the Boys tore up while on the road. "Everyone talked about it," she said softly. One day she was filling a minifridge in Vince's office with soda when she noticed a small vial of steroids. Now O'Shea was approaching the critical pass. Feinberg testified that on a half dozen occasions Zahorian used Federal Express to make a steroid shipment to Titan Tower. Vince would open it, separating out some vials for himself and some for Hogan. Then he'd ask his limousine driver to deliver them to Hogan wherever he was appearing. The first of these occasions was when they were filming *No Holds Barred* in Atlanta, but there were other times when he received them at the Nassau Coliseum, the Garden, or the Meadowlands in New Jersey.

As her testimony ended, O'Shea returned to his seat, sure that he'd now given the jury something to chew over. But under McDevitt's hostile, even insulting questioning, Feinberg's memory went hazy at the critical moment—when she was asked about the April 13 shipment to Hogan that was part of the indictment. Did Vince open the package in her presence? "I don't know," she said quietly. Were any of the contents delivered to Hogan? "I can't say for sure." Did the limousine driver deliver it to Hogan? "I don't know if it was one of those times." Did she send it to him via FedEx? "I don't recall." How about the October 24 shipment? McDevitt asked, referring to the second element of the distribution charge. O'Shea leaned forward. The prosecutor needed his witness to say that the limousine driver delivered the steroids to the Nassau Coliseum. Without that linkage, his jurisdictional raison d'être would evaporate. But at this critical moment, Feinberg looked into the distance, caught the sight of Linda fighting back tears, and replied, "I can't recall."

After McDevitt pointed out that the only WWF show at the coliseum was on October 20—and that the steroid shipment of October 24 couldn't possibly have reached Hogan that night—O'Shea let out a long, slow breath.

And so the stage was set for the last day of testimony, when the prosecution would call Terry Bollea to talk about his days as Hulk Hogan.

Hogan's last run with the WWF had come in June 1993 and was widely considered a flop within the industry. It had little impact on arena event business, and the buy rate of the *King of the Ring* pay-per-view had been below that of *Summer Slam* two months later, when Lex Luger replaced Hogan as the company's top act. Since then, Hogan had moved into television with a syndicated action show called *Thunder in Paradise*.

In court, Hogan knew he'd be pilloried for lying to the nation in his saccharine *Arsenio* appearance in 1992, so he quickly admitted that he used steroids as early as the mid-seventies and was equally forthright about the way he got them in the WWF. Testifying with immunity, he figured that he'd received steroids by mail ten times from Titan Tower and that he usually called Feinberg from the road, asking her to place his orders with Zahorian.

If this advanced O'Shea's case at all, the victory was short lived. That was because as the WWF's hired gun of a lawyer, a decorated former federal drug prosecutor named Laura Brevetti, supplanted O'Shea in the well, Hogan's memory deserted him completely, just as Feinberg's had the day before. He couldn't remember picking up steroids in April 1989, nor did he have any memory of Vince's limousine driver delivering a package to him at an arena. O'Shea tried to look unfazed, but the government investigator sitting beside him wasn't as unflappable. He threw his hands in the air, using the universal sign of the double cross.

O'Shea quickly leaped up, trying to salvage the day. "Was Emily Fein-berg or Vince McMahon a doctor?" the prosecutor demanded.

"No."

"But you got steroids from both."

"Yes."

"You got to be Hulk Hogan in part because of steroids!"

"In part."

"Like your twenty-two-inch arms?"

"Yes, thereabouts."

The damage was done. After Hogan was excused, one of the reporters who would plaster his confessions across the next day's news pages approached him with a roll of paper towels that mea-sured twenty-two-inches across. As he held it to Hogan's arms, it was clear they'd shrunk to a fraction of their onetime size. Like so much else about wrestling, Hogan's famous physique had become another cynical illusion that belonged to yesterday.

When Brevetti rose inside the courtroom and asked the judge to dismiss the distribution counts against Vince McMahon for lack of evi-dence, O'Shea and his team had to wonder if they'd been deceived by the con men of wrestling. Had all the Boys who'd encouraged them to go after Vince played them for suckers? In the end, neither Feinberg nor Hogan had established that Vince had tried to distribute any steroids in the Eastern District's jurisdiction. As a result, the trial judge had no choice but to dismiss those charges. The only thing left for the jury would be a single count of conspiracy.

O'Shea and his team were determined to make it stick. In a closing argument on a hot July morning, the prosecutor let his rage spill out. He called McMahon a "corporate drug pusher" who ran a business with a "corrupt underbelly." He glared at him when he raged, "We're not talking about the paltry profit Zahorian made. We're talking about the millions in profits that *they* made." Summoning the image of Pat Patterson asking Zahorian to call him back on a pay phone, he seethed, "That's what drug pushers do." All day Wednesday and into Thursday, O'Shea hammered the point. "This is a corporation of drug pushers trying to blame the little guy," he said, looking squarely at the jury. "This hugely successful money machine mixed up chemical cocktails to get wrestlers pumped up and keep them going. It's shameful and it's illegal."

Shameful? Maybe. Illegal? Well, said McDevitt, stalking the same floor, that was another story. The government couldn't prove its conspiracy, couldn't prove much more than a single conversation between Vince and the dirty doc. Certainly, it couldn't prove that Pat Patterson ordered Anita Scales to keep the osteopath on the WWF's payroll. Then, pulling out their ace in the hole, McDevitt said that the WWF didn't even hire Zahorian after Pennsylvania changed its law. And where's the cover-up? Zahorian destroyed no records. "As a cover-up," McDevitt scoffed, "this was a lousy cover-up. Every single piece of evidence is still sitting there…. This conspiracy idea is trying to create a crime when there wasn't one. They have the burden of proof. They didn't prove it. They didn't come close."

After being instructed on the definition of conspiracy, twelve federal jurors received the case late in the afternoon, eager to work past the dinner hour. They broke for the night just before ten o'clock, reconvening at nine o'clock the next morning. As the day wore on, they asked for read backs of three witnesses whose testimony was, at least in parts, damaging to Vince. And the strain showed on his face. As he sat with Linda and his kids, he prepared for the very real possibility he'd have to do time.

After this, no one could ever humiliate the McMahons again. No one could insult them. No one could criticize their tastes and make them care. After hearing what O'Shea had said about their father, no television critic or newspaper columnist would come close to mattering to Shane or Stephanie. Linda would become ice.

At four in the afternoon, the jury came back again, this time with a verdict. As Vince stood beside his attorneys, he kept his eyes down, his hands clasped. The foreman read it slowly, forcefully.

Not guilty.

NINE

THE PRESS HAD A field day attacking Hogan during his appearance at McMahon's trial. A tabloid television show, *A Current Affair*, breathlessly reported on a letter that O'Shea had written to the trial judge, accusing Vince of ordering an employee to substitute his own blood for Hogan's during an HIV test. But the story didn't have legs. The public was already tired of it. The man known to the public as Hulk Hogan hadn't wrestled domestically in more than a year. He was well into his transformation as a TV action star.

His latest vehicle, *Thunder in Paradise*, was a run-through-the-blender mix of *Baywatch* and *Knight Rider*, with Hogan starring as R. J. "Hurricane" Spencer, a former Navy SEAL who spent most of the hour catching waves, bad guys, and looks at his costar, the supermodel Carol Alt. Hogan couldn't have been happier. He was being paid handsomely and didn't have to travel to a different town every night. The show was shot on a beachside set at Disney World in Orlando, about an hour from the twelve-thousand-square-foot French-style country estate he was building out of the bricks of demolished European castles.

The set was also a few blocks away from MGM Studios, which Eric Bischoff, the thirty-seven-year-old new leader of WCW, was scouting as the new location to film his television shows.

A black belt martial artist with high cheekbones and fashionably long hair, Bischoff was a handsome up-and-comer in the Turner Broadcasting orbit. Unlike most of those around him, he dressed in khakis and sneakers instead of jeans and work boots and carried himself with an air of corporate worldliness. He came to WCW from Verne Gagne's American Wrestling Association, where he'd parlayed a job as a salesman into an on-air role as Gagne's right-hand man. From there, he'd tried to get a job at the WWF but was given short shrift, so he sent an audition tape to WCW and was hired as an announcer for its low-rated

Sunday night show. In the year and a half that he'd been in Atlanta, he'd sized up the competition and realized that he had as much to offer as any of the candidates vying to replace Cowboy Bill Watts. So he presented himself as the person who could wipe the southern yolk off WCW and make it a national entertainment company. After he came to an interview with illustrated storyboards showing his vision for a new, futuristic look, Bill Shaw was impressed enough to vault the newcomer over the more senior candidates who wanted the job of executive producer.

It was a good thing that Bischoff's hair had already gone gray because he quickly discovered that the best-laid plans meant nothing when you dealt with wrestling. In October 1993, he sent a WCW crew that included Sid Vicious and Arn Anderson, who'd been hired back after his firing by Bill Watts, on a flight to England. A chartered bus then met the plane to take them on a seven-hour ride to a show in Cardiff, Wales. After the show, the group started drinking on the bus ride home and good-natured ribbing turned into bickering. Vicious in particular got on Anderson's nerves by bragging that Bischoff was going to make him the company's new marquee attraction.

"You guys should retire so we can do business," he said, alluding not just to Anderson but also to Ric Flair.

When the group reached their hotel in Blackburn, England, and the drinking continued in the lounge, Anderson finally had enough. "You've never drawn a decent house in your life," he told Vicious. "If you weren't so juiced up maybe you could work a decent match."

Vicious started removing his watch.

"What are you going to do, beat me up?" Anderson asked.

"No, but if you don't get out of my face, I'll get you away from me," the six-foot-nine Vicious replied.

Anderson backed up a few steps, then threw a beer mug at Vicious's head, sloshing him with backwash. "I'll cut your guts out with that bottle," he told Vicious as the wrestler wiped his face.

Had things ended there, the night might not have been much different from the other three hundred they'd spent on the road. But on this night, after the men had been pulled apart and sent to their rooms, Vicious couldn't sleep. He sat in his room, staring at a hotel chair until it occurred to him that with its legs broken it would make a fine weapon. After he sheared them off, he went down the hall and banged on the door of Anderson's room. "Come on out, motherfucker," he yelled.

Hearing just silence on the other end, Vicious started away. Just then the door flew open, and Anderson lunged at him with a pair of scissors, nicking his hands but penetrating his stomach. Vicious managed to absorb the blow, and the scissors fell in the ensuing scuffle. Sid picked them up and started stabbing Anderson in the back. A pint of blood spilled from more than a dozen incisions in Anderson's chest and a five-inch gash across his throat. Anderson muttered, "You're killing me," and passed out.

The banner headlines in the London tabloids the next day forced Bischoff to suspend Vicious, which had the ripple effect of requiring him to find a new combatant for his top heel, a four-hundred-pound ex-lineman named Leon White, who used the stage name Vader. Vicious had been penciled in to take the belt away from White at the tenth anniversary of *Starrcade*. Since they'd booked Charlotte's Independence Arena, Bischoff decided to use Ric Flair, the city's most famous son, to wrestle Vader for the title instead.

The hastily rearranged program on December 27, 1993 showed the executive to be a resourceful producer. To intrigue the press, he'd announced that Flair had agreed to retire if he lost, and he opened the show with a soft-focus testimonial, complete with old headlines and slow-motion highlights. After a warm-up match, a closed-circuit interview with the dewy-eyed Flair reflecting on his possible retirement was piped into the arena from his home a few miles away. By the time the second undercard bout ended, the impeccably tailored wrestler was seen pulling into the arena in a stretch limousine, his arrival timed to coincide with a shot of Vader destroying a punching bag in his locker room. When Flair finally entered the ring, Bischoff's choreography had worked wonders, creating the kind of primal anticipation that WCW hadn't seen in some time.

Flair spent the early going absorbing what looked like every manner of pain from a monster who was nearly twice his 230 pounds, making sure he milked all the ardor the crowd had to offer before they reached their inevitable reversal of fortune. It came late in the match, when Flair mounted the tops of three turnbuckles, let out a wild *"Whoooo!"* and flung himself through the air, clipping Vader on the way down. The next series of moves—a flying forearm followed by five stiff chops that Vader shook off before swatting Flair back to the mat—built to the finish. With blood flowing from the split lip he'd gotten by running into one of Vader's clotheslines, Flair ran headfirst into Vader, trying to tackle the big man. Vader knocked him back, but the pace of the match now seemed to exhaust him and his right knee suddenly buckled. Seeing this, Flair moved in for the kill. Spitting blood, he leaned on the "bad" leg until he toppled Vader and pinned his shoulders to the mat with what little strength he looked to have left. Backstage, even the most jaded Boys had to admit it was a bravura performance.

The next day, Flair was icing his muscles at home when the phone rang. He picked it up to hear Hogan say: "You old SOB. You nearly had *me* crying last night."

Flair and Hogan weren't the best of friends, but they had worked together briefly during Flair's two-year stint in the WWF. Since Hogan had been putting out feelers that he might be interested in returning to the ring, he asked Flair what was going on in Atlanta. "We have a new guy who's got some ideas," he replied. Hogan said he was glad to hear that and told Flair that he should pass along his home phone number. Bischoff's phone rang at two o'clock the next morning. "Hogan here," said the voice on the other end. The two proceeded to talk for more than an hour.

While Bischoff continued his phone talks with Hogan over the next few months, he also presided over a move of the company's television tapings to MGM studios at Disney World. The move went over wonderfully with the Boys. Not only did they love the warm weather and nearby strip clubs, they went from being outcasts at CNN Center to theme park attractions in Orlando. As one of them remembered, "Half of us spent the time stoned out of our minds. Out of the ten days a month we filmed down there, we'd be on the beach for seven." Because the set was always air-conditioned, parkgoers grabbed up the free tickets to get out of the heat. It didn't matter that they didn't know a thing about what they were seeing: signs flashed to tell them when to cheer and boo.

In early April 1994—three months before McMahon's trial was to start—Bischoff flew down to Disney with an additional mission. His overtures to Hogan had developed to the point where they agreed they should meet, so he rented a car, picked up Ric Flair, and drove to the *Thunder in Paradise* set, where they found Hogan dressed in camouflage fatigues with greasepaint on his face. They watched him film for a short while, then, when the director yelled "cut," retired to the star's trailer. Bischoff opened by saying that he wanted Hulk Hogan to return to wrestling, and he wanted him to do it at WCW. The producer knew that Hogan wanted his future to be in film and episodic television and said that he was only looking for a six-month commitment. Hogan looked at Flair, wanting to know if the idea had his support. Flair nodded his approval.

Bischoff's power, however, was still limited. So he arranged for Hogan to meet Ted Turner, the only one who could approve a deal of the size they'd spoken about. The mogul's eyes lit up when he saw Hogan get off the elevator at CNN Center dressed in his yellow trunks, a pink shirt, and a bandanna. (When traveling, he made it a point to always leave home in costume.) And it was a look of genuine glee. As they retired into his corner office, Turner started talking about the old days, how wrestling saved the old Channel 17, and how much he'd always admired Hogan. The man was really a fan, Hogan thought. Turner showed how true that was when he turned to Bill Shaw and said, "Make this man a deal."

When Hogan left CNN Center that day, he didn't see how he could lose. Not only was the money sensational—$2 million for six months plus a cut of the pay-per-view take—a brief tour through WCW would give a huge promotional boost for *Thunder*, which had declined in ratings every week since its debut.

McMahon was at his weekend home in Boca when Hogan faxed over the contract to give him a chance to match it. On a quick read, it was obvious it had been loaded with ridiculous incentives that McMahon couldn't afford in the midst of preparing for his costly trial. Leaning into his living room couch, he shook his head and told one of his aides, "Let Ted have him. He's not worth it."

If Vince considered Hogan old news, Bischoff was mesmerized by the forty-year-old star. The two spent hours talking on his Viper boat and in the bakery he owned with his wife on exclusive Indian Rocks Road. With three movies and a TV show under his belt, Hogan was fond of saying that he was "bigger than the show." And from the moment they started working together, Bischoff treated him that way. He arranged a ticker-tape parade for his new attraction on the New York set of Disney World to announce his signing, hastily outfitting hundreds of parkgoers in Hulkamania memorabilia so they'd form a backdrop for his motorcade. To make sure that no questions about steroids intruded on the choreographed ceremony, phony reporters were planted at the postparade press conference to ask benign questions. Hogan was genuinely moved by the attention being lavished on him. At the end of the evening, he turned to his old friend and sometime manager, Jimmy Hart, and said, "Jimmy, this is our chance. We're starting completely over."

But ten years had passed since Hogan was fresh or flashy. For one thing, his last run in the WWF had been considered a flop within the industry. For another, the arena business was still mired in the recession that hit it in the early nineties—when the boom cycle of the eighties had finally played itself out. The McMahon trial was the curtain closer of that era, exposing all of its secrets and excesses.

In Philadelphia, an underground troupe called Extreme Championship Wrestling was making waves with wrestlers who put their bodies through punishment that bordered on self-mutilation. ECW was the brainchild of Paul Heyman—who'd been chased out of WCW during the Bill Watts regime when he'd worked as the manager named Paul E. Dangerously—and it owed more to gangsta rap and white hard-core music than anything that Hogan had ever done. Men with names like Axl Rotten and Balls Mahoney were fighting matches with flaming two-by-fours, or giving themselves contusions with tire irons. One of ECW's biggest stars, Mick Foley, was already a legend in Japan, where audiences expected their wrestlers to fight on top of thumbtacks and power bomb themselves into unconsciousness.

And that was still on the fringes of respectability. Away from those fringes, wrestling was often more disturbing. One reader of Dave Meltzer's *Wrestling Observer* wrote about channel surfing in Chicago, and stumbling on an episode of something called *Windy City Wrestling* in which a severely handicapped fan was put into the ring to give a plaque to one of the show's wrestlers. Apparently the fan had some form of autism, and he stuttered terribly as he read the plaque's message, much to the delight of those in the studio audience. Finally, the wrestler grabbed the plaque and ambushed the handicapped fan with it. "I couldn't believe what I was seeing," wrote the *Observer* subscriber. "The victim was obviously a wrestling fan. He agreed to it. And being part of a wrestling angle may have been one of the most exciting things to happen to him. But [the promoter] took someone who looked to be one step away from lifetime confinement in a wheelchair and used him to get a wrestler over as a bad guy. What's next?"

Hulk Hogan didn't have the answer to that question when he signed the deal that brought him to WCW. And judging from the reaction he received during a walk-on cameo at the *Clash of the Champions* show in Charleston, South Carolina, in June 1994, fans were going to make him pay for it. Monitors set up in the arena chronicled his limousine pulling up with a police escort, and as soon as the arenagoers saw him they began to boo wildly. The drumbeat grew louder as Hogan made his way inside for a few prepared remarks. The catcalls seemed to genuinely surprise him, throwing him off his usual cadence. His remarks were rushed and unclear, his manner unusually nervous.

Seeing that Hogan was embarrassed—and knowing that he would be embarrassed again when he would take the stand in Vince's drug trial in a few more days—Bischoff set out to drape him in even more celebrity scaffolding. Turner Home Entertainment spent $75,000 on a half-page ad in *USA Today* to hawk his debut match. There was a guest spot with Regis Philbin and countless print interviews. As for his WCW wrestling debut, it was to be held in Orlando, the heart of Hulk Hogan country. Bischoff designed the pay-per-view undercard so that heels would be put over in each of the other five matches on the card, leaving room for only one babyface to reign.

By the time the opening refrain of *2001: A Space Odyssey* was piped through the Orlando Arena on July 17, 1994, Ric Flair had made his peace with the fact that his job tonight was going to be making Hogan look his best. Once he'd worked a show in Texas with a wrestler who'd passed out drunk in the dressing room right before they went on, and the sold-out crowd never suspected a thing. This would be easy by comparison. For one thing, Flair knew that the WWF emphasized gimmicks rather than hard-hitting wrestling and that meant Hogan liked *working light*, or avoiding stiff contact. So, at the bell, he began by dancing and then circling inside to land a series of open-hand blows to Hogan's chest, each of which he held up just before they connected. Over the next ten minutes, Hogan thwarted everything Flair threw at him: his swirling chops, his suplexes, his trademark figure-four leglock. When Hogan began tiring, Flair locked his elbow around Hogan's chin, letting him take a break to get ready for the next flurry of offense. Hogan gasped for a minute, then powered out of the hold, hitting Flair with a pair of shoulder blocks and flinging him into the turnbuckle. It was one of Flair's favorite spots, and the two had worked out the details in their clench. Flair went upside down in the corner, falling back on his feet. Then he gathered himself and took off toward Hogan, leading with his neck so Hogan had a wide target for the clothesline. Just then, a new character intruded as a kind of bridge between two stanzas. She was one of Hogan's old sidekicks, a former women's champion named Sherri Martel who'd been cast as Flair's valet. An attractive woman in her mid-thirties, she started out in the business as Sensational Sherri, then morphed to Scary Sherri and finally to Sensuous Sherri—though with her garish *Road Warrior* makeup, the second appellation was more applicable. When she and Hogan started working together in the early nineties, Sherri would use her loaded pocketbook on Hogan, who'd hoist her into the air to give the fans a peek at her black lingerie before bringing her bottom-side down across his knee in a maneuver known as the *atomic drop*. This time, though, a new twist had been written into the end, one that was supposed to help Flair build to a big finish. As Sherri lay on her back from the drop, she threw Flair a pair of brass knuckles. Flair tried to use them to beat Hogan, but, to his enormous irritation, Hogan refused to sell the beating. After all these years, he silently observed, the guy still wouldn't give up his ego for the act.

Finally Hogan was ready to launch into his finish, the *Superman comeback*. Anyone who'd watched him for the better part of a decade knew its three basic elements, and he wasn't about to change them now. Hogan threw Flair into the ropes, put his boot on his face as he repelled back, and then dropped his leg across Flair's torso as the white-haired wrestler lay flat on his back, waiting for the three count. Once it was delivered, Hogan rose and cupped his ear to hear the rendering verdict of every last clap.

Thanks to the heavy publicity blitz, more than 238,000 homes ordered the show, the biggest turnout for a Turner wrestling event in four years. (Between the live gate and the PPV revenue, Hogan netted about $680,000.) And the upswing continued through August 24, when Flair and Hogan wrestled for the first time on free TV. Close to 3 million homes tuned in, the second-highest rating for wrestling on TBS. In November, Bischoff told Flair he wanted him to wrestle another retirement match, but this time lose. Flair grumbled, though a two-year contract extension convinced him to do the job.

By then, Hogan was firmly in possession of the company's star-making machinery. His contract may have let him skip most of the Orlando-based television tapings, but his fingerprints were all over them. Old friends started appearing regularly, among them "Hacksaw" Jim Duggan, an eighties' Stars-and-Stripes act whose most recent claim to fame had been getting busted for speeding on the New Jersey Turnpike with the Iron Sheik in the passenger seat and three grams of coke in the Sheik's shaving bag. Hogan also tried to land Jim Hellwig, the original Ultimate Warrior, though when he failed he settled for an independent named Richard Wilson, who worked as a knockoff Warrior called Rio Lord of the Jungle. Hogan gave him the stage name Renegade and within a month had Wilson contending for a title on one of WCW's cable TV shows. Steve Austin hated working with Renegade so much that he threw a whole day's television taping into chaos by refusing to lose to him. As a result, poor Renegade wound up wrestling someone named Tex in a match so nakedly awful that no one associated with it ever talked about it again.[1]

In the roundtable booking meetings, Flair warned that a dangerous schism was developing between the free and the PPV products. The quality of wrestling on the flagship *WCW Saturday Night* show had become atrocious. Fans wouldn't keep paying to see pay-per-views, Flair argued, if they kept getting fed a diet of shows leading up to them that featured hacks like Renegade.

He was right, of course. But he was also missing the larger point. The problem wasn't the way the shows looked, or even who wore the belt. The problem was that Saturday night had the lowest viewership among men of any night on television. USA, meanwhile, was breaking cable records with McMahon's *Monday Night Raw* by siphoning off male viewers who were used to being in front of their televisions for *Monday Night Football*. In May 1995, *Raw* did a 3.3 rating. The 3.9 that it

---

1. Though rarely used, he lasted at WCW until early 1999. Upon being given a pink slip, the thirty-three-year-old Wilson lapsed into depression and, several months later, killed himself with a shotgun blast to the head.

did the next month (with a match between the ghoulish Undertaker, Mark Calloway, and Memphis's Jeff Jarrett) set a cable television record. These weren't particularly great bouts. Vince always saved his best stuff for pay-per-view. But they indicated that a silent majority of young men were willing to abandon network television for cable in prime time.

Turner was watching the ratings, too, having been frustrated by his failed attempts to buy both CBS and NBC. Before he could think about another acquisition, his aides told him that he had to concentrate on shoring up his own stock price. The *Wall Street Journal* quoted an entertainment industry executive as saying, "They've got to show that they can make some money with what they've got."

It was against this backdrop that Bischoff happened to have his first significant meeting with Turner, having landed what he thought was the final piece that would put WCW into the black: a deal to beam its shows across China. Because the deal involved Rupert Murdoch's Sky satellite system, it needed Turner's approval. Bischoff had met the boss socially, but he'd never addressed him close up. He'd been working on his presentation for a month when he finally got word in July 1994 that Turner would see him.

As he was escorted into Turner's office he first saw Scott Sassa, the head of both TNT and TBS. Then his eyes reached Harvey Schiller, a former chairman of the U.S. Olympic Committee who was now overseeing all of Turner's sports properties. Schiller was no wrestling aficionado. In fact, his baptism in it came haphazardly—during a party at his Atlanta home. A guest couldn't stop talking about the prior night's WCW show, in which one of the wrestlers was carried offstage in a stretcher. Schiller hadn't seen the episode and was furious to learn something like that could happen on his watch without him being told. When he called Bischoff to demand an explanation, the producer seemed confused. "Uh, Dr. Schiller," he said. "You didn't believe that, did you?"

As all the men settled in, Bischoff started describing the China option. Then Turner held up his hand to bluntly ask, "Why aren't we doing better in the ratings?"

Bischoff froze. How hadn't he seen this one coming? Before he could catch himself, he blurted out, *"Because I don't have prime time."* As soon as he said it, he could feel Sassa's eyes on him. Sassa had done him a favor by getting him this meeting. He'd just sandbagged the man.

"How soon can you get it on the air by?" Turner asked, his face brightening.

"September at the latest," Bischoff replied, looking to the new 1995 television season.

Turner turned to Sassa and said, "Give the man two hours on Monday night on TNT."

On the way out, Bischoff expected Sassa to explode, but instead he just sighed with the resignation of a man who'd seen the mogul do this before.

As for Bischoff, it was a classic case of being careful about what one asks for. "I felt like I had a gun to my head," he says. "I'd just been handed two hours of prime time and everyone at Turner was watching me. Either I hit a home run or my career was pretty much over."

INSIDE TITAN Tower, where everyone had put the experience of Vince's drug trial the year before behind them, news reports of Turner's decision were greeted with contempt. "We were stunned they could be so stupid," one of his aides recalls. McMahon was irked by Hogan's attempt to re-create the old WWF lineup. It was stealing, when you got down to it. But he couldn't imagine that Hogan and this Bischoff newcomer could do serious damage to *Raw*. During the steroid controversy, much of the work had centered on Lex Luger, whom McMahon had spent a small fortune luring away from WCW to be the face of his WBF. When that folded, he went to enormous lengths to make Luger his next Hulk Hogan. On July 4, 1993, McMahon had clothed the muscular blonde in a stars-and-stripes body suit and dropped him from a helicopter onto the USS *Intrepid* for a bout with a six-hundred-pound Samoan named Yokozuna playing the role of a Japanese sumo wrestler. (Luger addressed him by saying, "What's wrong with America is bloodsucking, overstuffed, sushi-eating, rice-chomping leeches like you.") But it wasn't long before it began to dawn on Vince that no amount of money was going to make up for the wrestler's lack of charisma, and all the histrionics in the world weren't going to make him move any less stiffly. So when Luger's contract was expiring, and he wrote Vince to say he was considering himself a free agent, the promoter stashed the letter in his briefcase and promptly forgot about it.

On the evening of September 4, 1995, Vince settled into his living room along with the other nearly 2 million viewers to see what Turner had come up with. He was in a foul mood because the USA Network had preempted *Raw* for the U.S. Open tennis tournament, essentially inviting Turner to attack him unopposed. What he saw made his jaw drop. It wasn't just that Turner did better than expected. The feel was edgy, the crowd amped, and Bischoff, with his full-throated and peripatetic opening, "Welcome to *Monday Nitro,*" did a good job at creating a happening.

A half hour into the show, he was startled to see Luger on the other end of the television screen running across the WCW set. As far as he knew, Luger had wrestled a WWF show in Canada the evening before and was supposed to be en route to another one that night. Then he thought about the letter that Luger had given him, and he cursed.

The first shot in the Monday night wars had been fired.

TEN

THE SECOND INSTALLMENT OF *Monday Nitro* was held on September 11, 1995, in Miami. And though this was the first time that *Nitro* and *Monday Night Raw* aired against one another, both shows weren't truly live. As a cost-saving measure, Vince taped four weeks worth of TV in a single marathon session. Only the first hour was broadcast live. The other three were taped for subsequent weeks. Knowing in advance that the September 11 episode was taped, Eric Bischoff opened his show by crowing: "In case you're tempted to grab the remote control and check out the competition, don't bother. It's two or three weeks old. Shawn Michaels beats the big guy with a superkick that couldn't earn a green belt at a YMCA. Stay right here. It's live."

Vince had spent the summer denying that Bischoff could hurt him, and now he was paying the price. On Tuesday morning, the Nielsen overnights showed that *Nitro* had beaten *Raw* 2.5 to 2.3—a difference of a few hundred thousand homes. "Until then, there was the feeling that we didn't like these guys," remembers Michael Ortman, who was the WWF's vice president for distribution. "But we also had a sense that there was enough room for everybody under the tent. After Eric gave away the results of our matches, Monday night became a war."

Since the steroid trial, the WWF had been going through a very public repositioning, and Ortman was one of its architects. A canny tactician, he was troubled by the fact that Congress was taking up the issue of violence in the entertainment industry as part of an omnibus crime bill. If the rider that dealt with television passed, it would bump violent programming into the late evening, causing a massive drop in the preteen audience at a time when the WWF could least afford it. (The fallout from the trial included the dissolution of a licensing deal with Hasbro.) Concluding that the best defense was a good offense, Ortman suggested that they get ahead of the curve by positioning themselves as socially responsible. He helped create a corporate manifesto called *The Principles* that assured affiliates the WWF would ban a catalog of raunchy things during the peak hours for underage viewing, among them "the use of a foreign object as a weapon (i.e., the ring bell, chair or other props), blood employed for dramatic effect, and aggressive behavior toward women." As he saw it, congressional pressure would accumulate around WCW instead of the WWF, causing Turner to end up in trouble with the one constituency that mattered: his stockholders. McMahon endorsed the plan and promptly lent his name to a series of "Dear Ted" missives. As one of them began:

> On Sunday...Turner Broadcasting will kick off the cable industry's *Voices Against Violence* week by presenting its most violent pay-per-view ever—*WCW Uncensored....* This tasteless event is being marketed by describing how bones may pierce through skin, eyes might be displaced, a person's head may be dragged on asphalt from moving vehicle, and a leather strap could cut through flesh like a machete.
>
> The reputation of the company you built will be shaken if this event is allowed to go on as promoted. This letter marks my fourth written attempt to privately implore your company to reduce the incidents of gratuitous violence and unethical solicitation. While I initially held out hope that things were improving, I must now conclude that a consensus decision has been made by your WCW to fill a creative void with increased violent content. In order to further distance my product from yours, WCW's actions have left me no choice but to place your product under a more public microscope.

Since the trial, McMahon had weaned himself off his rope-muscled steroid gallery by using men like Canada's Bret Hart, the sultry and sneering Shawn Michaels, and Kevin Nash, who got his WWF start appearing as Michaels's bodyguard and was now drawing better reactions than Hart. To show he was now a promoter with a social conscience, McMahon even sent the three on a Christmas season "Wish" tour to benefit the Make-a-Wish Foundation.

Thinking that the tour was a good way to tout his company's new direction, Ortman met several of its Canadian business partners at the US Air Arena, which was just a few miles from his Baltimore home, in November 1995. An antiviolence campaign by the Quebec-based Coalition for Responsible Television had just helped get *Power Rangers* thrown off the air. As he pulled up to the arena in an Acura that he'd fitted with *NEW WWF* license plates, Ortman wanted the Canadians to feel comfortable with the product so they could defend it at home.

The undercard contests were hard fought and exciting, and the main event pitting Hart against Nash was a perfect example of the license plate's message. The men didn't have to rely on violent gimmicks because they were athletes. But then something happened to make Ortman shift in his seat. Hart pulled out a chair and leveled Nash with it. In response, Nash rose to his feet and ripped a TV monitor loose from its sockets to go after Hart. Ortman pretended to be nonplussed, mentioning to his guests that pay-per-views, unlike broadcast shows, were supposed to be a bit edgy. But after the show he cornered Vince backstage. "Just give me the words to explain to those folks what I just saw," he said.

"Two guys just got carried away," Vince replied. Then he wrapped a thick hand around Ortman's shoulder and added, "It won't happen again, Mike. I promise."

On Sunday, December 17, Ortman was in his home when he flicked on the follow-up pay-per-view, *In Your House*. Once again, the matches unfolded as expected until Hart met his real-life brother-in-law, Davey Boy Smith. Not a minute into their bout, Hart fell on a raft of metal stairs and split his forehead. With blood streaming down all sides of his face, he continued to wrestle. No sooner had he won than Linda called Ortman to say, "Vince knew you'd be upset, Mike. But we didn't have anything to do with Bret cutting his head. It was an accident, and we still had a half hour to go with the show."

While that may have been true (and there is ample reason to believe it wasn't, that Hart had bladed himself), the McMahons couldn't have been unhappy with the result. Footage from the match was edited into *Raw*'s opening sequence, and a memo was distributed through Titan Tower warning that while they had a "responsibility to exercise appropriate restraint when younger, unsupervised viewers may be watching," the company's shows "may include elements which are consistent with the time period." *Nitro* was in its eleventh week, and the two shows were even in the ratings. To Ortman, the memo suggested that the WWF could no longer afford to have principles.

In January, Vince announced he wanted to do a series of skits lampooning Turner. Aides tried to talk him out of it, reminding him that he had a long-standing policy of never acknowledging the competition. But he dismissed their concerns. "It's going to be the funniest thing we've ever done," he said.

The first episodes, which started airing in January 1996, *were* funny. An actor in a terrible toupee and a cheap suit portrayed Turner leading a roundtable meeting of his top acts, which included a white-haired Huckster and his portly sidekick, the Nacho Man. In one skit, as images of Vince's current acts flickered onto the boardroom projector screen, the limp-skinned Huckster sighed and said, "No way can I do that, brutha. At my age my feet don't even leave the ground."

But over the next six weeks, the vignettes went from funny to malicious. In a draft of one script entitled "TV Trivia," Turner was depicted as a game show contestant playing beside a dizzy blonde. As the host introduced a Jeopardy-like category called "Pompous Quotes," the draft called for this dialogue:

HOST: Who made the racial comment, "As for blacks, well, most of them are not black anyway. They're brown. Well, aren't they? It's very seldom you see a black black."
TED: Michael Jackson. (buzzer)
GIRL: That's funny, Billionaire Ted.

HOST: Right! Next question. What famous person said this? "King Henry VIII didn't get divorced, he just had his wives' heads chopped off.... Now, that's a good way to get rid of a woman—no alimony."

TED: Why that was my buddy, O.J. (buzzer)

GIRL: (To Ted) Shame on you, Billionaire Ted. (Ding ding ding.)

HOST: Yes! The correct answer is Billionaire Ted....

The more elaborate the skits, the more Vince became willing to stop the company's work to produce them. Employees were sent e-mails directing them to drop what they were doing because extras were urgently needed in the WWF's in-house production studios. But what little humor was left in the rivalry disappeared when McMahon directed his legal staff to send a brief to the Federal Trade Commission, arguing that merger talks between Turner and Time Warner be stopped because Turner was "engaged in a systematic plan to destroy the WWF."

That was too much for Kay Koplovitz. The president of the USA Network had been following the Time Warner talks, too, and though she and Turner were fierce rivals when it came to programming, she had to be more circumspect where Time Warner was concerned. After all, the media giant owned cable systems around the country that accounted for about 10 million of USA's 70 million viewers. While Koplovitz usually didn't interfere with what the McMahons broadcast, the Billionaire Ted skits put her in an indelicate position. After the March 18 episode of *Raw* featured Turner as the Jack Nicholson character in *A Few Good Men*—thundering the famous line, "You want the truth, you can't handle the truth"—Koplovitz decided things were going too far. Something had to be done.

The word came to Ortman in a phone message from one of Koplovitz's top aides: Not only would there be no more Billionaire Ted skits on USA, the network wanted to see advance copies of his scripts and have a representative at all future creative meetings. It was more than just the skits that worried the network president. *Raw*'s ratings were as low as they'd been since the show was launched. And other strange things that Vince was trying weren't working. Doink the Clown, for instance, was introduced as kind of a slasher-film villain. He'd chase fans into the audience, later bringing his midget assistant, Dink, into the act. It was as if Vince's dark side was spilling out without any of the perspective or filters that had carried him to the top of the business in the eighties. Koplovitz thought that Vince was letting the strain get to him. She'd seen it before in Hollywood. He was losing his balance. He needed someone to keep him in touch with the outside world.

The person she chose to pair him with was Wayne Becker, a former golf programmer who favored double-breasted suits and presented himself as an urbane insider. He was fiercely loyal to Koplovitz, who he viewed as a genuine pioneer. As he put it later, "As far as we were concerned, the WWF was low maintenance as long as Vince was behaving himself. But the whole FTC thing really changed that."

Going to midwestern arenas to monitor the WWF shows was slow torture for Becker, who was used to the more genteel world of PGA clubhouses. But he dutifully did it, and what he saw genuinely opened his eyes. "Vince is very hard to deal with because he's such a character," says Becker. "There are times where your greatest challenge is trying to decide whether his view of reality is the same as yours because he is so into what he was doing. I never knew if I was dealing with Vince the person or the character because he'd waffle back and forth."

Of all the things the WWF did, nothing struck Becker as more darkly confusing than an androgynous character named Goldust. As played by Dustin Runnels, the son of Virgil Runnels (Dusty Rhodes), Goldust was a giant wink to the gay community, though it was hard to imagine many found it all that fun to watch him beat rivals with the kinds of homoerotic advances that sent them out of the ring screaming. Dustin spent hours in makeup, streaking his long and puffy face with golden paint and black lipstick, then framing it with a platinum blond wig that dipped past the shoulder pads of his massive pantsuits. Once he disappeared into character, he was willing to do anything to shock, including running his hands over his breasts and crotch in the ring and making bondage part of the act by wearing dog collars and spiked bras. What struck Becker wasn't just that Goldust sprang from the minds of men who had some pretty fucked-up ways of amusing themselves. What struck him was that Dustin was running his career into the ground—as a wrestler, he'd never quite recover from the act— simply to spite his father. Becker also thought that McMahon seemed to take special delight in stoking the family feud, which as best as Becker could tell involved Dustin's marriage to an ex-cosmetologist named Terri Boatwright, who vamped around as his cigar-smoking manager. (In a speech that he gave in full costume one evening on *Raw*, Dustin showed how many levels wrestling scripts could operate on when he spoke directly to his father through the cameras lens. He said: "All those years I looked up to you, you were bigger than life, and I wanted to be just like you. I wanted to live like you. So I became a professional wrestler.... There is no one on the planet who can do Goldust as well as I can. I hope you're proud of my family and myself. I'm very proud of them.")

But as uncomfortable as Goldust made Becker, he also realized he was a stranger in a strange land and had to proceed cautiously. He had to earn Vince's trust. It was something of a breakthrough, then, when Vince approached him one day to solicitously ask for a piece of advice. On *Raw* that night, he wanted one of his wrestlers to refer to Goldust as a queer. Becker knew that Vince had already made up his mind to do it, but he acknowledged the gesture. When he was told that Goldust would fight back, he agreed. It may not have been a huge step in the cause of human rights, but it was a small step in the cause of Wayne Becker's gaining the trust of Vince McMahon.

The effect of that night's show, and others like it, was evident in a focus group that USA commissioned. A tape of one of the sessions showed a group of fourteen- and fifteen-year-old boys gathered around a conference table behind a one-way mirror. Asked about their favorite viewing habits, they ticked off a long list of sports. When one mentioned wrestling, they all quickly agreed that, yes, they watched it, too. Their favorite show? *Raw,* they all answered. Then the moderator asked each to pick a character they didn't like. "Goldust," said one boy in a down parka with a pair of headsets dangling from his neck. "He's a queer." But, interrupted another kid, "he's got a chick." The reference to Dustin's real-life wife prompted a lusty debate among them that was finally settled by a third boy. "Nah," he concluded. "She's a lesbian."

It scarcely mattered to the McMahons that Goldust was giving millions of teenagers their first images of what gay men acted and sounded like. He was a heel, and in the moral nexus of Vince's world, there was only one way to deal with someone like that. You had to beat the shit out of him.

That job fell to Roddy Piper, who was making a return to the WWF in *Wrestlemania XII* at the Pond in Anaheim in March 1996. In a pre-taped vignette at a nearby lot, Piper waited for Goldust in a white Bronco, clutching a baseball bat. When Dustin, made up as Goldust, arrived at the lot in a speeding gold Cadillac, Piper cut him off with his Bronco, leaped out of the car, and started madly smashing the Cadillac's windows. As glass shattered everywhere, Dustin ran for cover, and then Piper hunted him down.

In any other context, it would have been called a hate crime. But what Ortman had come to accept, and what Becker had discovered, was that the rules were different when you called it wrestling.

ELEVEN

THE EXECUTIVES AT THE USA Network weren't the only ones who were uncomfortable about Goldust. Before Roddy Piper was penciled in to fight him, Vince had asked a veteran of the game, Scott Hall, to do it.

Hall freely admitted that he'd be living hand to mouth—rather than in a five-thousand-square-foot Orlando-area home—if not for McMahon, who allowed him to develop into Razor Ramon, a James Dean knockoff with oily black hair and a stubble-covered jaw. Despite a terrible Puerto Rican accent that sounded like it belonged in a high school production of *West Side Story*, Razor Ramon became one of the icons of the so-called new WWF and a member of a circle of top acts known around Titan Tower as the Clique.

The Clique was more than a catchphrase. The alliance—comprised of Hall, Shawn Michaels, Kevin Nash, Sean Waltman, and Paul Levesque (Hunter Hearst Helmsley)—was a strong-willed, frequently vindictive group that used their collective mastery of wrestling politics to forge a kind of shadow government in the WWF. All five had close ties to McMahon and used them to obtain special meetings in which they called their own shots and, on occasion, influenced the careers of others. Their swagger was evident on a tour of Germany when one of them, reportedly Michaels, taunted the blond manager Tammy Lynn Sytch by putting feces on her plate during a preshow buffet. Sytch fell apart and left for the States. When her boyfriend, wrestler Chris Candido, subsequently got into a fight with Michaels about it, he was promised that he'd be stripped of his half of a tag-team belt when they all got home. Sure enough, he was.

But in this instance, Hall's membership in the Clique didn't help him much. What Vince was asking him to do with Goldust left him facing an impossible choice. "What do I do when my kid goes to school and hears from the other kids that his daddy is a queer?" he asked, genuinely distraught that a long-term angle with Goldust might raise the wrong kinds of questions about his own predilections. Lines had to be drawn, especially when the moral issues got intertwined with the financial ones.

Vince's contracts featured downside guarantees allowing wrestlers to count on a minimum salary. But the real money to be made was in salary-boosting incentives. If a wrestler worked hard at building his character's popularity, it could lead to a pay-per-view appearance, which was the Holy Grail. Because talent got a percentage of the gross revenues, a star like Hall might make six figures for a night's work. The problem was that after a strong year in 1995, Hall had found his hours cut in the general belt-tightening that accompanied Raw's ratings doldrums. His $400,000 downside guarantee had been cut by a third. Hall feared that if the Goldust act didn't go over—if the macho Razor Ramon was suddenly viewed as, uh, fruity—he'd irreparably damage his character and the chance to star in lucrative pay-per-views.

Like many wrestlers, Hall had kept his wife largely in the dark about his business affairs. So when he'd started complaining about his salary, she asked, "How can Vince be that unreasonable? Let me talk to him." Dana, Scott's wife, didn't believe all the cynical things that people said about Vince. In fact, she thought the drug tests that he'd put in place after his trial were helping to keep Scott, an addictive personality, clean and sober. She also knew that other wives had gotten involved in their husbands' negotiations and had found the owner to be reasonable. She was sure that if she could just sit down and talk to him, she could straighten things out.

But before she could reach Vince, Eric Bischoff at WCW had gotten word to Scott that he stood to make three times his salary if he crossed over to TBS. Hall didn't breathe a word about the overture to anyone in the WWF until the day before he decided to leave. After a television taping in West Virginia on February 20, 1996, he leaned over to his best friend, Kevin Nash, in the showers and said, "I'm gone when my contract is up in two months, brutha. I'm breaking up the Clique." Nash was stunned, but no more so than Hall's wife. After emerging from his private study in his home, where he'd dictated his termination notice and sent it to Vince, he told her that he was heading to WCW.

When Vince arrived at his office and read the telegram with Hall's termination notice, his blood pressure started to rise. Hall had been two inches from his face the night before in Huntington, West Virginia, and hadn't said a word about it.

McMahon sat down to dictate his own missive. Effective immediately, it read, Hall was suspended for failing a drug test for marijuana several weeks earlier. He'd be out of work for six weeks. When his contract expired after that, he could do whatever he wanted, so long as he left the name Razor Ramon—and all the character's gimmicks—with its rightful owner.

LIKE HALL, Kevin Nash had spent his share of journeyman years in woeful costumes. The worst was when he worked under Jim Herd at WCW and had to wear a hideous rubber mask with a cone on his head, wrestling as the caped Oz. His entry into the WWF in early 1992 transformed him into "Big Daddy Cool" Diesel, a *monster heel* whose entrance on stage was usually accompanied by a film clip of an 18-wheeler rumbling down the highway.

"When I started there, we were all young and hungry," he'd say years later. "If Vince had told us women weaken the legs, we probably wouldn't have gotten laid. We were trying to get the business back on its feet because it had been strip-mined by the old-timers for so long. And I'll always love him for helping us."

But in February 1996, even Nash was beginning to understand the ground was changing underfoot. Vince was relying on smaller and more agile wrestlers, which is why he'd asked Nash to *drop the strap*, or lose a title match, to Bret Hart. Before Hall had made his decision to break up the Clique, Nash was in Phoenix, driving to a restaurant to have a Valentine's Day dinner with his wife, when he got a call on his car phone. It was from Bischoff's next-door neighbor and emissary, a bar owner turned wrestler named Diamond Dallas Page.

Page pushed hard. Exciting things were happening at WCW, he insisted, and Nash should be a part of them. Then, in a moment of spontaneity, he gave the wrestler a private number for Bischoff and implored him, "Call Eric right now."

Bischoff was surprised to hear from Nash and greeted him warily. Even though Page had set up the call, Bischoff still considered Nash a loyal Clique member. In fact, he'd boasted that he'd get a sex change before he returned to WCW. And from the long pauses in their conversation, Nash could tell that Bischoff was suspicious. When Bischoff threw out a figure that Nash considered too low, Nash joined the game of playing hard to get. Thanks for the interest, he said, but I'm not really job hunting.

The truth was, though, that both men wanted to do business. At thirty-seven, Nash had a new wife, a baby boy, and a questionable number of years left as a headliner. As for Bischoff, he was forming the outlines of a plan that the two WWF stars would come in handy in implementing.

IN JAPAN, where professional wrestling is at least as big as baseball, the most respected and innovative company is called New Japan. Under the guidance of the senator and wrestling legend Antonio Inoki, New Japan was drawing NFL-size crowds. Bischoff flew to Tokyo as part of a regular exchange of talent. At the time, another Japanese wrestling company was struggling and needed help, so Inoki brokered a deal in which they would face one another in an interpromotional rivalry. Two companies going to war with one another, the equivalent of a wrestling World Series, had never been done before on such a grand scale, and the response was fantastic.

By the second New Japan/UWFI (Union of Wrestling Forces International) show in January 1996, Tokyo was abuzz with the rivalry, and Bischoff decided to adapt the gimmick for his American audience. The only question was how to do it when he didn't have a rival like the UWFI willing to cooperate.

Recruiting Scott Hall was a first step. Convincing Nash to follow put the final piece in place. Nash was in a Florida motel room, on the road with the WWF, when he decided to accept the six-figure deal that Bischoff finally offered. "It was the hardest thing I'd ever done," he'd say. "Though it was my sweat, it was Vince's opportunity that made me. I'd slept on Vince's couch and by his pool. I hung out with his son, Shane. I tried writing a letter to him in my motel room, but I started crying so much I had to get my wife to type it. Then I called Vince in the office because I didn't want him to get the letter first. He didn't sell anything. He was like, *Fine*."

If McMahon knew the way Nash would be used with Hall, he wouldn't have been so calm. Hall gave an early indication of the bumpy road that lay ahead when he worked his last WWF match on May 19, 1996, at Madison Square Garden. (Once Hall served out his suspension for marijuana use, McMahon decided to bring him back for the final weeks on his contract, hoping in vain that the wrestler might decide to stay.) The night had an edgy feel, and Hall heard it in the crowd's chant of "You sold out, you sold out." Yes, he did, and he was proud of it, and before he wrestled his old friend Helmsley he looked squarely in the fans' faces and snapped, "So what?" (The power to his microphone was cut before he could say more.) Later in the evening, Hall decided to make his last act as a Clique member a memorable one. After Michaels won his cage match with Nash, Hall made an impromptu appearance in the ring and spontaneously wrapped his arms around Michaels in a good-bye hug. Helmsley was so moved that he ignored the fact that he was supposed to be feuding with Michaels and joined them. Next they approached Nash, who was still laid out unmoving, and got him to rise up with them. It was the rarest of moments: four wealthy men who'd sworn allegiance to a life of pretend were putting their friendship before the business.

McMahon was furious at the breach of kayfabe,[1] but at least the hug was part of a dark match, not meant for television. The same couldn't be said of Hall's shocking appearance the next week on *Nitro*. At 8:34 P.M. on May 27, the first night that *Nitro* was scheduled to expand to two hours, Hall swept through the Macon Civic Center in Georgia, interrupting a WCW match in progress by declaring, "You know who I am, but you don't know why I'm here." Bischoff pretended to be stunned, and the confusion on his face was the confusion he wanted the audience to feel. What was Hall doing there? Who was he working for?

In Internet chat rooms, tens of thousands of fans exchanged their thoughts, most divided into two camps, *smarts* and *marks*. Smarts were fans who thought they were so sophisticated they could never be fooled. Marks were the rubes. Those who weren't smarts by definition were marks. But as soon as Hall made his debut, even the smarts got marked, or duped. Were they seeing a WWF-WCW war? Or, even more astoundingly, were they seeing the beginning of an era of cooperation?

It was a canny move. In effect, Bischoff was forcing McMahon to play an unwitting role in a WCW story line, a character employed against his will. And he succeeded in making the whole episode murkier by

---

1. McMahon's anger came spilling out backstage, and he confronted Michaels about it. But Michaels was one of his biggest attractions, so McMahon couldn't punish him. And there was nothing more he could do to Hall and Nash. The only person he could punish was Helmsley. In a fateful move, he told the wrestler that he would not be making an appearance in the finals of the upcoming *King of the Ring* pay-per-view. Instead, that spot would go to Steve Austin. Had Helmsley not been punished, and had Austin not been put in his place, Austin might never have met Jake Roberts in the finals and come up with the "Austin 3:16" monologue that launched the company's comeback.

using a friendly Pittsburgh sportscaster named Mark Madden to float misleading information on a 900 phone recording that charged for "inside information." Hall wasn't working for WCW, "so what's he doing here?" Madden wondered. (Merely referring to Hall by name was an innovation. Once, wrestlers hid behind the impenetrable walls of kayfabe. But since Bischoff couldn't legally use the Razor Ramon name, he did away with their idea of stage names entirely. Scott Hall became Scott Hall. The more real things seemed, the better.)

McMahon was furious. It was one thing to steal Hogan, who hadn't worked for the WWF for a year when he was hired at Turner, or snare past-their-prime acts like Randy Savage. It was another to take current performers and misrepresent them as still working for the WWF. He instructed aides to go undercover to WCW shows with cameras to film Hall and Nash performing, hoping to catch them using the trademarked names Razor Ramon and Big Daddy Cool Diesel. (The performers didn't have to; fans shouted the names for them.) When that didn't work, he expanded the scope of his search, looking for evidence that Turner was forcing WCW's shows down the throats of syndication affiliates by withholding his other program offerings until stations bought wrestling, an illegal practice known as *block booking*. When he couldn't find any evidence of that either, he turned to his lawyers to find something he *could* sue for.

The result was a sweeping piece of litigation that alleged a kitchen sink of wrongs, from copyright infringement to tampering to defamation. Essentially, the WWF position was that any attack on it was illegal. It claimed that Turner interfered with its contracts by offering Hall and Nash a combined $4.5 million over three years. Acting as if there was something untoward instead of robustly competitive about airing *Nitro* on Monday nights, it accused WCW of trying to "dilute the viewership of the WWF." It insisted that "TBS utilized *Nitro* as a vehicle to disparage, defame, and libel the WWF," sidestepping the issue that the Billionaire Ted skits could be seen as doing much the same thing. It defended those skits as being part of the WWF's "competitive strategy" to deal with "the unfair and anti-competitive tactics of WCW."

In other words, when McMahon skewered Turner it was David battling Goliath. When Turner used his checkbook to buy ratings, something that everyone in Hollywood tried to do, it was anticompetitive.

SHORTLY AFTER Nash joined Hall on *Nitro* in early June, the WCW's website and 900 lines began to plant the seed that a third ex-WWF wrestler would soon be joining the two-man invasion squad dubbed "the Outsiders."

Hulk Hogan hadn't been a heel since his first stint working for Vince's father at the World Wrestling Federation that ended in 1981. The closest he came was a brief flirtation in the fall of 1995, when he donned black gloves and a black rag on his head during a *Nitro* show and declared, "I just might hang on to the black gloves, brother, because everyone knows what a man with a pair of black gloves and a black rag on his head is capable of doing, dude." (When the tactless allusion to O. J. Simpson bombed, he shed the dark image and asked the fans for their support back.)

But as the summer of 1996 dawned, Hogan wasn't as quick as he might once have been to reject the idea of stepping into the role of the third man. For one thing, his movie career was on the skids. The new vehicle he was filming, *Santa with Muscles*, would get such bad reviews ("Call it the movie equivalent of coal in a Christmas stocking and you won't be far off the mark," huffed *Variety*) that it would only be the thirty-sixth-highest grossing film on its opening weekend. For another, he was below his natural weight of 240 pounds and showing every bit of his forty-two years. Even towns that were reliably supportive of him were starting to yield such loud boos that his closest friends had begun to suggest that he turn heel.

With his contract running out, Hogan saw that Hall and Nash were becoming the company's new creative force. With each passing week that *Nitro* beat *Raw*, Bischoff became more respectful of their judgment. Hogan could see the expediency of attaching himself to them. He'd look younger and hipper trading his yellow shirt and trunks for biker black. And once he got a toehold, he'd be in a better position to muscle them aside.

On July 7, 1996, the plan was for Hogan to come to the Ocean Center in Daytona, Florida. He flew into town that morning on his Lear jet and remained in seclusion most of the day, shunning the local hotel where the rest of the Boys stayed. Neither Hall nor Nash knew for sure who their new partner was going to be, although they suspected. Everyone suspected.

Bischoff was giddy about this element of surprise, but he was also nervous. What if Hogan was setting him up? In this business, you could never tell. So in the event that Hogan pulled a double cross and backed out at the last minute, he had Sting standing in the wings, ready to take his place.

It wasn't necessary. Fifteen minutes before show time, a stretch limousine pulled into the back of the Ocean Center and idled with its tinted windows up. Once Hogan was assured no one was looking, he was hustled out of the car with a towel covering his head and ushered into a private dressing room. There he stayed over the next two hours, until the show was nearly over. The last match of the night featured Sting, Randy Savage, and Lex Luger against Hall and Nash and the unadvertised partner making his debut as the Third Man. Hogan watched on a backstage monitor as Luger got knocked out and the tide turned twice, first to the advantage of the babyfaces, then the Outsiders. It was at that point that a backstage aide knocked on his dressing room door.

Hogan walked out, strode to the side exit, and stopped at a curtain that opened onto the walkway. There he knelt down and dropped his head, as if in prayer. A moment later, he lifted his head, made a fist, pounded the table twice, and walked through the curtain to do what he'd avoided doing for fifteen years.

With the audience expecting him to rescue Sting, he walked between the ropes. Then he looked around and laid a prompt legdrop on his old friend Savage. For a moment, there was silence. Then Hogan let his face turn a couple of shades of mean.

In creating the Outsiders, Bischoff had created a new kind of genre: reality-based wrestling, in which threads of reality were woven into the world of pretend that promoters once took pains to paint as real. And the act of turning heel and telling the truth seemed to inspire Hogan, who was at the crux of it.

"The Outsiders are the men I want as my friends," he scowled, pointing at his new allies. "They are the new blood of professional wrestling. And not only are we going to take over the whole wrestling business with Hulk Hogan and the new blood, we will destroy everything in our path..." Given that preamble, only a sweeping name for their coalition would do: Hogan called it the New World Order, or nWo.

As fans started pelting Hogan with ice, paper cups, and garbage, Bischoff took off the headset he'd been listening on backstage and heaved a sigh of relief. "Congratulations," one of the show's producers told him at the postshow party. "Everybody's going to remember you as the guy who turned Hulk Hogan."

But the brotherly scene of Hogan, Hall, and Nash joining hands masked the paranoia, mistrust, and jealousies that would inevitably erupt. Hogan would come to despise the fans who booed him and the wrestlers who criticized him. Nash would get tired of Hogan's incessant meddling and power plays. And Hall would find that his wife was right, that success would be a curse.

For the moment, though, all that mattered was the picture of the three stars together and the weekly ratings victory that it provided.

TWELVE

AS ERIC BISCHOFF'S SUCCESS with the nWo proved, family wrestling, at least as a marketable concept, was a bust. While the nWo was turning into a licensing juggernaut, the WWF couldn't land a major toy company contract for its action figures. One licenser put a fine point on the problem when he told a WWF pitchman, "Forget it. You guys are a dead brand."

What Vince needed was a new cast of characters, and to assemble one he turned to his talent director, the oval-faced Oklahoman Jim Ross. Having risen through the ranks as Bill Watts's right-hand man in Tulsa, and later the vice president for broadcasting at WCW, Ross knew everyone there was to know. Just as important, he had the same hard-on for Bischoff as Vince did. Bischoff had just forced him out of WCW in a management purge. By offering Ross a soft landing in the WWF, McMahon got a pipeline to all the disaffected WCW players and one of the shrewdest judges of talent in the business. Ross proved it by making Steve Williams, the Texas backwoodsman whom Bischoff had also just fired, one of his first hires.

When he shaved his head and put on a bad-boy attitude, Williams could have been any truck driver drinking bad Scotch before dawn. But that never quite came through when he wrestled in WCW as half of a tag team called the Hollywood Blonds. And McMahon didn't do much better when he initially introduced him as the Ringmaster, a bland, costumeless character. (Vince had so little faith in Williams's interview skills that he gave him Ted "Million-Dollar Man" DiBiase as a manager and had DiBiase do all the talking.) But Ross knew the wrestler had more to offer and gave him the latitude to shape his own persona. First, Williams designed the Stone Cold Steve Austin character out of the shards of his own dyspeptic past. Then, in June 1996, while he was getting his lip stitched from a gash he'd suffered in one of the early matches at the *King of the Ring* pay-per-view, he began to think of the final bout he was scheduled to have with Jake "the Snake" Roberts, a recovering crack addict who was making a comeback under the guise of having given his life over to Christ. Roberts had been invoking *John 3:16* during his ring entrances, and Austin decided to play on the verse by coining his own phrase, "Austin 3:16." After he'd pinned Roberts in less than five minutes that evening, Austin announced that he didn't want to hear any more biblical bullshit because "Austin 3:16 says I just whipped your ass."

"Austin 3:16" was one of those catchphrases that hit the zeitgeist at a perfect moment, and McMahon threw his hungry marketing machinery behind it, churning out T-shirts, posters, and Styrofoam middle fingers like the one that Austin gave crowds. Austin was exactly what Vince needed to build his new cast around. All that remained was finding a foil. Austin had far too much visceral intensity to be paired with just anyone. McMahon needed someone who looked at the world just as diffidently, a partner who could radiate the same blue-jeans cynicism.

One of Ross's favorite acts was Brian Pillman, a Cincinnati street fighter with a vicious temper whose twisting corkscrew jumps off the ropes earned him the nickname "Flying Brian." Well before Hall and Nash coalesced in the nWo or Austin coined the phrase "Austin 3:16," Pillman was using a novel titled *The Big Con* as a blueprint for the canniest confidence games to ever be pulled off in a business that was built on them.

In February 1996, Pillman had been penciled in to lose on a *Super-Brawl* pay-per-view bout with Kevin Sullivan, the old ring hand who was pulling double duty behind the scenes as Bischoff's chief booker. Sullivan had written a script that called for Pillman to lose a leather-strap match in which the loser had to surrender by shouting, "I respect you." Sullivan was at least ten years past his prime while Pillman was lithe and tanned, and the crowd had every reason to expect youth to prevail. As expected, Pillman came roaring out to dominate Sullivan. But suddenly he dropped his arms, dropped his strap, and in a wrestling version of *no mas,* spat the phrase, "I respect you, *booker man.*" The last two words were more than an improvisation; they were an attack on sixty years of dogma. Maintaining the illusion of wrestling meant denying that bookers or any of the business's other puppeteers even existed. By outing Sullivan, Pillman was taking it on himself to tear down the industry's wall of silence. Sullivan stood dumbstruck in the ring while Pillman stomped backstage, entering into a furious shouting match with Bischoff.

"What the hell's wrong with Pillman?" Hulk Hogan asked. And before anyone could think of an answer, Pillman blew past him and through the arena doors, where he got into his car and burned rubber out of the parking lot, clipping a parked Caddy on the way.

Pillman's behavior in the weeks that followed made him the most talked about wrestler in the business. He arrived at an independent show produced by Philadelphia's Extreme Championship Wrestling and had to be restrained from taking out his penis and pissing in the ring. He did a guest stint on a right-wing Cincinnati radio show and hung up on callers. At strip clubs, he cursed fans who stopped by to say hello. Wrestler Terry Funk didn't know what to think when Pillman mused about chaining himself to the goalposts during the Super Bowl. That the whole thing was an act—privately blessed by Bischoff—occurred to almost no one. Wrestlers always conned the fans. But what was the point of conning each other? There wasn't any. Which, in its own way, made the self-promotional lunatic charade even shrewder. Act or no act, Brian's friends assumed that he was headed for a breakdown.

THOUGH HE seemed to walk lightly through life, the boy from the working-class side of Cincinnati spent most of his childhood in and out of hospitals, battling throat cancer through thirty-one operations. His mother, a waitress, hit up everyone she knew to pay for them. Most children would have withdrawn after that kind of ordeal, conditioned to baby their bodies. But Pillman went the opposite way: to the streets, where he carried the vain but well-earned belief that he could win any fight he found thanks to his ability to withstand pain. That reputation caught the eye of a coach in suburban Norwood and led to a high school football career.

Still, he was small for college ball—just five-foot-ten—and had to walk on at Ohio's University of Miami to land a spot on the starting squad. There, he made as much of an impression off the field as on, once astounding his roommates by having sex with a woman who was hanging upside down from a chin-up bar while wearing gravity boots. After his graduation, the irrepressible athlete tried out for the Cincinnati Bengals and—impressively, considering his size—won a spot as a linebacker. But his pro career was short lived. He was traded to the Buffalo Bills the next year and cut when steroids were discovered in his locker. It was a quick hop from there to wrestling, where no one cared what he was using to pack 210 pounds of muscle onto his slight frame.

With deceptively sweet looks, Pillman was cast as a babyface at WCW, hitting the road as a dependable player with a weak spot for seducing the mothers who brought their kids backstage for autographs. (Whenever possible, he pawned the kids off on stagehands while he took their moms to hotels that charged by the hour.) Of the bevies of women he bedded, however, none was more complex than Shawn Rochelle Floyd, a heart-stopping blonde he met in a one-gas-station town called California, Kentucky. After a whirlwind romance, Floyd became pregnant and the couple moved in together. Unfortunately, it didn't take long for their relationship to sour. Rochelle, as she was commonly known, was a heavy cocaine user and disappeared for long stretches at a time. One day, Pillman had to drive through the crack ghettos of Cincinnati with her picture, asking every street peddler with a Raiders jacket whether he'd seen her. The local cops wound up busting him, figuring *he* was the one trying to buy drugs. Rochelle turned up in Florida, partying in a car with strangers.

When he'd had enough, Pillman took their daughter, Brittany, and began a new relationship with a Penthouse Pet who'd just ended a stormy relationship with Jim "Ultimate Warrrior" Hellwig. A soft woman with two children from a past relationship, the future Mrs. Melanie Pillman kept her distance from Rochelle. But that became impossible when the newlyweds sued for custody of Brittany. On the day that a family court judge approved their petition and said there would be no change until Rochelle went into rehab, Rochelle called the Pillman home, threatening to kill herself. Melanie tried calming her, but soon the two women began fighting over the best interests of the child. At a particularly pitched point, the line went dead and Melanie tried dialing the number displayed on her caller ID box, only to get a busy signal. Rochelle had called her mother and shot herself in the head while crying about her failures.

Wracked by the guilt of having played a role in the suicide of his daughter's mother, Brian doubled up on the pills he was taking to keep up his work schedule. He'd started taking so many Vicodins and Percocets that he had to rotate among forty pharmacists in Cincinnati just to keep any one of them from getting suspicious. One evening at the dinner table, his wife noticed that he was trying to bring the fork to his mouth and was missing it completely. He didn't do it once, but several times. "Brian, what are you doing?" she asked. He slurred his words, then nearly fell over trying to get up. At a hospital later that night, the examining doctor told her that Brian had ten times the recommended dosage of pain medication in his stomach. "You wouldn't have any idea why he'd be taking so much, would you?" he asked. Melanie just shrugged.

By March 1996, Brian had created the loose cannon act from the fraying threads of his personal and work lives. By skirting the edges of what was fact and fantasy, he'd built a cult of personality around himself, though not the kind most wrestlers encouraged. It was a morbid cult filled with rubberneckers just waiting for him to take the final lunge into complete madness.

Vince didn't know Brian and wasn't sure what to make of the whole thing when Ross convinced him that they'd found the perfect foil for Austin, but he offered him a deal that more than doubled Pillman's

WCW salary. Bischoff, not eager to lose a homegrown star, sweetened his own offer until it got up to $400,000. Over forty-eight hours in early April, Pillman stayed up trying to figure out which one to accept until, finally, he grabbed his car keys and took his Humvee on a deserted road to clear his mind. As he rounded a sharp bend, he felt his eyelids get heavy and his hands slip from the wheel. In that second, the truck drove straight off the road and over a tree trunk, shooting him like a missile out the front window while it sailed into a field, flipping four times before coming to a rest.

There would be considerable debate about what exactly had happened, and Pillman's crazy/not crazy act didn't help matters. After the accident, he confided to a friend that at the very moment his eyes closed he'd seen Rochelle's face in his rearview mirror. It was just as possible that the excitement over signing a new contract triggered a recurrence of the manic depression he'd battled since childhood. Whatever the cause, he woke up from the crash with a face broken in so many places that it needed four steel plates to be reconstructed and a right ankle crushed to the consistency of eggshells.

It was the ultimate con. The man who'd fooled his fans and friends into believing he had a death wish had nearly gone ahead and done it. He'd nearly killed himself for real. And now, despite being on crutches, his loose cannon bit was hotter than ever.

After he had his face repaired and a rod inserted into his ankle, Pillman left the hospital and signed a deal to become Austin's foil at the WWF, creating a rivalry between two antiheroes that McMahon hoped could be his answer to the nWo.

IN NOVEMBER 1996, USA decided to move *Raw*'s time slot up an hour, to eight o'clock, so it could air head-to-head with *Nitro*. For the debut show, one of Vince's writers suggested a script based loosely on a film he'd just seen, *Cape Fear*, which involved an ex-con terrorizing a public defender. Vince liked the idea of doing a remote shot from Pillman's Cincinnati home and flew there to discuss its details. The shoot would have to be done live. That was certain. What they needed was a back-story to set up the action. They came up with the idea of telling the show's viewers that Pillman was going to be interviewed live on *Raw* and that Austin was in the neighborhood, rumored to be eager to settle old scores. The Pillmans loved the idea, and Melanie went so far as to fix the guestroom so their old friend Austin could spend the night after the filming ended. The only thing they had to worry about, Vince joked, was some Kentucky hayseed interrupting the show because he thought the whole thing was real.

AT EIGHT o'clock on November 7, 1996, a black screen appeared on USA warning viewers that what they were about to see was both graphic and violent. It was the only time it would be shown over the next hour and was the last thing shown before the scene switched to Brian Pill-man's stately colonial home in Walton, Kentucky, thirty miles from Cincinnati.

A graphic in the upper-left corner was stamped "Live!" and a reporter stationed in the driveway was there to set the stage for those unfamil-iar with WWF product: A hobbled and frightened Pillman was trapped inside, he said, waiting for Austin to make good on a threat to kill him.

Pillman was introduced while lying on his couch, his ankle in a cast from the operation he'd just endured. "Don't you feel like a hostage in your own home?" Vince asked through a remote hookup. "Austin is a dead man walking," Pillman replied on cue, unsheathing a Glock pistol and cocking it confidently. "When Austin 3:16 meets Pillman's nine-millimeter gun, I'm gonna blow his sorry ass straight to hell!"

Later, Vince would insist the scene was no different from the stan-dard fare in police shows and cable movies. But he'd have a hard time explaining why, if his audience was really adults, a Milton Bradley rock-em-sock-em Karate Fighters commercial preceded the next piece of footage—arguably the most violent thing that he'd ever put on television.

When the program resumed, Austin had arrived outside the Pillman home to force his way past three plainclothes "guards" (actually extras from a nearby wrestling school) on hand to protect the feeble Pillman. In street-fighting style, he punched and clawed and used children's toys (a hockey stick and Radio Flyer wagon) to barge past them. In the ugliest moment, Austin forced the head of one of the men into a car door and slammed it as the victim wailed. Finally, with the guards subdued, he disappeared into the dark—a jackbooted intruder bent on terrorizing a typical suburban couple with kids toys in the driveway and a loaded Glock in the basement.

If this was the new WWF, it had to coexist jarringly with the old WWF because the action quickly switched back to matches that had been previously recorded in Fort Wayne, Indiana, including a bout featuring, of all people, the Iron Sheik, the very symbol of Vince's eighties heyday. It was a head-spinning juxtaposition—the old naïveté next to the new noir. Even Vince seemed a bit unsettled by the new ground he was plowing. "There's a very uncomfortable feeling in that live shot we just saw," he said, as much to himself as to his audience.

He was right to worry. Whatever it looked like on paper, whatever it sounded like in the writer's room, there was no way he could have known the next scene would look like this: Pillman, trapped in his basement, holding his gun over his head. Suddenly, a hand breaks through a glass door. Melanie screams. Brian, his eyes as wild as downed power lines, cocks the gun. Austin lunges. And then the video feed is cut, the screen goes gray, and Vince intones, "Quite frankly, a publicity stunt has gone too far and our hope is that nobody has been hurt."

For most of the next hour, periodic attempts to "restore" the feed were tried. Each effort "failed," however, with the on-site director insisting his men were afraid to get out of the truck. To make sure new viewers tuning in at nine o'clock were kept in the loop, the incident was replayed twice more, interspersed with the more conventional Fort Wayne matches. Finally, at 9:55 P.M., the video feed was "restored" in time to capture a scene out of *Cops*. As Pillman tried to leap up and chase Austin, his bodyguards held him down. The handheld camera shook so as not to give any clear idea of who was shouting. "Did anyone fire a shot?" "Is anyone hurt?" "Do you know where Austin is?"

And then: "Oh my God, he's back."

Melanie cried, "Will someone call the police."

Austin taunted, "Shoot me!"

Vince yelled from the studio, "Grab the gun! Will someone please call the cops."

And then Brian Pillman cocked his Glock, aimed it squarely at Austin, and screamed, "This son of a bitch has this coming. Get the hell out of the fucking way. *Get out of the way.* Let him go!"

The screen went gray again, and a gunshot rang out.

WATCHING THE show in his Connecticut home, Wayne Becker sank back into his chair. Did he just hear the word *fuck* go out over his network's airwaves? Yes, he was sure he did. Without missing a beat, he called USA's control room in Manhattan and ordered that a copy of the show be on his desk by the next morning.

By Tuesday afternoon, Kay Koplovitz had already heard about it. The complaint lines of the network had lit up with parents whose kids mistook what they saw for real news footage and with advertisers who were aghast. This was more than bad-boy Vince pushing the envelope. This was an out-and-out betrayal of her trust. She told Becker that she wanted him to thoroughly examine USA's contract with the WWF and report back on their options. Becker thought that if they wanted they could get Vince on a standards-and-practices issue. Koplovitz considered it, then said, "Get Vince down here. I want him to know that."

When McMahon finally arrived at USA's offices, he was led to a conference room with windows that overlooked Rockefeller Center. There was a screen behind Koplovitz's chair, and Becker had prepared a video to show. The video had everything he thought could be construed as violating McMahon's contract: from Goldust's homoerotic gyrations to

Steve Austin giving his middle finger to a crowd. In short, the whole ugly New WWF canon.

After he played it, Koplovitz leaned forward. Though there were half a dozen people in the room, she looked at Vince as if they were the only two in the world. "Vince," she said with a controlled evenness that gave Becker a shiver. "This is not fun. This is not for kids. And this is not what we are going to be doing. It has to be lighter. It has to go back to the original formula."

Vince played the contrition card and promised to make a public apology, which he did the next Saturday on the WWF's *Live Wire* show, addressing his audience by saying: "In an effort to draw attention to our new time slot at 8 p.m., there is no doubt we went overboard. We humbly apologize. The actions and the language were reprehensible and this will never ever happen again in the WWF."

But apology or not, Vince was sure he was onto something. His competition wasn't WCW, he decided, but the rest of what America was watching at night: *NYPD Blue, Homicide, Cops, Law & Order*. All of a sudden, the scripts emerging from the creative meetings got strikingly darker.

They included the Nation of Domination, a black-power gang that taunted their rivals by telling them to kiss their "black asses;"[1] Degeneration X, the white-trash successor to the Clique, which popularized the crotch chop—an open-palm chopping gesture toward a thrusting pelvis—and the "Suck It" war cry; and the Hart Foundation, a Canadian heel group that drew patriotic jeers by calling the American cities that they visited "toilets."

The overall tone for the show was set by Jerry Lawler, who sat at the announcer's table alongside Ross during *Raw*. One night in Evansville, Indiana, he referred to the feud between Dusty Rhodes and his son,

---

1. The group included a young Rocky Maivia, a third-generation wrestler who'd entered the WWF a year before as babyface and was now doing a heel turn. Because he loathed the racial overtones of the group, he lasted only a few months before emerging on his own as The Rock.

Dustin, who was in costume as Goldust, by saying, "Your father doesn't love you because you put on a woman's wig and went around kissing men like a flaming fag." If Koplovitz continued to be appalled by what she was airing, the inescapable fact remained that *Raw* was still the network's highest-rated show, outdrawing the drama that followed it, *Le Femme Nikita*, by a two to one margin. So in February 1997, Koplovitz felt compelled to listen to aides who argued for expanding *Raw* to two hours and moving its start time to nine o'clock.[2]

The first show in the new time slot aired after the two-week stretch when *Raw* was preempted by the U.S. Open. McMahon was inconsolable. Each year, he muttered that the people at USA had no appreciation for how hard it was to get an audience to come back after it had lost the thread of a soap opera. This year was even worse because *Nitro* had shattered all previous records by luring more than 3.5 million homes to its shows, creating an astounding 4.97 cable rating. To hook his audience back quickly, Vince and his writers concocted a story line featuring Pillman and one of his old flames, Dustin's wife, Terri.

Winking at a past sexual relationship, the WWF writing group came up with an angle that paired Brian and Terri—who now used her husband's birth name, Runnels—in a love triangle. It started when Pillman pinned Goldust at a Louisville show and, as a spoil, earned her "services" for a month. Over the next four episodes of *Raw*, Brian tormented Dustin. (This was another uncomfortable inside joke, since the real-life marriage of Dustin and Terri Runnels was in shambles.) In one episode dubbed "Brian Pillman's XXX-Files," Terri lay in bed next to him in a seedy motel, handcuffed to the headboard. In another, he led her into the ring while she was hunched over, announcing that he'd "given

---

2. For years, one of the things that severely irritated Vince about his deal with USA was Koplovitz's insistence on running *Murder She Wrote* as a lead-in to *Raw*. Its audience of middle-aged women turned off their TVs as soon as their show ended, forcing him to build his young male audience from scratch. This time, however, Koplovitz agreed to insert the demographically friendly *Walker, Texas Ranger* as a prelude instead.

it to her." The end of the arc was set for October 7, when Terri's thirty-day sentence was to be finished. The script called for her to renew her vows with Dustin live on *Raw* that night, only to ditch him at the last minute and run off with Brian.

Pillman was ecstatic enough about being back in the center of the action that he upped his dosage of pills so he could ignore the pain of wrestling on an ankle held together by fused bone and steel. "One night, me and him, Bret [Hart] and Davey Boy [Smith], were sitting in a room getting dressed," says Del "the Patriot" Wilkes. "It wasn't a TV show, just a house show.[3] And he'd just come back from a match. He was skinny looking, unhealthy looking. He'd lost a lot of weight. I said, 'What are you going to do tonight, Brian?' He said, 'I'm gonna go out and get so drunk that somebody will kill me and put me out of my misery.' It was very obvious that he had just given up. In those last few months he was just one pathetically miserable human being."

As far as drug testing was concerned, things had eased up at Titan Tower since the dark posttrial days when the McMahons monitored everyone under their roof. But deciding that something had to be done for Brian's own good, Ross gave him a test that he failed. "As long as nobody pushed the envelope, Vince was willing to let dope smoking or casual coke use ride," says another wrestler. "But Brian threatened that whole status. Two of the Boys took him out back and roughed him up, you know, saying stuff like, 'Listen asshole, don't you fuck it up for the rest of us. We know how to handle it. Don't screw us just because you don't.' Everyone knew what was going on with Brian. They were just afraid to do something about it."

His "Rehab Is For Losers" shirt pretty much said all there was to say about his attitude toward going straight. One of the few times he agreed to seek a doctor's advice was after he took his kids to a

---

3. *House shows* are arena shows staged for ticket revenue but not broadcast over TV. Their results are usually considered meaningless. As the old expression in wrestling goes, "If it didn't happen on TV, it didn't happen."

Chuck E. Cheese's and drew the attention of a cop because he was stumbling like a drunk. After that, Melanie became worried enough that she told Brian she wanted him to get life insurance for the sake of the kids. He agreed, only to balk when he later learned that he'd have to take a drug test to qualify. A tester arrived at his home four times, and each time Brian refused to submit. On the fifth occasion, the tester said he wasn't coming back. Brian relented and gave blood. But after the man left, he turned to his wife and said, "Well you can kiss that million dollars good-bye."

On Sunday, October 6, 1997, Melanie was at home, cooking dinner for the kids and wondering how to break the news to Brian that she was pregnant once again, when a road agent from the WWF phoned to ask if she knew where he might be. He'd missed his early Sunday shuttle to the Twin Cities airport and hadn't shown up at the *Badd Blood* set in the Kiel Center in St. Louis.

Melanie was more mad than worried. When he'd slipped back to his motel room Saturday night, he'd left her an answering machine message saying that he was going to bed. He probably took too many pills and overslept, she thought. Or maybe he'd smashed up another rental car. After she hung up the phone, she called a friend and said, "Brian's doing this to spite me. He's on so much shit, he probably *wants* to lose his job."

The words had just left her lips when the doorbell rang. She pulled aside the curtain to see a police officer on her doorstep.

The news that the policeman was delivering—that Brian had died of a heart attack in the middle of the night—reached the Kiel Center at about the same time as it reached Melanie.

Three wrestlers were sitting in a room, trying to figure out a finish to their match when a ghostly white Owen Hart walked in and said, "Guys, they just found Brian dead in the hotel room."

One of them, Leon "Vader" White, looked at his colleagues, then paused. "We can worry about that after the match," he said. "I've got to come up with a *fucking finish!*"

As word of the discovery spread, the confusion surrounding the way Brian lived shrouded the way he died. Was it a simple heart attack, caused by the stress his chemically inflated body put on his heart? Was it a suicide? There were bottles of pills and muscle relaxers around his bed. Or was it just an accidental overdose? Vince dreaded that thought. That would be all he needed—something else to start a whole new inquisition, a whole new round of ratings-killing press.

The irony, of course, was that Pillman was one of the few people the WWF actually tested for drugs. The problem was that they let him keep working even though he'd flunked. Referee Ed Sharkey would tell the *St. Paul Pioneer Press* that he last saw Pillman sleeping on the floor of the locker room Saturday night, curled into a fetal position.

After huddling with his advisers, Vince decided to go on the air before *Badd Blood* to announce the death and acknowledge the chance that it might be drug related. That, at least, would explain Brian's absence. But by the light of the next morning with another show scheduled later in the day in Kansas City, it was clear that wouldn't be enough. A tribute film was quickly stitched together and a decision made to toll a bell for the sellout crowd at the Kemper Arena in Kansas City while the WWF cast stood for a moment of silence during *Raw*. But was even *that* enough? Didn't he have a responsibility to do more? For his fans? For his wrestlers? For his ratings? The way he saw it, his competition wasn't just *Cops*. It was *Dateline* and *PrimeTime Live*, too. What would Jane Pauley or Diane Sawyer do?

That one was easy. Put the widow on the tube.

And that was where things got weird. Because shortly after the opening credits rolled, shortly after the ten-bell salute to Pillman clanged, it was clear that wrestling was about to cross a very shaky bridge, leaving the faux world of kayfabe behind for good. Vince was going to give *Raw*'s fans a real-life, grieving widow less than forty-eight hours after she'd been left with five orphaned children and another one on the way. To make sure no one missed the exclusive, he hyped it before every commercial break, sending his viewers to the Pillmans' empty family room where it was announced Melanie would soon appear. When she finally made her way to the couch—the same one on which Brian had gone wild during the home invasion angle nearly a year earlier—Vince's voice filtered into her earpiece. "You sure you want to do this?" he asked. "Really, it's not too late to back out."

"Yes, yes, I'm sure," she said, waiting for a video game commercial on *Raw* to end.

When the show resumed, Vince appeared dressed in a black army-like jumpsuit with the *Raw* logo embroidered above the breast pocket. He opened the interview in a stilted tone that chafed against the confessional nature of the moment. "Melanie, I'm sure you're distraught, shocked, dismayed over this, and we thank you very much for joining us tonight," he started. "There's always a great deal of speculation when a thirty-five-year-old man who's in competitive condition passes away. Can you, please, tell us what you've been told about Brian's death?"

"Apparently there was a problem with his heart. Uh, apparently his heart had been under a lot of stress..."

"There was some speculation last night that Brian, because of his injuries, had to take a great deal of medicine," Vince continued. "There was some speculation that he may have taken too much."

Melanie expected this question, but the speed at which Vince leaped to it surprised her. Her face curled up in a look that was more disgust than despair. Seeing that, he backed off. "Is there anything you want to say to aspiring athletes who get hurt and may have to resort to prescribed medication, pain pills?"

"I can't really comment," she replied, sniffling. "My husband, not only was he an athlete but he was involved in a car accident and had extensive injuries from that and, uh, it was hard on him." Then, looking into the camera, or perhaps past it, she added, "I just want everyone to know it's a wake-up call. For some of you it could be your husband. Or it could be you. And you don't want to leave behind a bunch of orphans like my husband did."

"How are the children taking the news?" Vince pried, a bit too eagerly to sidestep the Tuesday morning critics who'd call the whole affair exploitative.

"Little Brian doesn't understand why Daddy's not coming home," she said. "But Brittany...she screamed for fifteen minutes." Melanie suddenly looked exhausted, as if whatever energy she had three questions ago was completely gone. But the impulse to go for one last piece of emotional punctuation proved too great for Vince to resist.

"Have you had a chance to think about what you as a single parent will do to support five children?" he asked, not really needing an answer to bring the segment to a close.

Melanie was back to staring at the floor. She mouthed something about being grateful for the support she'd received from fans and the company, then sighed. "I don't know, Vince. I don't know."

THIRTEEN

LIKE EVERYONE ELSE WHO knew Brian Pillman, Eric Bischoff was angry with him for dying. But Bischoff was also more than a little afraid that the next one to go might be under Turner's roof. So on October 13, 1997, a few days after he'd returned from Pillman's funeral, he gathered the Boys together before airtime at the Ice Palace in Tampa and let them know that anyone who needed help kicking a habit could take the time off, no questions asked. He needed them healthy, he said, because WCW was poised to expand to a third hour on Monday nights and get a beachhead on Thursday nights on TBS. They were all making more money than any of them dared to dream. But nobody should be confused about what Ted Turner wanted. He was sick of the raunchy language, the crotch chopping, and the sexual innuendo. Then, as if to send a heat-seeking missile, he scanned the group of faces, settling on Scott Hall and Kevin Nash. "There are only three wrestlers in this company who've ever put asses in the seats," he said. Then he named Hulk Hogan, Randy Savage, and Roddy Piper.

The line was a near-verbatim recitation of what the old guard had been saying since Hall and Nash arrived to create the illusion of an in-house war and succeeded beyond their wildest dreams. "I'm not a Hall fan," Piper would say. "Personally, I think he's a piece of shit. And Nash, well, at least he shows up. But I've never seen either of those guys draw a dime by being a single main event anywhere. I've done that so many motherfucking times—I have no idea how many times I've done it."

Piper was right, but he was also ignoring the obvious. Hall and Nash had spent the last sixteen months storming across the landscape as a pair of rat-pack bullies who smirked their way into the hearts of teenage boys everywhere. They were emotionally stunted million-aires—petulant, crass, leering. And they glided high above the company's rank and file, determined to get the kind of star treatment that had been reserved exclusively for Hogan.

In their rat-pack roles, Hall was the hothead while Nash was the acid-tongued comic who did more with his wits than his fists. After forty-one-year-old Arn Anderson retired on *Nitro* because neck surgery had left him unable even to button his shirt, Nash skewered the ceremony, tucking his long brown hair into a bald mask and wearing a neck brace to lampoon Anderson's sentimental good-bye. Anderson had no words when his wife called him backstage because their twelve-year-old son was in tears at home as he watched his father portrayed as a womanizing alcoholic surrounded by senile old wrestling buddies like Flair.

"What was the point of trying to make me look bad?" he'd say later. "I'm retired. What kind of person makes fun of someone else's genuine emotions?"

Hall made the Boys nervous because there was no telling what he might do at any minute, drunk or sober. One night he hit a wrestler named Jerry Sags so hard with a series of chair shots that he gave Sags a concussion. When the pair met a few weeks later at a *Nitro* taping in Shreveport, Louisiana, Sags was particularly careful about rehearsing a moment in the match when he'd throw a chair into the ring to set up an attack. "Go easy with that thing, okay?" he said to Hall. "You nearly fucking killed me last time." Hall mumbled agreement, but when show time came and Sags threw the chair to the ring, Hall grabbed it and flung it back, knocking Sags in the head again. Furious, Sags broke character and jumped into the ring, loosening one of Hall's teeth and puncturing an eardrum in the ensuing scuffle. (Sags subsequently filed a lawsuit, claiming that the cheap chair shot caused a recurring neck injury that led to his WCW contract not being renewed.)

Hall and Nash, the dark soul of the nWo, were just living in the world that Bischoff created for them, a cash-rich world of hard drinking and easy women. (In the prostitution trial of a strip club owner named Steven Kaplan, an exotic dancer would testify that Bischoff's wife paid her to return to a hotel for a threesome. Taking the stand later, Bischoff would say that he'd drunk at least a dozen beers and called the whole thing "a bit of a blur" while he watched the two women have sex.) Whether one considered them cool or vulgar, the fact remained that they were increasing the number of eyes watching prime-time wrestling.[1] When *Nitro* debuted in 1995, the total number of homes tuning into wrestling on USA and TBS on Monday nights averaged 4.5 million; now it was 5.5 million. And with the higher ratings, Bischoff was convinced that he was within striking distance of forcing McMahon out of business. In fact, when he gathered the Boys around him at the Ice Palace in Tampa after his return from Pillman's funeral, he even made a prediction: McMahon and the WWF were going to be out of business within six months.

ONE OF the faces looking out at Bischoff when he made his speech at the Ice Palace was Bill Goldberg, a rope-muscled former Atlanta Falcon whose career had been shortened by a tackle that tore the abdominal muscles near his groin in a 1994 preseason game against the Philadelphia Eagles. Goldberg understood pain and drugs. He took Vicodin and needed Sunday-morning needles to get through the rest of that season. But no matter how much he took, he wasn't agile enough. The Falcons put him into the expansion draft and the Carolina Panthers took him; he showed up to camp so lame that he was made the team's first-ever cut. After that, the son of a concert violinist and a gynecologist hung around Atlanta, running through the last of his NFL salary while he worked out at a local gym that he soon discovered was owned by WCW wrestlers Sting and Lex Luger. A quick friendship followed, and Goldberg found himself being introduced to other wrestlers, including Diamond Dallas Page.

---

1. According to a ratings study by Dave Meltzer, the gross number of viewers was substantially unchanged from years before. The difference was that the audience was now watching in prime time.

In the course of downing shots at the Gold Club strip bar in Atlanta (later made famous by its sex and mob-related scandals), Page suggested Goldberg try wrestling. But Bischoff was noncommittal when they met, suggesting they simply stay in touch. So Goldberg placed a call to a fellow Oklahoman, Jim Ross, and received an invitation to Titan Tower. When McMahon learned Bischoff was on the fence about hiring the six-foot-three, 285-pound stud, he offered him a contract on the spot. Goldberg demurred, asking for enough time to hear back from WCW. Weeks passed without word, and it wasn't until Goldberg decided to go to work for McMahon that Bischoff came through with a last-minute offer, which was accepted.

As the producer scanned Goldberg's face at the Ice Palace, he still wasn't sure what to make of the man. The instructors at WCW's training facility, the Power Plant, usually hated football players; most arrived thinking they could breeze through the three-day tryout and wound up leaving it exhausted and puking. But Goldberg was different. He came with a remarkably clear sense of who he wanted to be—a mix of football player, kickboxer, and street fighter. The package came together in his two-part finishing move. Drawing on his knack for headfirst tackles, he learned to ram his head full speed into rivals' stomachs and then, when they were off balance, hoist them upside down and bring them crashing to the mat. Needing a moniker for his finisher, he remembered the stage name his stepmother wanted him to use: Jack Hammer.

The way Goldberg evoked Steve Austin was uncanny, that much Bischoff could see. And while he wasn't as darkly nuanced or nihilistic as Austin, he was a primeval mountain of muscle who grunted and groaned, snapped his thick neck in a frightening twitch, and had a truly unnerving habit of head-butting concrete walls. Bischoff saw that watching him in his first few dark matches—ones performed at television tapings for the audience after the cameras were turned off. The producer measured the reaction a wrestler received from the fans in the front row, and he'd been impressed at how Goldberg held their attention without music or pyrotechnics. Though he showed up at his first televised match in Salt Lake City on September 22, 1997, with little fanfare—even announcer Mike Tenay, a walking encyclopedia on wrestling, admitted he didn't know much about the newcomer—he leaped off the screen in a way that screamed pain, making quick work of a pudgy but agile 325-pounder named Hugh Morrus. He won two more matches by the time the company reached Tampa, where he was scheduled to win TV match number four.

In pushing Goldberg, Bischoff forced men who'd spent years perfecting their own finishing moves to sacrifice themselves for the sake of a rookie whose long-term corporate potential was still uncertain. Nor was he particularly graceful about it. When a tough-guy Brit named Lord Steven Regal got penciled in as Goldberg's forty-third victim (the numbers rose without much rhyme or reason), Regal tried to retain some respect by throwing in a flurry of offense during their meeting. Unfortunately, it left Goldberg looking lost and confused. After the match ended, Bischoff cornered Regal in the rafters. "What the hell are you doing out there," he screamed. "You made the man look like a fool."

Wrestling ratings, like economic indicators, don't always show the present reality. Loyal fans continue their viewing patterns for months after a show has started to wane. In the case of WCW, that kept the ratings hovering around the 4.5 mark even as Bischoff and his writers flogged the nWo concept past its natural shelf life.

More troubling, the numbers also masked a fundamental turnaround at the WWF. At CNN Center in Atlanta, Turner's old wrestling hands watched with concern as Vince's shows became tighter. Somehow, the notoriety of the Pillman escapade had given him his timing back. The pace of his shows was frequently brilliant now, with five to ten well-crafted story lines—involving everything from sex to satanism—woven through a two-hour episode. The cliff-hangers were dead-on, and the plot turns all came at exactly the right moments. It was, WCW executives decided, a bad sign. Whatever Bischoff thought, Vince was too dangerous a man to let get up off the mat.

To make matters worse, Scott Hall, a third of the core of the nWo, picked this very moment to let his life unravel. Hall's wife of eight years decided to call it quits on their marriage, and Bischoff had to suspend him for going on the air drunk. A third stint in rehab did no good. A few weeks after he was released, the thirty-nine-year-old crashed his Pathfinder near the Cocoa Beach home he used when he was separated from his wife and was found by a cop sleeping in the wreckage. Later, when the car was towed to a garage, a woman in the parts department who asked for an autograph claimed he'd grabbed her and pressed his penis to her groin, mumbling, "I'll be whoever you want me to be, baby." Bischoff could only shake his head at the ensuing lawsuit and at the fact that three days later Hall wrecked his rented Cadillac in a highway spinout, claiming he'd fallen asleep at the wheel.

IT WAS raining on Monday, April 13, when Bischoff flew to Minneapolis for that night's *Nitro*. He was in a particularly bad mood. The 1998 NBA playoffs were about to start on TNT, which meant that *Nitro* was going to lose its hold on its Monday night for the duration, giving McMahon a major advantage at a moment when the producer wanted to surrender it least. The WWF had just scored the publicity coup of the year by getting Mike Tyson to referee at *Wrestlemania*. Because of that, *Raw*'s ratings had started to nudge up. The prior Monday's *Raw*—the second show to air after the Tyson *Wrestlemania*—was the closest call yet: *Nitro*'s advantage was less than two-tenths of a rating percentage point.

When Bischoff landed in Minneapolis, a steady spring rain was falling, the kind that made a tired man ache. To most of the Boys, the strain on the boss's face had become apparent. Though he dyed his hair black in an attempt to take a few years off his looks, there was no mistaking the worry lines around his eyes or his quick temper. His trusted emissary, Diamond Dallas Page, warned him that he was losing the Boys. In Page's words, they thought he was "becoming an asshole." It had been six months since he had given the Ice Palace speech. He decided to give another one when he reached the Target Center.

For one thing, he wanted to clear up rumblings that had been spreading over his handling of a recent tempest involving Ric Flair. Flair missed a TV taping of *Thunder* in Tallahassee the prior Thursday night because he was watching his nine-year-old son wrestle in a tournament in Detroit. In other times, it would have been forgotten. Certainly, it was no worse than any of the unpredictable things Hall did. But Bischoff was so irritated with Flair that he'd sent word from Japan, where he was traveling, that if he missed the Tallahassee show he'd be fired. Flair went to Detroit, anyway, and by the weekend assumed that he was no longer working at WCW. He didn't even bother showing up at Minneapolis's Target Center.

The problem was that Flair was a native of Minneapolis and his fans had bought seventeen thousand tickets in less than four hours, expecting to see him. Bischoff rubbed his temples. He had a month of NBA finals ahead of him that were going to bump *Nitro* out of its time slot and he had only this show to use in creating a favorable impression that would linger with the viewers in the interval. Now that Flair was a no-show, he'd have to create that impression using a pissed-off crowd that was going to be dead for the cameras. Marvelous. Just marvelous.

About an hour before show time, he gathered the company before him. Nodding toward Page, he admitted that he'd become a bit short-tempered and promised to be better about it in the future. He also knew they'd all been talking about what had happened with Flair and he wanted to address it head-on, before Flair had a chance to spin his side. His position was simple: Flair's contract stipulated that he had to be at television tapings, and the company was well within its right to hold him to it.

Bischoff watched the Boys shift uncomfortably. "Look, Ric Flair is a liar, but everyone lets him get away with it because he is Ric Flair," he said, trying to bring them around to his side. Well, so be it. He had enough. "Let him be Ric Flair. I'm gonna sue his ass into bankruptcy."

At that, a kind of stunned silence swept the room.

"Ric Flair set the standard for work ethic," one of the men in the room would later say. "And here's Bischoff saying he was going to sue him. You could hear everyone thinking, 'If he can do that to a world champion, what can he do to me?'"

If the point of the meeting was to reduce the paranoia and apprehension that was creeping through the locker room, the producer failed miserably. And, as he feared, his eighty-three-week run of ratings wins would end that April 13 night.

FOURTEEN

IN THE SPRING OF 1998, Jim Cornette left a booking meeting in Vince McMahon's office feeling as if a nervous tic was starting to develop over his left eye. He was worried that McMahon was panicking, reacting too much to what was happening down in Atlanta. Granted it was hard not to worry when, as recently as the summer of 1997, *Raw*'s ratings had dipped below the 1.5 mark and the company was losing $135,000 a week. It had gotten so bad that watercoolers were taken out of the executive offices. But Cornette was sure that things would turn around without turning *Raw* into an apocalyptic freak show.

And that's exactly what he feared was happening as McMahon began to take more cues from a pushy new writer. Vince Russo was one of the WWF's most ardent defenders in New York when he worked as the host of an AM radio show that covered wrestling, and he'd managed to parlay that support into a job writing for the WWF's magazines. A driven man with long hair, lean features, and a tough-guy accent, he would sit for hours outside his boss's office, waiting for him to come out so he could pitch ideas.

And what Russo was pitching seemed to be working. As *Raw*'s ratings drifted into the 2.0 range in late 1997, he became the staunchest advocate of introducing homosexuality, gang culture, broken marriages, racism, and cross-dressing into the program's scripts. "I'd get a headache and a nervous tic trying to explain to him why you couldn't have the guys in some kind of explosive goddamned barbed-wire, AIDS-infected needle cage match," Cornette recalls. "And I would end up with no voice."

Cornette was particularly appalled when Russo's deputy, a onetime comedy writer named Ed Ferrara, booked a miscarriage angle involving Dustin Runnels's now *ex*-wife, Terri. "Let me ask you a fucking question," Cornette asked Ferrara. "How many tickets did that sell? And tell me, Ed, why anyone should give a fuck? The only thing that did was piss off anybody who's ever had that happen to them. Personally, if it happened to my girlfriend and I knew you wrote it, I'd come over and punch your fucking teeth out."

At USA, the network of Wimbledon and the Westminster Kennel Club Dog Show, Kay Koplovitz had learned enough from the Brian Pillman affair to know she couldn't trust Vince's writers to work alone. That's why she insisted they run their scripts by a new liaison, Bonnie Hammer. (Wayne Becker had left by then, exhausted by the experience of working with the McMahons.) The fashionably prim native of Manhattan's Upper East Side couldn't have been more different than the tough-talking Russo. She'd begun her career at the Boston public television station WGBH and more recently produced a public-service documentary series for Koplovitz titled *Erase the Hate*. She was mortified to learn that her new assignment was wrestling, yet she took it on with the same intensity that she took on everything else. When she traveled to Stamford for her first meeting, McMahon barged into his conference room impatiently, as if anything having to do with USA was a chore. Sizing up the moment, she decided to be blunt. "Vince, I hadn't ever watched your show until a couple of weeks ago," she said. "I don't know what your business is about and I don't care. But I do know how to make good TV. And I want to get you out of the twos and into the threes."

Some of the changes were technical. For example, they used smoke machines but didn't have gadgets to clear the residue; as a result, the rest of the show was filmed in a haze. But the biggest problem Hammer saw was that it was hard for a newcomer to pick up the stories in midstream. "If I can't understand what's going on in the first five minutes of the show, then we're in trouble," she told Russo. "You have to get viewers in right away, tease them." She developed what she called "hot minutes" at key channel-switching times, like ten o'clock. She also tried to help him round out his characters to give them more depth.

Hammer's intervention came at a critical time for *Raw*. The WWF's three-year contract with USA was due to expire in May 1998, and Vince wanted more than just money in a new deal. He wanted influence. He wanted an expanded role in a network that he felt had underappreciated him for too long. Hammer became a vocal advocate for him within USA. She discussed ideas like a late-night show about the Las Vegas strip and a series on USA's sister Sci-Fi Channel that would involve the Undertaker. But the truth was that no one at USA was ever going to give the McMahons more power. The network president had just hired a new entertainment chief from CBS, Rod Perth, and he was making deals for big-budget, prestige miniseries like *Moby Dick*, *Huckleberry Finn*, and *Treasure Island*. Koplovitz's secret prayer seemed to be that those and other new shows would do well enough that she could eventually dump *Raw* entirely.

Then, two weeks after Brian Pillman's funeral, the terrain shifted completely under everyone's feet.

Barry Diller, the fifty-five-year-old former head of Paramount and founder of the Fox Network, paid $1.2 billion in cash to buy USA. In a deal that startled Hollywood by virtue of its scope, Diller also gained control of the Sci-Fi Channel and the television production studio of USA's parent company, Universal. When added to the two home shopping channels that he already owned, the purchase positioned Diller as a new major player in cable television. The dust hadn't even settled when he told reporters that he found USA to be "under-strategized," an allusion to its lack of a strong identity. But he was circumspect about his own plans. Was he going to keep going highbrow, continuing the arc initiated by Koplovitz and Perth? Or was he going to go back to what he'd done at Fox and fill its lineup with funny but crude shows like *Married with Children*?

"Diller was like *The Wizard of Oz*," said one high-level employee who worked there at the time. "You always heard he was around, but you didn't know what he was planning."

. . .

WITH THE announcement of the deal just days old, Vince was getting his pompadour touched up at a Manhattan barbershop when his cell phone rang with a call from Bret Hart.

Hart was a humorless millionaire who regarded himself as an icon of the business and had been with Vince since the beginning—or at least since Hart's father, Stu, sold his Calgary-based territory to the WWF in the early eighties. A stooped man with a butcher's handshake, Stu and his wife raised twelve children in a gabled mansion that had a classically haunted, B-movie look. It had twenty rooms and a labyrinth of a yard piled high with the husks of beat-up cars. The heart of the house, where Stu taught his craft, was a basement dubbed "the dungeon." Billy Graham, who'd left a bouncer's job in Phoenix to pursue what he thought would be easy money with Stu's traveling road show in 1969, recalls that "it was really a classic, hard-core dungeon. I literally walked into a room with no door to close behind me, mats on the floor, and three walls covered with blood, snot, and saliva. Stu liked to make you moan and groan when he got you down there. I was a bouncer in a lot of bars and I dragged a lot of drunks out by their feet, but I was never in positions where I couldn't hear anything but groaning from my guts."

The Hart boys—Smith, Bruce, Keith, Wayne, Ross, Dean, Bret, and Owen—spent their time wrestling in the rings that lay in the backyard. Smith, Bruce, Keith, and Dean were the first to enter the business. Bret, however, was the one who was able to make the transition to the States when Stu sold his territory to Vince. With slicked-back hair and sunglasses, he rose through the WWF's tag-team ranks as part of the Hart Foundation with his brother-in-law, Jim "the Anvil" Neidhart. The combo held the WWF's tag-team title belts through most of 1987 and again, more briefly, in the fall of 1990. After that, Neidhart was shelved so Bret could be tested as a singles act.

Because he was six-foot-one and 230 pounds, he was small by the standards of the early nineties. But after the WWF's steroid scandal—when Vince was forced to lessen the visibility of his doped-up muscle men—technical proficiency became more important than size.

Boasting that he was the "excellence of execution," Hart rode a lengthy title reign in which he became instantly familiar to fans everywhere and tried to follow Hogan into acting. He landed a guest spot on the miniseries *Lonesome Dove* and bit parts in other series, and in so doing became convinced that his future lay as a small-screen action star. After losing the WWF title to Shawn Michaels at *Wrestlemania XII* on March 31, 1996, he took a sabbatical from wrestling, but he soon found that it was harder to land parts than he first imagined. In the fall of 1996, with the competition between WCW and the WWF at a fevered pitch, he decided to return to wrestling.

Rather than see Turner get his hands on one of the WWF's last bankable stars, McMahon offered Hart an unprecedented twenty-year contract. Negotiated in October 1996, it gave Hart a seven-figure salary for three years, during which Hart promised to keep wrestling, and a six-figure paycheck thereafter, when he would ascend to the booking committee and have a key role as a scriptwriter. But now, a year into the deal, Vince regretted his impetuousness. For one thing, Hart hadn't spiked the ratings as had been hoped. For another, McMahon had begun talks with a Manhattan investment house about taking the WWF public, and he'd been advised to limit any long-term obligations on his balance sheet. So before a show in Madison Square Garden, McMahon told Hart that he could no longer afford the deal they'd struck. He should feel free to pursue his fortune at WCW.

While Hart probably could have gone to court to enforce the contract, he sought out Bischoff. The call Vince received in the barber's chair was Bret reporting that he had a deal on the table worth $2 million a year. Was Vince sure this was what he wanted? A few half-hearted options were explored but none amounted to much of a counteroffer, so Hart said that he was accepting Turner's offer.

As he walked through the cool air of a Manhattan fall and into a waiting limousine that was about to whisk him to the movies with Linda, Vince was already thinking about how to make money off Hart's departure. His next pay-per-view, the *Survivor Series*, was due to air on November 9. He told Hart he wanted him to lose the belt to Shawn Michaels.

Michaels and Hart disliked each other as much as two men could. Hart came from a legendary Canadian wrestling family. Michaels was the son of a military man, born on an air force base in Scottsdale, Arizona, and reared in San Antonio, Texas. He had no patience for the pretentious Harts and their stuffy claim to being the self-appointed guardians of tradition. When Hart took his brief hiatus from the WWF to pursue an acting career, Michaels moved into the company's top slot. He was understandably piqued, then, when Hart returned to bump him down a notch.

From his vantage point, Hart saw Michaels as a low-class player who was lucky to have gotten as far as he had. "In my absence," he once wrote in a Calgary newspaper column, "the WWF had been overtaken by a prima donna of unmatched proportions." For his part, Michaels argued to McMahon that there was no way Hart was worth roughly twice the salary. Michaels was younger and a harder worker. Most important, he claimed, he was on message. So he wanted a raise or he'd walk. When Vince refused to let him out of his one-year contract, Michaels vented his frustrations by showing up at a Mobile, Alabama, taping of *Raw* barely able to stay on his feet and needing directions to the ring. Once inside of it, he let his anger fly by drunkenly quipping that Hart was seeing "a lot of Sunny days lately." The allusion to an affair that Hart was widely rumored to be having with the buxom Tammy Lynn Sytch, who appeared under the stage name Sunny, was a low blow. If there's one pact among wrestlers, it's that what happens on the road stays on the road.

When *Raw* visited the Fleet Center in Boston the next week, Hart let Michaels know just how much trouble he'd caused by following him into a bathroom and starting an argument that escalated into a floor-rolling brawl. After Hart wound up with a fist full of his hair, Michaels stormed out of the building, muttering, "Fuck this shit, Vince, I'll never work for you again."

That was in May. Now it was November, and Hart told Vince that he'd never give up his belt to Michaels. For as long as he'd worked in the WWF he'd done as he was told, but this time Hart wanted to call his last shot.[1] He'd lose to anybody, he said, except Michaels. And he didn't want to lose in front of his fans in Canada. With the pay-per-view days away, a series of negotiations forced Vince to relent. The Montreal match could end in a disqualification, he agreed, and instead of dropping the strap, Bret could hand it to Vince the next night at the episode of *Raw* that they were taping in Ottawa.

But as his flight landed in Montreal on Saturday, Vince had already decided that the plan was too risky. Word was out on the Internet that Hart was heading to WCW. With the ratings gap finally closing to within a percentage point, he couldn't stand the idea that Bischoff would show up on *Nitro* crowing that he'd hired the WWF's reigning heavyweight champ. No. The only way that Hart could leave Montreal on Sunday was without the strap.

Hart arrived in Canada on edge as well. At a house show in Toronto on Saturday night, he approached the referee who was scheduled to work the *Survivor Series* match, a longtime McMahon deputy named Earl Hebner, and asked if anything had changed. No, Hebner replied, the finish was still the same. Michaels would bump Hebner and knock him out, then be placed in Hart's finishing move, the *sharpshooter,* an updated version of the old *Boston crab.* Because Hebner wouldn't see Michaels submitting to Hart, Michaels could escape the loss and Hart could save face before his hometown fans. In the confusion, there would be run-ins by Degeneration X and the Hart Foundation, leading to the disqualification. Seeing the worry on Hart's face, he added, "I swear on my kids, I'll quit before I double cross you."[2]

Hart was still jittery when he landed in Montreal, but backstage at the Molson Center he started to relax. After going over their spots in an agreeable fashion, he and Michaels dressed quietly, without much

---

1. This wasn't purely a request. Hart had a clause written into his contract that gave him creative control over his character for thirty days before his departure from the company.

2. This quote, along with many of the details of the incident, was included in a chronicle of the events in the November 17, 1997, issue of Dave Meltzer's *Wrestling Observer.*

drama. Vince changed beside them, seemingly in a good mood now that all the details had been worked out.

When it finally came time for the match to start, Michaels played it straight, just as he said he would in the locker room. In fact, as the men brawled their way into the crowd, Hart thought he was putting on a hell of a show. For the better part of five minutes, they flung each other up and down the aisles. When they brawled their way back to the ring, Michaels gave Hebner the timely bump that knocked him out and set up the series of spots that started with him placing a submission hold on Hart. Because they still had eight minutes to go, Hart let Michaels mount his back and relaxed a bit, grabbing a few deep breaths to conserve his energy. He was still gathering strength when, out of the corner of his eye, he heard a director yell, "It's time! Get up!"

Hart saw Hebner rise and felt Michaels tighten his grip. Then he heard the words "Ring the *fucking* bell!" And that was when Hart understood what was happening. Later that night, Michaels would insist that he knew nothing about the deception, and the look of surprise on his face lent him the benefit of the doubt. In fact, he seemed disjointed when Vince barked at Hebner, "Give him the belt!" and he had to be told by road agent Jerry Brisco to raise it over his head, thereby letting the crowd know he was accepting the title. Hart had his own way of acknowledging the double cross. Meeting McMahon's stare, he spat at his boss, streaking his face.

The backstage area was chaos. While Hebner was being whisked to a waiting rental car, Michaels waited in the locker room for Hart. "You weren't in on that?" he was asked when Hart finally stormed in.

"I had no fucking idea," Michaels replied. "As God as my fucking witness. My hands are fucking clean on this one. I swear to God."

Vince had retreated to his own locked office backstage when the WWF's locker-room leader, Mark "the Undertaker" Callaway, rapped on his door to say that the Boys were angry (many had threatened to boycott the next night's show in Ottawa) and had decided that Hart was owed an apology. Seeing the politics of the situation, McMahon nodded in agreement and walked into the dressing room area flanked by his son, Shane, and road agents Brisco and Sergeant Slaughter while Hart was toweling himself off. Hart called his ex-boss a liar, warning Vince that if he didn't leave the area before Hart finished dressing, "I'm going to punch you in the fucking mouth." But Vince insisted on explaining himself. Yes, he'd lied to Hart, but weren't they all going to be rich in the end? Wasn't that all that mattered? Hart answered with his fist, landing a hard blow to Vince's right temple. Shane jumped on Hart's back, but by then it was clear the long night was over. "Get this motherfucker out of here, or I'll hurt him," Bret said, controlling what was left of his voice. Vince staggered to his feet and left limping down the hall, a dark bruise on his lower lip.

By the next morning, the episode had sparked a furor on the Internet sites and chat rooms, and the WWF was in turmoil. Staffers stayed up half the night quelling a threatened boycott. In a high-stakes meeting with his talent before the taping of *Raw* on Monday evening in Ottawa, McMahon insisted that Hart was jeopardizing the company, that he'd taken the punch for all of them. (The only on-air mention of the match came from Michaels, who won few friends by coming out with the belt and crowing about how he'd run Hart out of town. Vince kept his bloodied face off camera, never once mentioning the events of the night before.)[3] When he finally decided to address

---

3. A year later, a documentary about Bret Hart, *Wrestling with Shadows*, would rekindle the controversy surrounding the Montreal double cross, featuring tapes of conversations between Vince and Bret, some of which McMahon did not know were being recorded. It shows Pat Patterson going over details of the finish of the match, which he obviously knew wasn't going to happen. It also shows Bret talking to his wife and telling her Vince had agreed to the disqualification finish, to which she responded, "I don't believe it." In a conversation before the match, Bret was filmed saying, "I'd just like to get through today. Then tomorrow I should just forfeit my title. It allows me a chance to leave with my head up, leave in a nice way. I don't have to beat Shawn. We can have a schmooze or whatever you want." To that Vince replied, "I'm open to anything. As I said before, I'm determined for this to wind up the right way."

the issue for the TV audience the next Monday, he had started believing it himself.

"Some would say I screwed Bret Hart," he began. "The referee didn't screw Bret Hart. Shawn Michaels didn't screw Bret Hart. Bret Hart screwed Bret Hart." Then he issued this warning: "If we're going to have problems along those lines in the locker room or anywhere else, okay, we're going to have them. But no more free shots."

MCMAHON SEEMED to take sustenance from the double-dealing image that he flew home with from Montreal. He'd unwittingly given his audience a peek inside his backstage world, and they wanted more. He could feel the crowds urging him on.

At first, he wasn't sure how to react. After all, he'd spent thirty years believing he was best suited as an announcer. But those around him pushed him to strike while the iron was hot. *Raw* was delivering more twelve- to thirty-four-year-old viewers than the big three networks on Monday nights. And repackaged versions of *Raw* that were appearing on Saturday and Sunday mornings were heating up his licensing sales. "You're your own best act," Hammer told him.

So in the days after Montreal, he started to build a faux rendition of himself that played to those expectations. He started appearing in backstage vignettes that drew inspiration from the events of Montreal. In an episode of *Raw* that aired in early December, for example, Vince was seen scheming to screw Steve Austin out of his upcoming title match with Michaels.

The events of Montreal also gave his wrestlers the heady sense that they could keep pushing the envelope. Koplovitz was on her way out at USA, and there was no telling what Diller would or wouldn't allow. One night Michaels felt giddy enough to perform a scene in which he stripped down to his shorts while playing poker and reached to do something that looked very much like shaking his dick.

The last thing that McMahon needed was to have to defend an action like that. But the *Los Angeles Times* forced his hand. He could remember the problems he had with advertisers the last time that the *Times* devoted a cover story to the WWF during the depths of the steroid scandals. This time around, he wanted to get ahead of the curve. So on December 15, he rushed an interview into production that would come to be known as the "New Direction" speech.

Stepping out of his Montreal mode with a softer, more deliberative tone, Vince appeared on *Raw* to say that he was taking it in a more "contemporary" direction, something akin to the *Jerry Springer Show*, which Diller now owned. "This is a conscious effort on our part to open the creative envelope, so to speak, to entertain you in a more contemporary manner.... We in the WWF think that you, the audience, are quite frankly tired of having your intelligence insulted. We also think you're tired of the same old simplistic theory of good guys versus bad guys. Surely the era of the superhero that urged you to say your prayers and take your vitamins is passé. Therefore we've embarked upon an innovative, contemporary campaign that is more invigorating and extemporaneous than before. Due to the live nature of *Raw*, however, we encourage some degree of parental discretion when it comes to the younger audience allowed to stay up late." In other words, the TV-14 tag was on and the gloves were off. Later that night, the wrestler Billy Gunn would make his debut as Bad Ass Billy Gunn, soon to be changed to the simpler Mr. Ass.

The reinvention of *Raw* reflected McMahon's restlessness. As with *Springer*, the shows were becoming increasingly interactive as he shortened the matches and extended the time his acts used to taunt the crowds. In the week before Christmas, drunken fans in Little Rock and Memphis hurled bottles and lit firecrackers at the wrestlers, causing the main events in both cities to be canceled. And yet it was evident that the WWF was filling up seats again. Not only had pay-per-view revenue rebounded and the ratings started to nudge up, the live gate from November was $2.4 million. "That's the best month for business since we started keeping a monthly tab on things in 1992," wrote Dave Meltzer in his *Wrestling Observer* newsletter.

With the *Royal Rumble* coming up next, and the Austin title turn on the horizon for March, the mood in Titan Tower was electric. To keep the momentum going, all Vince needed was a gimmick to bridge the divide between the *Rumble* and *Wrestlemania*.

Thanks to a spending spree that involved the purchase of ten Beemers, four Rolls-Royces, several Bentleys, and a mansion in Las Vegas, Mike Tyson had awoken to find himself $11 million in debt to the Internal Revenue Service. His promoter, Don King, went to Showtime to get a $5 million advance on Tyson's next fight. But the network balked, as did WCW when King offered them the champ for the same price. By the time Vince and Shane got involved, the asking price was down to $3.5 million.

Left to his own devices, Tyson would have probably considered doing it for free. As a boy in Brownsville, Brooklyn, he studied the image of Bruno Sammartino at eleven o'clock on Tuesday nights on Channel 47 (WJNU), the Spanish-language station. As he told the writer Mark Kriegel, he made championship belts out of discarded canisters of Pillsbury dough, turning the flashy foil sides out and stringing them together around his waist. Now there was just one problem. He was due to appear before the Nevada State Athletic Commission in June 1998. Fortunately, the commission's director, Marc Ratner, was a huge wrestling fan, in no small part because his commission regulated wrestling events and got a 4 percent tax on the gates. McMahon and Ratner knew each other well enough for McMahon to call and say that that he was thinking of using Tyson in a parody of the infamous "bite fight" with Evander Holyfield. "No, no," Ratner said quickly. The commission would go crazy if Tyson ridiculed something they were still pissed off about. The idea of him wrestling was off limits, too; Tyson had to show he was willing to behave for a while. Finally, McMahon asked whether he could referee a match between Austin and Shawn Michaels. "That's probably okay," Ratner said. "I just hope it will be in good taste."

Tyson started paying for himself right away when his appearance at *Rumble* in early January helped spike the buy rate to the tune of an extra $750,000. When he was introduced the next night in Fresno and got into a mock scuffle with Austin, the combined audience watching *Nitro* and *Raw* was 8 million homes, a record for wrestling and for cable television. "His journey is endlessly entertaining because it is half-tragedy, half-cartoon," wrote *Chicago Sun-Times* columnist Rick Telander, echoing sports pages across the country. But wasn't the reverse equally true, that Austin and Michaels had become real enough to meet the champ halfway in the public's mind? Wrestling gave Tyson a structure and context that he couldn't find in the real world, and McMahon was pushing hard to exploit it.

McMahon tried to convince the ex-champ that he should make the relationship more permanent by using the WWF as his sports management agency. In a nifty bit of gamesmanship, McMahon even helped edge King out of the picture by sending a copy of the WWF licensing deal that King had negotiated on Tyson's behalf to the champ's home in Las Vegas. Tyson's wife, Monica, was furious when she saw that her husband had signed away the rights to his own likeness and that the cash registers k-chunged for King every time the WWF sold a Tyson T-shirt. In early February, Tyson got into a furious fight with King over the arrangement at a Bel Air hotel, slapping his longtime promoter before firing him. As it happened, the incident caused a media frenzy at roughly the same time that the WWF was holding a press conference to announce Tyson's role as a referee at *Wrestlemania XIV*. Twenty-seven cameras and dozens of out-of-town reporters overran the All-Star Café in Manhattan to find out what was going on. Tyson didn't address it. To Vince's delight, all he did was turn to Steve Austin and deliver the line, "You do anything to Shawn Michaels and I'll knock your teeth out. And by the look of things, you can't afford it."

Tyson was worth twice what Vince paid him that day. By agreeing to join Degeneration X and become a thousand-watt shill for Suck It T-shirts and Mr. Ass dolls, the biggest draw in the pay-per-view universe singlehandedly brought the mainstream press back to wrestling. Many at the All-Star Café that day would insist they were shocked at what wrestling had become since they last looked. But the fact was that for all its R-rated flirtations, the WWF wasn't pushing the envelope alone. In fact, it was getting pushed.

PUDGY AND balding, thirty-something Paul Heyman had been around the business for years, first as a manager of a group called the Dangerous Alliance and later as an announcer at WCW. After a run-in with Cowboy Bill Watts led to his firing, the native of an affluent suburb in New York's Westchester County took control of a Philadelphia-based wrestling company, Eastern Championship Wrestling, and renamed it Extreme Championship Wrestling. Because he had enough friends at every level of the industry, he was able to hire a solid though unorthodox group of performers and build a small but loyal following throughout the Northeast. ECW played at bingo halls and bowling alleys and mixed the atmosphere of a cockfight with the violence of a Mexican snuff film. And at no time was that feeling more pervasive than the night that ECW came to a dog track in Revere, Massachusetts.

Jerome "New Jack" Young, a former bounty hunter who once shot and killed a man during a bust, was supposed to wrestle an ECW regular named Axl Rotten, but the latter was a no-show. When his absence was announced, a seventeen-year-old novice named Erich Kulas approached Heyman. Kulas had been using a Ralph Kramden–bus driver act with a pair of midgets at small-town shows and had come to Revere looking to step up. After he convinced Heyman that he was nineteen and had been trained by Walter "Killer" Kowalski, the owner let him stand in for Rotten.

Young—known for hauling shopping carts to the ring loaded with foreign objects and routinely stapling opponents' heads with a staple gun—was under instructions to draw blood that night. But Kulas wasn't a veteran and didn't have the soft and porous skin that bled easily when nicked. His was virgin skin, hard and thick. So after Young hit him with a chair, a guitar, a toaster, and crutches, and then sank an X-Acto knife into his scalp, the teen screamed and started gushing an alarming amount of blood. Though his father stood up and yelled, "Lay off, he's only seventeen," the four-hundred-pound volunteer stayed in the ring, accepting more punishment until he finally collapsed in a thick puddle. As paramedics rushed in, soaking up the gore with towels and shirts, a drunken fan shouted, "You fat fuck!" Kulas gave him the finger, prompting the audience to roar "E-C-W! E-C-W!" and Young to declare: "I don't care if that motherfucker dies."[4]

Heyman's rogues' gallery also included the twenty-six-year-old drug addict and former WWF pinup Tammy Lynn Sytch. It didn't matter that her face was drawn, or that her stage name, Sunny, had become a cruel joke after her life unraveled and she became so desperate for cash that she auctioned her breast implants off on eBay. Heyman put her back on television, letting her bare all her secrets about her battle with alcohol and painkillers and depression. To be fair, he also demanded that she enroll in college and go through counseling as a condition of her employment. But within a month, she'd passed out on a chair in the ECW locker room, claiming that she accidentally sipped someone else's drink that was laced with the designer drug GHB. She was fired after that, though not before Heyman let her embarrass herself one last time by getting her bare ass spanked by an equally buxom wrestler, as fans yelled, "Show your tits!"

Most old-timers would rather have read *Ulysses* than get stuck in a room with Heyman, but he had an influential admirer in Vince Russo, the head writer for the WWF. In late 1997, Russo began pressing McMahon to adapt some of ECW's hard-core stylings and hire the

---

4. Claiming long-term emotional and physical damage, Kulas pressed criminal assault charges against Young, but the wrestler was cleared in 1999 when his six-person jury viewed a tape of Kulas pressing together his lips and puffing out his cheeks—an action to make the blood flow more freely—and decided that Kulas was a willing participant.

wrestlers who could pull them off, in particular Mick Foley. Though his body looked like it trained at Taco Bell, Foley's gift for absorbing pain was so remarkable that he reinvented the standard by which high-risk wrestling was judged shortly after arriving at the WWF under the ring name Mankind. Meeting the Undertaker at the King of the Ring pay-per-view in a match dubbed *Hell in a Cell*, Foley did a suicidal sixteen-foot pratfall off the top of a steel cage suspended above the arena's floor, timing it so exquisitely that he narrowly avoided hitting the cold concrete and crashed backfirst through his target, a wooden announcer's table. After being attended to by medical personnel for ten minutes, he rolled off the gurney and once again scaled the cage. This time, however, the plan went awry: After he got choke-slammed onto the roof of the cage, a weak spot in the mesh snapped under his three-hundred-pound girth, sending him hurtling backfirst to the canvas below. "Good God almighty," Jim Ross intoned. "With God as my witness, he's been broken in half." Amazingly, the first two bumps hadn't been enough to write Foley into history: He rose from the ground a third time, dumped thousands of thumbtacks onto the mat, and let himself get slammed into them. The bruised kidney that he ended up with was the least of his worries. He also left that night with a dislocated jaw, his tongue sticking through a hole under his lip, and a tooth sticking out of his nose.

With the promise of mayhem like that, five thousand fans—many of them high school kids skipping classes—descended on a plaza by the Boston Holocaust Memorial to see a public photo-op with Tyson, Austin, and Michaels four days before *Wrestlemania XIV* on March 29, 1998. *Raw* was still behind *Nitro* in the ratings, but anyone who scanned the crowd could see the tide had turned. These were new converts coming to see an arena show that was only partly about wrestling. One New Hampshire man who bought tickets for his kids told a *Boston Globe* reporter, "My wife says I'm stupid for coming to this, but I look at it just as a performance. If you want to watch *Fiddler on the Roof*, go watch it. I'm not a *Fiddler on the Roof* kind of guy."

From the opening of the show, McMahon was determined to give the anti-*Fiddler* man, and those who thought like him, something gaudy and glittery. The opening battle royal had so many costumed bodies in the ring it looked like a Rock and Roll Hall of Fame jam session. Hunter Hearst Helmsley came out for his "European title" fight costumed like Cher. Sable and Luna were dressed like sex club swingers. And the penultimate match between the Undertaker and Kane was taken right out of *Phantom of the Opera*, wrestling wrought on a Broadway-style scale.

In addition to all its other uses, *Wrestlemania* ends one booking year and sets up a new one. The job of this particular show was to employ Tyson to help close the book on the Shawn Michaels era and hand the belt to Steve Austin. With all that was riding on the evening, the two main eventers could hardly be expected to back out, though Austin had suffered so much neck pain that doctors were warning him against wrestling again—ever—and Michaels was popping pills to numb the pain of the disks he'd herniated getting pushed into a casket during a match months earlier.

During the weeks before the show, Tyson had been aligned with Michaels and his group, Degeneration X (DX). Now the champ was used to warm up the crowd, introducing a montage of Michaels's career that showed him at his arrogant best. As Michaels watched it backstage, he knew he'd never look like that again. Still, the night's match was booked to go twenty minutes, and he was determined to throw himself into every minute of it. When Austin tossed him through the ropes and caused him to crash on the concrete, Michaels could barely feel his feet but got up anyway, holding his back as he grasped the ropes for leverage. Each move caused pain to rip up his spine and explode in his brain. By the last series, he was nearly immobile. He shoved Austin into the ropes and extended his legs, preparing to kick the Texan. Instead, Austin blocked the kick so he could go into his finisher. It was a simple move: Austin grabbed Michaels by the neck and fell with him hard to the mat. But Michaels nearly blacked out from the impact and was grateful to see Tyson jump into the ring, hit the mat three times, and hoist Austin's arm in the air. All that was left was for Tyson to set up the surprise ending by taking off his DX shirt to reveal one that read "3:16". Under the guise of being furious that Tyson would switch allegiances so fast, Michaels poked Tyson in the chest weakly and took a swing. When Tyson connected in return, Michaels had never been happier to get hit in his life. As he lay on his back staring up at the lights of the Fleet Center, Tyson gave him a wrestler's good-bye: He took his T-shirt with the new champion's slogan on it and laid it across the old champion's face.

THE NIGHT after *Wrestlemania* traditionally garnered strong numbers for *Raw*, but not many expected those numbers to hold up during the following weeks. However, the WWF did what most analysts would have considered impossible just a few months earlier. The March 30 episode of *Raw* from Albany, New York, beat *Nitro* in five of the eight quarter-hour rating periods where they faced one another. Overall, it lost the nightly competition by just two-tenths of a ratings point. (Had it not been for the fact that WCW, sensing that *Raw* was closing in, scheduled a pair of pay-per-view-caliber matches during *Nitro*'s final two quarters, the night surely would have gone to *Raw*.) The April 6 episode proved it was no fluke. It cut the previous week's gap in half, and it did it with a show that had been taped a week earlier.

Vince's writers came up with a clever skit to nudge him further into the center of things during that show. Austin appeared on camera in a suit and tie, suggesting that in the weeks since his reign as champion started, he'd been transformed into a blithe corporate mouthpiece. But then he ripped the outfit off and kicked the perfectly pressed promoter in his stomach, dropping him to his knees. The expression on McMahon's face was an exquisite blend of confusion, powerlessness, and rage.

The final stage of Vince's transformation into the star of his own show came complete with a new look for its opening on April 13. Banks of TV screens flashed images of Steve Austin marching to a pulsing score through streets that had been set ablaze, followed by fiery rockets screaming in the air and an explosion. Before viewers could even think about changing channels, Jim Ross announced that Austin would be settling his differences with McMahon at some point in the show.

The next 120 minutes was another textbook example of how to produce wrestling. Interspersed between vignettes showing Vince in a warm-up suit, training for the big showdown, he delivered up his new soft-core cast. There was a sweaty Val Venis on the giant TitanTron, wearing only a towel and telling the audience, "I've got a rocket in my pocket that will take each and every one of you women on the face of this planet to new and exciting heights." There was a Degeneration X match between Owen Hart and "Bad Ass" Billy Gunn in which Hart yanked down Gunn's tights, exposing his buttocks. (In the wings, DX cohort Hunter Hearst Helmsley asked, "Doesn't he know crack isn't good for you?") There was Rocky Maivia, who was still part of the Nation of Domination, but would soon approach Vince with the idea of becoming a new millennium version of Ric Flair—complete with $500 shirts and shoes—and morph into The Rock.[5] And there was the requisite appearance by Goldust, dressed in a leather bra and panties set.

Finally, at 9:50 P.M., the fifty-two-year-old McMahon strutted into the ring, demanding that Austin make good on his boast to beat him with one hand tied behind his back. "Come on, hotshot," he said. "You got any guts?"

In fact, with just a few minutes left, he had no intention of wasting a valuable match on free television. That was the difference between the WWF and WCW. An increasingly desperate Bischoff was giving away pay-per-view quality matches in a bid to boost his ratings. But that was what you did when you dealt from weakness. Dealing from

---

5. Maivia, who was known as Dwayne Johnson when he played linebacker for the national champion Miami Hurricanes, assumed the stage name the Rock as a tribute to the two generations of wrestlers in his family. His father, Rocky Johnson, worked in the WWF under the name Soul Man. His maternal grandfather, High Chief Peter Maivia, was a top Samoan wrestler during the sixties and seventies. With genes like that, no one at the WWF was surprised when he progressed so fast that the Rock became a breakout star by the age of twenty-seven.

strength meant having a star like Foley emerge from the wings to suddenly drag Austin out of the ring as the show was going to black.

If anyone had the slightest doubt about McMahon's drawing power, it was shattered the next afternoon. *Raw* had achieved a 6.0 rating in that quarter-hour—an all-time high in their head-to-head competition. When all eight quarter-hours were added together and *Raw* averaged a 4.6 rating, *Nitro*'s streak of eighty-three straight Monday night wins had come to an end.

FIFTEEN

THE WAR BETWEEN THE WWF and WCW was entering a new phase now, one in which both companies were abandoning any reservations about explicitly attacking one another. On April 27, 1998, in Virginia—where the rivals had scheduled shows within thirty miles of each other—Vince rented an army jeep with a mounted bayonet and sent Hunter Hearst Helmsley and the rest of his Degeneration X crew to the Scope Arena in Norfolk with it. At the gate, Helmsley aimed the gun barrel at the marquee and fired a blank shot, proclaiming it the maiden shot in the Monday night wars. Because *Nitro* aired in an hour version that started at eight o'clock (so the NBA playoffs could begin at nine), *Raw* ran unopposed in its nine o'clock slot. That meant the stunt was seen in 4.1 million homes—helping the show to post a 5.7 rating over the full two hours that broke its former record, set two weeks earlier, by a full point. Emboldened, Vince sent Helmsley back on the road to Atlanta a couple of weeks later with Sean "X-Pac" Waltman, a wrestler whom Eric Bischoff had hired away from the WWF and then subsequently fired. As they arrived at WCW's corporate offices in suburban Atlanta, Helmsley lingered out front while a cameraman trailed Waltman into the lobby, where he told a security guard that he wanted an explanation for his firing. Not surprisingly, Waltman was turned away. With nothing else to do, they took their jeep to the CNN Center in downtown Atlanta and pretended to fire another shot. When editors at *Raw* spliced in footage of a building collapse, unamused Turner lawyers had a cease and desist order on McMahon's desk within days.

Bischoff, however, loved the warfare. On television the next week from Kansas City, he hyped a forthcoming pay-per-view by suggesting that if Vince really wanted to find him that badly they should simply meet in the ring. The prospect of more stunts drove ticket buyers to the box office of the Georgia Dome for a show whose lineup wasn't even announced yet. More than fourteen thousand tickets were sold in just less than five hours, a company record for first-day sales.

The heat was so intense that Bischoff was able to sign Karl Malone to wrestle Dennis Rodman as part of a tag-team match after the Chicago Bulls met the Utah Jazz in the NBA finals. David Stern, the league's commissioner, wasn't happy when he got wind of the stunt. Rodman didn't help matters by skipping a Bulls practice between games two and three so he could show up, cigar in mouth, at a *Nitro* taping in Detroit. When the Bulls forward scrambled for a ball with Malone in the sixth and deciding game of the finals, a disgusted Bob Costas suggested that they save the theatrics for their "bogus match." But Malone, like so many in sports, was tired of being told how to act to keep corporate money (read: white money) pouring into luxury boxes and season ticket plans. A reporter came up to him before his bout with Rodman and mentioned Costas's remark, causing him to snap, "Fuck Bob Costas. For a long time I've lived my life for the media. Now let me live it for me."

In other words, wrestling was the distraction du jour for the sports world's elite, all the more desirable because the sanctimonious press hated it so much.

But within the WCW offices, there was growing concern that the expensive stunt looked too derivative and wasn't going to have the same ripple effect as Tyson's ratings revelation at *Wrestlemania*. On June 1, 1998, the day Michael Jordan propelled the Bulls into the finals and the buildup to the pay-per-view started, the episode of *Nitro* that aired was the lowest-rated one of the year. By June 30, when the finals were over and anticipation for the show should have been red hot, *Nitro* had fallen a ratings point and a half behind *Raw*—the biggest disparity since the wars began.

If Bischoff was worried, he didn't let his staff see it. One day Nick Lambross, a smart young lawyer who'd been installed as a kind of second in command to oversee the business side, sat listening to the producer talk about the flying lessons that he was taking so he could shuttle between both coasts and the home he was building in Cody, Wyoming. "I'm going to be just like Ted," Bischoff crowed.

"The difference between you and Ted," Lambross replied dryly, "is that Ted sits in the *back* of the plane."

IF THERE was one match the producer knew he could still bank on, it was Bill Goldberg versus Hulk Hogan. The two biggest names in his company had yet to meet. When they did, many thought it should be at a pay-per-view, where the anticipation would have been enough to produce a multimillion-dollar payday. But a week before the next *Nitro*, Bischoff was driving through Marina del Rey, California, when Hogan reached him on his cell phone. "What do you think about letting me work with Goldberg and having him win the strap?" he asked. Bischoff pulled off the highway to think about it. The Georgia Dome show was a sellout and would be held in the backyard of CNN Center in downtown Atlanta. He knew that Hogan, who'd been running on fumes lately, wanted the station's brass to see that he could still put on a big-time show. But as self-serving as Bischoff knew the idea was, Hogan had a point: It was the one match of the year that everyone would talk about, the one that would take Goldberg over the top. He'd lose a small fortune putting it on basic cable, sure, but with *Raw* routinely beating *Nitro* in the ratings now, Bischoff decided it was a gamble worth taking. After he told Hogan that he'd do it on Thursday, July 2, he called one of his road agents, J. J. Dillon, and told him to go on television that night—on a new show they'd started called *Thunder*—to announce that Goldberg would be squaring off against Hogan for the title four days hence.

Bill Goldberg was watching that show in his living room in Atlanta. No one had breathed a word about it to him. Somehow, it wasn't the way he thought he'd hear about his first meeting with the biggest money earner of all time.

On July 6, Goldberg arrived at the Georgia Dome to find the whole cast of WCW being pressed into service to make him a star. Even Karl

Malone was on hand to hype the following weekend's pay-per-view match with Rodman (who no-showed because he'd spent the previous night crashing the stage of a Pearl Jam concert in Dallas, shoeless, shirtless, and chugging wine from a bottle). The buildup unnerved Goldberg, and the hours to the main event seemed to drag on forever. When it finally arrived, he found it hard not to be unsettled by the full-throated crowd's chanting of his name or the fear that somehow he might hurt Hogan.

A year on the road had helped Goldberg perfect his entrance; he walked out with his head bowed as if in prayer, looking almost peaceful as fireworks and fog sprayed over him. Though the sparks burned his skin, he never let on that it hurt because he knew it seemed more authentic when he finally uncoiled and began his full-throated scream. Hogan had seen the move before, but with forty thousand fans roaring "Goldberg" in unison, even he allowed himself to be a little impressed.

Just as the match had been laid out, Goldberg dominated early, overpowering Hogan in a battle of strength. Hogan, dressed in his nWo black, acted the part of the heel, poking Goldberg's eyes, raking his back, and whipping him with a weight-lifting belt. The key spot of the first series was when Goldberg grabbed the belt away. Feigning surprise, the older wrestler shook his jowls like a dog shaking off water, then played to the crowd with a wide-eyed "Oh-oh". He tried falling on Goldberg with a series of painful-looking elbow drops, but each time Goldberg rolled over, leaving Hogan to rub his right elbow in apparent pain. The match had a bare, stripped-down feel, and it continued when Hogan launched into his own offense, grabbing Goldberg, lofting him upside down, and dropping him headfirst onto the mat. As the ex-tackle lay there, his chest rising, Hogan sprung into two leg drops, seemingly gathering strength.

It was at this point that a prearranged distraction turned the tide of the action. Curt Hennig, a second-generation grappler once known as Mr. Perfect, appeared from the wings, ready to help when he was suddenly intercepted and dropped by Malone at ringside. With Hogan watching Malone, his back to center ring, Goldberg assumed a combat crouch. Every soul in the Georgia Dome knew what was coming next. Just as Hogan turned around, Goldberg speared the golden champion with his head, then launched into the most ferocious-looking jackhammer he could summon. At that moment, as all of Atlanta seemed to be rocking, reporter Dave Meltzer looked in his notebook and wrote:

> Make no mistake about this…WCW is now Goldberg's company. Not Hogan's or anyone else's…. When the story is written years from now, people will be shocked that Goldberg's first world title win wasn't something planned in advance, and came simply because a company was desperate.

In WCW's offices on Tuesday morning, no one was thinking about the long run. The overnight ratings showed that *Nitro* just scored its first victory in fourteen weeks—a 6.9 rating that continued the upward rating arc for wrestling. If they had been thinking longer term, they might have paused before their next move.

GARY CONSIDINE, the executive producer for NBC Studios, had helped book Hogan and Diamond Dallas Page on *The Tonight Show* in advance of one of their pay-per-views and was impressed at the way they'd helped NBC get an edge over CBS's *David Letterman Show*. So in mid-July, Considine invited Bischoff to his office in Burbank to ask whether WCW might want to expand the relationship, perhaps even get Jay Leno involved in some kind of angle. Bischoff replied that he had the perfect vehicle—the *Road Wild* pay-per-view in August. Leno loved bikes. It was a natural fit, even more so because he had the perfect way to cast it: He and Hogan would wrestle on one team, Leno and Dallas Page on another.

Leno threw himself into the role. A regulation-sized ring was moved into an empty union hall on the NBC lot, and Leno and his musical director, Kevin Eubanks, went there to practice after every show. Chris Kanyon, a native New Yorker who learned the business in a basement gym in Manhattan's Lower East Side, was given the assignment of training the comic. Kanyon thought Leno was taking his training seriously, maybe too seriously. As they went through their steps, Leno was so businesslike he was almost boring; he refused to crack a smile or show much personality. It wasn't until Kanyon went to a *Tonight Show* taping that he understood Leno became a different man when the camera's light blinked red.

To weave Leno into *Nitro*, Bischoff had written an angle that essentially staged a war of talk show hosts. He had Considine fax him Leno's monologue from the Friday before and then unveiled a replica *Tonight Show* stage on the *Nitro* set from Salt Lake City, from which he repeated the monologue word for word. At first the crowd started to rustle, then jeer. Finally, it booed with outright hostility. But the producer was elated when he finished. As far as he was concerned, Leno was the best thing to happen to him in Hollywood, the apotheosis of what he'd been building toward. Unfortunately, the same reaction wasn't shared inside TBS. As Bischoff drank coffee in his hotel room the next morning, working on the script for the Thursday taping of *Thunder,* he got a call telling him the Standards and Practices Board of TBS wanted to see him right away. He went through the past few months' worth of shows in his mind, wondering what for, and was astounded when he was told the company's lawyers were balking over the Leno monologue. Of all the things he could get called on, it would amaze him that it was a Monica Lewinsky blow-job joke, and a used one at that. But that was just the beginning. He was also told that he had a new guideline: He couldn't present anything that wasn't suitable for a first-grader. "I should have seen the writing on the wall and resigned then," he'd say later.

Instead, he traveled on to Sturgis, South Dakota, for the annual Black Hills rally, a weekend that wound up lifting his spirits. It was beautiful on August 8, and a hundred thousand bikers gathered in the center of town to rev their engines around the makeshift set that the WCW crew had built. Bischoff had suggested that Page team up with Leno because he didn't want to trust such a delicate assignment to a newcomer like Goldberg. And as the match began, he was glad he did. Page carried the load with Hogan like a pro, leaving Leno the light duty of delivering the few spots he was given with energy and humor. The *Tonight Show* host taunted the principals, struck a few muscle poses, and twisted a couple of arms. Then, ten minutes into the match, his band leader, Kevin Eubanks, made a cameo appearance designed to give Leno an efficient exit. He ran in, took down Bischoff with a maneuver he learned from Page called the *Diamond Cutter*, and left Leno the perfunctory work of rolling over and pinning Hogan to win the match. Afterward, waves of relief gave way to good feelings. The biker crowd partied well into the night at a country music concert that featured Travis Tritt, while the wrestlers retired to the parking lot of a Best Western that had been decorated to celebrate Hogan's forty-fifth birthday. It was the kind of party that everyone attended—if only because it was good office politics to stay on Hogan's good side.

Kevin Nash stayed in his room, however, brooding. He couldn't get his mind off what the photo in the next day's papers would look like: Leno wearing baggy sweats, pretending to strangle the bug-eyed and bald Hogan. It was a giant fuck you to the audience, he thought, a sign they were all just winking their way to the bank. Though they'd worked together closely, Nash couldn't say he'd ever actually *talked* to Hogan. That was how distant he could be. But tonight, Nash was determined to have himself heard. So after showering he went down to the party and buttonholed the tanned star. They wound up talking for nearly an hour, sitting on the bumpers of parked cars. Nash told Hogan that the show they'd just done was a perfect example of what was wrong with WCW. He understood Hogan's income was heavily influenced by the buy rates of the pay-per-views he worked. But no other wrestler could build a following, or add to the company's depth, as long as Hogan kept using his power to assure that each of the monthly story cycles climaxed with him in the forefront of the action.

Hogan listened patiently, more patiently than Nash expected. But at the end of the hour he concluded, "Brother, what you want is gonna cost me money." Nash looked at him. "What could I say?" he'd recall.

Hulk, after all, was just reciting the code of the Boys. So Nash shook his hand and walked away saying, "Okay, dude."

JESSE VENTURA never had much use for Hogan, going back to the days when Hogan snitched him out to Vince McMahon for trying to unionize the WWF's talent prior to the second *Wrestlemania* in 1986.[1] He thought less of Bischoff, who fired him shortly after taking over WCW.

By the late fall of 1998, Ventura was putting them and the rest of the wrestling world behind him. Against all odds, his long-shot campaign for the governorship of Minnesota was actually gaining converts. A Minneapolis ad executive named Bill Hillsman, brought into Ventura's campaign to help sharpen its message, had ignited it with one of the more unorthodox political commercials of the campaign season. He wanted an ad that could be produced cheaply and placed on the air fast, so he sent his creative team to a local Toys "R" Us to get an action figure that resembled the candidate. Studying the shelves, they selected a G.I. Joe doll for the stoic expression on its face. The only problem was its body was too small for it to resemble Ventura. They solved that by buying a muscular Batman and gluing G.I Joe's head onto it. As a member of Hillsman's team put it, "We wanted him to look like the governor and be taken seriously. But still, you didn't want Ken's wimpy body on him." The commercial they ended up with featured one boy playing with Evil Special Interest Man while his friend played with a Ventura doll that groused, "I don't want your stupid money."

As the first statewide candidate of Ross Perot's Reform Party, Ventura leavened his campaign with quotes from Jerry Garcia, conservative fiscal policy, and a pledge to keep government out of voters' bedrooms. But the thing that helped him most was a Minnesota law

---

1. In his book, *I Ain't Got No Time to Bleed,* Ventura wrote, "Hogan had been a friend of mine—or so I thought—for six or eight years at that point. He was the last person I would have suspected.... It turned out Vince was taking care of him very well, and I guess he didn't want to share that with any of the other wrestlers."

that allows voters to register at the polls instead of months in advance. For wrestling fans, turning out to vote was the equivalent of rolling up to an arena to buy tickets to a show, albeit one that would last for four years and be filled with more surprises. So many new voters registered that Minnesota's turnout rate was 61 percent, the highest in the nation. By evening, a majority of them had elected a wrestler as their governor.

Ventura was understandably proud of what he'd accomplished, so he was more than a little irritated when Bischoff and Hogan mocked him on the November 9 episode of *Nitro*. After the show opened with a band playing "Hail to the Chief" and shots of flags waving outside the White House, they emerged from behind the tinted glass of a limousine and, once in the ring, offered perfunctory congratulations to the governor-elect. But it was obvious they were setting him up. As hundreds of red, white, and blue balloons fell from the rafters, Hogan looked into the camera and crowed, "I'm going to rock the world, just like Jesse did." He elaborated on what he meant during a Thanksgiving appearance on the *Tonight Show*. Dressed all in black, he told Leno that he was retiring from wrestling. (Leno had seen Hogan work a crowd before and put his spiel in perspective, asking the balding star, "You're not going to come back in six weeks and say you're back?") "This helps me segue into being the next president of the United States," he said. "In fact, I'd love to run against Jesse because that would be really easy pickings. Everything I've always done against Jesse I've always won. That would be fun to beat him one more time."

Hogan and Bischoff were too arrogant for their own good, Ventura thought as he watched from his library at home. He was going to relish watching them get speared by their own egos.

IN EARLY November, WCW was well on its way to having a record year. Ratings had doubled, and with twenty-three straight sellouts the company was on pace to post a $55 million profit on $200 million in revenues. There was even talk about a series of prime-time specials for

NBC to fill in for the striking NBA. But Bischoff was starting to wear down; he even began to resent the Boys who he'd made rich. To be fair, they were *all* tired. To get through their days and stay bulked up for the cameras, many of them ordered steroids through the latest Dr. Feelgood to worm his way into the business, an Indianapolis physician named Joel Hackett.[2] A joke that made its way around the WCW locker room went, "I've got to get back to the hotel room and call my doctor. I just can't *Hack-ett* anymore."

Backstage, meanwhile, the Hogan and Nash factions continued to regard one another warily, if not with outright hostility. As for Ric Flair, he wouldn't go away, even as the writing crew tried to literally bury him by having him suffer a heart attack on live TV. But what could Bischoff do? He'd put himself in a box. Thanks to the guaranteed contracts he'd negotiated, his talent could call in sick whenever they felt like it. Kevin Nash had already infuriated him by no-showing a pay-per-view at the last minute. Bischoff knew that Nash didn't want to lose to the overweight and sluggish Paul "The Giant" Wight. But it was low to wait until the weekend of the show began and then leave a message saying that he thought he was having a heart attack. It was a not-so-subtle reminder about who really held the power.

Nash, however, was more than happy to show up for the December 27, 1998, version of Starrcade, booking himself to win the world title while unceremoniously ending Goldberg's victory streak. The dethroning, the equivalent of demoting the lead actor of a hit show, was the worst birthday ever for Bill Goldberg, and a nasty turn of fortune for the company.

---

2. Hackett's name was found on the bottles of drugs that lay at the bedside of a young WCW wrestler named Louis Spicolli when he overdosed in 1996. Scott Hall's wife, Dana, also remembers routinely receiving "boxes of stuff" from him at their Florida home. "I asked him, 'Do you realize my husband is an alcoholic, and he's not supposed to be taking these things? Do you know that he's washing these down with beer?'" she'd recall. "But he still gave Scott whatever he asked for." Hackett had his license suspended by an Indiana medical board and was facing thirty-eight counts of writing bogus prescriptions in late 2001.

But what could Bischoff do? Despite appearances to the contrary, the Turner brass was keeping him on an ever tighter leash, increasingly suspicious of the direction things were taking. He pressed them to sign the deal he'd done with NBC, but they stalled. When David Stern and the head of the NBA Players Association locked themselves in the league office and came out twelve hours later with a deal to end the lockout that had delayed the 1998–1999 season, the hopes Bischoff had pinned to a high-profile berth on prime-time network television died. He was frustrated and running out of ideas. "The numbers were still holding up," says a member of the company's road crew. "But you could feel that things were changing. Vince was beating us with a lot less talent, and that wasn't a good sign."

Eager to start 1999 with a bang, Bischoff brought Hogan out of "retirement" for what looked to be another sensational gate at the Georgia Dome on January 4. The main event had been advertised as a title rematch between Nash and Goldberg, but the latter was surgically excised by a script that had Atlanta cops carting him to jail under the guise that Randy Savage's ex-wife, Elizabeth, had accused him of stalking her. Goldberg wasn't happy, but at least the original angle had been scrapped—the one in which he was accused of rape.

Not only were the forty thousand fans in the arena furious to find that Goldberg had been removed from the match, the substitute bout was an example of the paralytic state of affairs: In a bid to make peace among the warring Hogan and Nash camps, the two principals agreed to reform the nWo in a way that neither made Hogan look good nor Nash particularly bad. Hogan would lightly poke Nash in the chest, Nash would take a dive, and Hogan would walk off with the belt. The entire charade would last less than two minutes and keep the peace.

What was worse, advance word about the finish had leaked out and was posted on the Internet. Although the *Raw* match had been taped on December 29, 1998, in Worcester, Massachusetts, McMahon did his voice-overs live. Seeing a delicious chance to tweak Turner, he told Jim Ross to announce over the air that Nash was going to lay down and hand the belt to Hogan on TNT. Bischoff, who always monitored both shows from backstage, lost his composure when he heard that. Grabbing a headset, he screamed at his own play-by-play man, Tony Schiavone, to retaliate by telling their audience that Mick Foley was about to win the WWF's title from The Rock.[3] Schiavone winced. This was Foley's first world title win. He knew that viewers would probably turn the channel in droves to watch the belt change hands. And when he did as he was told, he was proven right. Thousands of viewers switched to see two of the hardest-working men in the business, instead of two of the laziest.

Over the next six months, Bischoff began to spend nearly all his time in Los Angeles, where friends introduced him as the "man who helped save wrestling" while he tried to fill the void left by the NBC fiasco. But it wasn't until the end of May, when he was headed to LAX to pick up Bret Hart for an appearance on *The Tonight Show*, that the full weight of what he'd helped turn the business into finally settled on him. Owen Hart had fallen from the rafters in Kansas City that night, and Bischoff had raced to the airport to tell Bret. Hart would be getting some information in the air, but Bischoff worried that he'd think it was a prank. Some months before, a crude joke had been played on Bret by another wrestler, who called an arena where he was performing to say his father had died. When Bret stepped off the plane, Bischoff sadly assured him that it was no prank. The men talked awhile. Then, during a moment of reflection, the producer turned to the star. "Do you ever wonder if it's worth it anymore?" he asked.

---

3. The Rock had won the WWF world title belt for the first time five weeks earlier, when he was the last man standing in a fourteen-man elimination tournament at the Survivor Series pay-per-view in St. Louis.

SIXTEEN

AFTER HE LISTENED TO the details of his youngest brother's fall, Bret Hart pulled himself together and flew on a chartered plane back to Calgary to rejoin his family. He dreaded seeing what the death of Owen would do to his parents. On Owen's last trip home, the clan's light-hearted son had been uncharacteristically moody, telling his folks that he did not want to talk about wrestling, that he was sick of it. Bret would think about that as he held his seventy-five-year-old mother's hand and watched his father sit in stony silence.

The media fallout the next morning was like nothing anyone involved in wrestling had ever seen. As the WWF business staff in Stamford was poring over the morning's headlines—"Death in the Ring," screamed the front page of the *New York Post*—Vince huddled with his creative team in St. Louis, trying to plan a response. He'd been hammered when he put Brian Pillman's heavily sedated widow on the air nineteen months earlier; he wasn't making that mistake again. Instead, he decided they would try to produce something tasteful. All the company's wrestlers would stand silently in full costume as a short video tribute was aired. Then they'd engage in the tradition of tolling a bell ten times.

"What I experienced that night couldn't have been done any better," recalled Jeff Jarrett, Hart's tag-team partner. "Was it shameless? Not at all. What we do is sports entertainment, and that's how sports entertainers pay tribute. We're not baseball players. We're not actors. We're the hybrid."

Yet if wrestling was on trial—as Owen's brother accused it of being—it was hard to call the evening tasteful. When Jerry Lawler, who cradled the dying Owen in his arms the night before, tried delivering his own homage, he had to deal with a group of drunken men behind him who were sloshing beer in plastic cups and waving a Styrofoam middle finger.

Precisely because the broadcast on Monday, May 24, drew a 7.24 rating, Martha Hart angrily dismissed it as a sanctimonious exercise in conscience cleansing. "Had Owen talked about discomfort with the increasing complexity of the stunts that wrestlers are asked to do?" the host of *Good Morning America*, Charles Gibson, asked her when she made the talk show rounds the next morning.

"Well, yes, we did discuss this stunt," she replied. "And, you know, I did voice that I wasn't comfortable with it and that I thought it wasn't safe. And I did say that there should definitely be safety nets. He never liked the format of the wrestling business, the way it was going. He was just trying to fit in as best as he could so…"

Gibson interrupted her so he could probe further, "What do you mean by feeling uncomfortable with the way it was going?"

"Well, he was just a solid wrestler, and he wasn't into all the sex and violence and everything that it was promoting. He always said that he, you know, it was definitely not appropriate for children."

Gibson turned to Bret, who was seated beside her, to ask if he thought his brother's death would prompt any changes.

"You know, this family, our family, always prided ourselves on wrestling being a fun thing to do," he replied. "We're not dead set against the business. We're just disappointed in the drastic turn that it's taken in the last two years." Then he paused, as if wondering whether he should say the thing that was really bothering him. "It's a shame," he said, frowning. "Because the fans have become wild dogs. They just want more and more and more all the time."

To be sure, McMahon had become totally seduced by the loud, angry circus he'd created. In February, he wrapped up the feud he'd started with Steve Austin at *Wrestlemania XIV* by making his own wrestling debut at the Pyramid Arena in Memphis. He ordered a steel cage installed over the ring for the occasion, then came out to chants of "asshole." He let Austin chase him up the side of the cage, hammer his head into the wire mesh, and throw him fifteen feet down to the arena floor, where he crashed through a gimmicked announcer's table. "Is the son of a bitch still breathing?" Austin growled as faux paramedics tried to lift Vince away, tipping the gurney so he tumbled to the cold floor. As he lay crumbled in a heap, he signaled his intention to give up every inch of his body by flipping Austin a middle finger. After he'd been beaten to what looked like an inch of his life, he gave Austin the finger with *both* hands.

But on May 31, it was a different Vince who sat in the last pew of the McInnis & Holloway Funeral Chapel in Calgary. He sat still and silently, aware this wasn't friendly turf. Martha was no Melanie Pillman, no grieving wife willing to suffer her loss within the context of a larger family. She resented her in-laws for not denouncing the WWF (Bret was one of the few Harts who could afford to turn his back on the business and rally to her side) and bridled at the organization's attempts to project an image that had them all grieving as one. When she arrived at the chapel and noticed a huge floral heart by the casket with a WWF logo on its side, she grew so angry that she told one of the funeral directors to "get it out of my sight." When it came time for the eulogies, she was in no more of a mood to forgive the business for what it had become. "I'm not bitter or angry, but there will be a day of reckoning," she said. "I promise that."

ONE OF the top executives in the WWF, a former *Muppets* executive named Jim Bell, liked to preach a cardinal rule about business: It's easier to apologize for something after you've done it. That was an aphorism Vince and his writers took to heart as they continued to ratchet up the sexual content of *Raw*. As the head of licensing, Bell had few complaints about the show's tone. Having been in children's programming for much of his career, he took the same position as Bonnie Hammer, who'd worked in public television in Boston before coming to USA: If parents didn't want their kids to watch, they were in the best position to stop it.

Sure McMahon and his writers went over the line. Like the episode of *Raw* that aired the prior January in Beaumont, Texas, where Mark Henry was portrayed as being so desperate for a blow job that he accepted the advances of a character portraying a transsexual. Yet as Bell saw it, a little controversy wasn't necessarily a bad thing. When he first arrived at Titan Tower in 1996, licensers told him that the WWF was a dead brand. Now it was being called *edgy*.

The WWF marketed that edge to companies such as M&M Mars—which agreed to shell out $1 million to sponsor the upcoming *Wrestlemania*—with a variant of the military's don't ask, don't tell policy. The WWF's version went something like don't watch, don't ask, and it promised to deliver young demographics so long as advertisers didn't spend too much time looking into the details of how the McMahon's got them.

As Harvey Schiller, who was overseeing Turner Sports at the time, puts it, "Vince was using sex to fight us at TBS because he knew that we weren't allowed to do that kind of thing. So they got all these fourteen-year-old boys to lock their doors and tell their parents it was just wrestling, and because those parents remembered wrestling as Hulk Hogan and the Iron Sheik, they said, 'Sure, yeah, fine.'"

Most could be forgiven for assuming that wrestling dealt with sex in a harmlessly burlesque fashion. Those who grew up in the 1950s may have remembered the way Lillian Ellison appeared as a slave girl, wearing a revealing leopard-skin dress, to escort Elephant Boy to the ring. The WWF had a brief flirtation with feminism in the Cyndi Lauper years, but Vince made his feelings toward that side of the business clear when Wendy Richter, Lauper's confederate, pushed him to expand his ladies' division. Irritated, he stripped her of her title. Through the early 1990s, the largest part for a woman belonged to Randy Savage's demure wife, Liz. When Liz followed her ex-husband to the WCW, the WWF's hemlines came up with Tammy Sytch, who distracted opponents by wiggling her breasts or hiking up her skirts. But it took the arrival of Rena Mero to cause the WWF to lose what little innocence it had left.

Mero was the born-again Christian wife of Marc Mero, who erased his past as the son of a Jewish detective from the Bronx when he reinvented himself as a Little Richard look-alike named Johnny B. Badd.

With a heavy tan that he deepened with skin creams so he could pass for black, he became a modestly successful midcard act at WCW. He was driving through Jacksonville on the way to a show one day when he stopped at a restaurant and laid eyes on his future wife.

Rena grew up as one of six kids in a crowded, working-class Jacksonville home, which she left in tenth grade to become a teen bride. She was widowed with an eight-year-old daughter, and was making money by modeling, when Mero passed a note to her table asking for a date. A whirlwind courtship followed, and the two married. Marc was so devoted to Rena that he slowly let his feelings toward her, and toward the born-again faith that they shared, interfere with his work. Things came to a head when he refused to do a sexually charged angle with Dallas Page's wife and later no-showed a special appearance Bischoff had booked him for; after that, Bischoff suggested that WCW might no longer be the place for Mero. The wrestler agreed. Soon thereafter, he turned up at Titan Tower with Rena looking for work. McMahon was so taken by Rena that he offered them a double deal: While Marc wrestled, his wife—who would be renamed Sable—could linger at ringside as his valet.

Engaging and articulate, Rena became a favorite of Bonnie Hammer, who thought *Raw* needed a strong-willed woman, and of Vince Russo, the head writer who was grateful to have a bombshell who wasn't on drugs. When Marc blew out his knee on a show one evening and Sable was left with no one to valet, Russo let her headline a series of matches with Luna Vachon, the Gothic-garbed daughter of Paul "the Butcher" Vachon. (Because she was afraid of falling on her implants, Sable was introduced in a series of evening gown matches that required the tearing of more clothes than limbs.)

Sable provided a potent new weapon in the ratings war. Just as Mick Foley redefined athleticism, she became the prototype for the aerobicized temptress in ass-hugging spandex—a category that would grow to include Terri Runnels, the pert and pouty wife of the androgynous Goldust; Debra Marshall, who wore gray-flannel micro-miniskirts with square-cut jackets that opened to her bra; and Jacqueline Moore, an African American black belt in tae kwon do who was hired to be Marc Mero's girlfriend after an on-air "split" with Sable. As a group, the women wrestled one another in mud, cottage cheese, vats of oil—whatever was good and greasy. They pounded each other's chests, ripped off each other's clothes, squeezed each other's heads between their thighs.

The lone exception was Joanie Laurer, who was neither pristine nor innocent, and had the muscularity to wrestle for real. With a string of stepfathers that caused her to consider making a career out of kicking men's asses at an early stage in life, Laurer was serious about her athleticism. And having chucked a job as a singing telegram girl to train with Killer Kowalski in Boston, she had no interest in the women's division. She wanted to fight men. By mixing equal doses of *Carrie* and *Charlie's Angels* to develop the character known as Chyna, Laurer set herself apart as a kind of New Age feminist. She even argued that she was advancing the cause for sexual equality by delivering the first blow, and then letting men hit her back without being viewed as wife beaters or misogynists.

But for every pile driver that Laurer took for womankind, Sable and her imitators were there to make sure that no one got the wrong idea about what the WWF was selling. A report being prepared by the Federal Trade Commission showed that major movie studios were targeting R-rated movies to kids as young as nine. And the WWF was indisputably in the trenches with them. At one house show in Texas, Sable wore so little that she popped out of her top lunging for Luna, causing a stir when stills were bootlegged on the Internet. In the summer of 1998, she and Jacqueline were paired in an angle that culminated with a pay-per-view bikini contest that Sable won by strutting out with painted palms on her otherwise bare breasts. A couple of months later, the two brought their show-and-tell act to live television. In an evening gown match, they went at it so hard that Sable popped Jacqueline's breasts from her dress and took a victory strut around the ring in her lingerie.

Though the "accident" couldn't possibly have surprised anyone in the WWF, McMahon was sheepish about owning up to it, asking the *Rocky Mountain News* in Denver, "Is that appropriate at 8:45 P.M.? I dare say it's not even appropriate for 10:45 P.M. It's just not what we want to do." But the truth was that selling sex was *precisely* what the WWF wanted to do. One only had to listen to the announcers, who watched the action like horny uncles, elbowing their nephews (or in this case, the 36 percent of *Raw*'s audience that was under the age of eighteen) with an endless supply of one-liners like "She certainly seems comfortable with that microphone up at her mouth like that."

By the start of 1999, it was pointless to ignore the obvious. A study of fifty episodes of *Raw* from the prior year released by Indiana University counted 1,658 instances of crotch grabbing, 157 obscene gestures, and 128 instances of simulated sexual activity. What McMahon needed was a way of acknowledging the success without seeming to be gloating about it. (And there was a lot to gloat about. His 1998 cable TV ratings were up by 50 percent over 1997; attendance increased by 72 percent; and pay-per-view buys had climbed by two-thirds.) His solution came in a brilliantly conceived, unflinching commercial that cost $1.6 million to air during Fox's coverage of the Super Bowl. It showed Sable walking through the WWF's offices and passing, among other things, a couple who seemed to be hard at sex on a desk. The spot, which was designed to get viewers to watch a WWF halftime show on USA, wasn't without a sense of humor. By its end, a melee broke out on one of the upper floors of Titan Tower while McMahon stood outside, watching as a fireball flew out of the building and a hapless office worker plunged to the ground. The signature line came when he smirked and said, "Get it?"

A New York–based watchdog group called Morality in Media didn't get it. The group called the sixty-second spot "one of the most vile commercials ever aired on network TV" and begged the FCC to investigate whether it violated decency laws. (No action was ever taken.) Writing in the *New York Post*, Phil Mushnick asked:

If McMahon is so proud of what the WWF presents, why hint at it in a commercial? Why not show today's Super Bowl audience exactly what the WWF now regularly presents to kids? Why not show clips from recent shows, perhaps the crucifixion angle, or the castration angle, or the transsexual oral sex angle? Perhaps some of the negative stereotype ethnic angles, or racial gang angles, or the weekly sexual degradation of women, women now known to young WWF audiences as *hoes*.

Ironically, neither Mushnick nor the self-styled cultural cops from Morality in Media caused as much trouble for McMahon as Sable. Bell used his friendship with *Playboy* publisher Christie Heffner to land Sable a deal to pose in the April 1999 issue. The success of the issue, which sold a million copies (only Cindy Crawford, Katarina Witt, and Farrah Fawcett sold more copies of a magazine in the nineties), brought with it a slew of new demands. One was that she no longer wanted to work house shows. Another was that she didn't want to wrestle on *Raw*. The only times she'd get down and dirty, she said, was on a pay-per-view where she stood to get a cut of the gross.

Her diva act began causing backstage problems with the other girls, and Russo complained that it was irritating for him to submit her lines to her husband for approval. Finally, McMahon had enough. He decided to bump her down in the pecking order by taking the women's title away. But everything about the match gave him headaches. The Meros insisted the rules had to be written out in advance and that they include a promise that the Sable character "not be degraded." Vince agreed, only to set his announcers loose on her when her match with Debra Marshall aired live on May 10, 1999, from Orlando. As the women clawed at one another, Lawler asked Shawn Michaels, who was making a cameo appearance at the announcer's desk, "Do you think she is horizontally accessible?"

"She's accessible every which way from what I hear," Michaels replied.

Mero would quit shortly after that appearance—the third of four episodes that helped *Raw* account for the four highest-rated shows on cable during the May sweeps period.

The fourth one was the memorial episode for Owen, whose death on May 23 prompted Martha Hart's promise that there would be "a day of reckoning."

Between the two eventful episodes, Vince and Linda found themselves signing a deal that would bring them to broadcast television for the first time since the days of NBC's *Main Event*.

IN THE spring of 1999, Dean Valentine, the president of UPN, was struggling with his future. After five years of dismal ratings his network was on track to lose $180 million, and Valentine's bosses at Paramount were breathing down his neck. What was most embarrassing was that Warner Brothers, with its WB Network, UPN's archrival, was scorching him with teen hits such as *Dawson's Creek*, *Buffy the Vampire Slayer*, *Felicity*, and *Charmed*. As the forty-four-year-old Valentine looked at his forthcoming fall schedule, about all he saw was a *Moesha* spin-off called *Mo'Nique* and a sitcom with a grown-up Jaleel White (better known as Urkel of *Family Matters*).

Then the network CEO had a brainstorm, or at least the kind of clearheaded thought that precedes most near-death experiences. Instead of attacking the fem-friendly WB directly, why not go the opposite route and target the corresponding male audience that the WB was writing off?

The idea reflected the fundamental shift in the way television was being programmed. As a network vice president told *Entertainment Weekly*, "Demographics are the currency of the business now. Household ratings are a holdover from an era when demos were not available on a daily basis." In other words, it didn't matter how many people were watching, but what kind. NBC may have won the November 1998 sweeps, but Fox could argue that it was the real winner because its audience was more heavily weighted toward the young males that advertisers coveted (since they were the ones most likely to be willing to experiment with new brands and products).

There was a second issue for Valentine as well. Unlike Fox or NBC, his network was relegated to the high country of the cable dial; its average channel position was 29. Viewers had to really want to see something if they were going to surf that high. But he couldn't invest a whole season, or even half a season, in building a hit that would lure them that high up the dial. He didn't have the time. He needed to land something that had a built-in audience.

Over dinner at the Hollywood restaurant Patina, Valentine was explaining his dilemma to a friend who mentioned that his teen sons were addicted to wrestling. In his day, Valentine had also been a huge wrestling fan. Growing up in New York, he'd worked as a bellhop at the Hotel Holland on Forty-second Street, which lay across from the Port Authority bus terminal and was where the wrestlers stayed when they played the Garden. Valentine not only remembered helping Andre the Giant and Bruno Sammartino with their bags; those memories were some of his fondest from childhood.

Yes, he agreed, wrestling was a perfect fit. Moreover, if he acted fast, he could get something on the air that would announce his repositioning intentions before the annual "up-front" meetings in May, when all the networks debuted their fall lineups to advertisers. Valentine had met Vince McMahon briefly a year earlier, when Vince was afraid Barry Diller might cancel *Raw* and he'd need a new home. At the time, Valentine listened politely but said they didn't have an opening. Now he couldn't get the WWF on the air fast enough.

The two-hour WWF special that aired at the end of April was a smashing example of narrowcasting, luring more young male viewers than *Monday Night Football*. And so it was that when Valentine faced fifty of his advertisers at the Manhattan Center Theater on a bright mid-May day in New York, it was to announce a new Thursday night show called *WWF SmackDown!*

"It's hard for a lot of people to get the idea that most guys would rather put a bullet in their brain than watch *The Practice*," Valentine crowed with The Rock and several of the WWF's other most recognizable faces surrounding him. "Vince gets it. His genius is that he's an out-and-out populist."

Thanks to its futuristic new sets and a hard-core soundtrack, *SmackDown!* turned into the fourth youngest–skewing show on television. And with an average viewer who was thirteen years younger than the ones who watched *Friends,* it continued Vince's improbable comeback as the Pied Piper of teenage America.

BY JUNE 1999, Eric Bischoff was disappearing further and further into the Los Angeles music industry. Midway through the month, the rap impresario Percy "Master P" Miller convinced him that they could marry wrestling to an urban dance crowd. It was a dubious premise considering that both WCW and WWF had spent decades feeding their audiences a steady diet of antiblack stereotypes. Nonetheless, Bischoff struck a million-dollar deal to make Miller's posse, the No Limit Soldiers, a hip-hop version of the nWo. Inevitably, the whole thing turned into a disaster when they were thrown into a rap-country angle with a heel group called the West Texas Rednecks. The black rappers wound up getting jeered so heavily by WCW's young country-loving audiences that they were gone from the program within a month.

Was it wrestling? Did Bischoff even know what that meant anymore? His job had become an endless series of arguments with his new masters at Time Warner, with the irreconcilable factions in his locker room, even with himself. He should quit; he shouldn't quit; he should let the Boys he'd made rich go ahead and screw themselves right into the ground. Let Hogan and Nash finally have it out—for real, on pay-per-view. Wouldn't that be something? Then again, maybe not. Maybe all they'd do was threaten one another with lawyers. After all, they'd all gone soft, the whole lot of them. Dennis Rodman, brought out for another five-week stint that July, showed the cynicism permeating everything when he told *TV Guide:* "It's money. That's all I'll say. I just don't know why I have to do that damn wrestling shit. I just want to show up." Even Bischoff would admit that he was going soft. He could feel his middle, see the results of too many lunches like the one at the Beverly Wilshire Hotel, when Gene Simmons, the brains behind Kiss, convinced him to support the band's upcoming tour by using wrestlers on *Nitro* who wore the band's makeup. The idea excited Bischoff. It was a perfect launching pad for the music label he envisioned building. He was just as excited by the news that David Arquette, the *Scream* movie actor, had signed on to star in a wrestling movie that he was executive producing at Warner Brothers.

Unfortunately, while he was spending Time Warner's money to play West Coast mogul, he'd lost sight of how to fight the war they'd hired him to win in the first place. For one thing, he hadn't created a successful new act since Bill Goldberg. It wasn't that he hadn't had opportunities. He had a great talent in Chris Jericho, but the charismatic youngster left after being held back by the Hogan and Nash factions and was now blossoming into a star in the WWF. What was worse, the aging stars who held Jericho back were themselves out of control. When Randy Savage decided that Hogan was trying to sabotage his career, Savage boycotted high-profile shows in San Francisco, Reno, and Los Angeles, where his role in a tag-team match had been heavily hyped. The crisis forced Bischoff to throw Bret Hart into the breach, ruining a long-term plan to have Hart and Hogan—who'd never met in the ring—do so for the first time in the company's upcoming *Fall Brawl.*

It was this kind of last-minute madness that caused the white-haired producer to explode in the locker room before a *Nitro* taping in Las Vegas, where they'd flown after the Los Angeles show. The previous week had been an embarrassment, he hollered. Scott "Raven" Levy, a midcard wrestler who'd publicly complained about Hogan on a Chicago radio show, could get the hell out if he didn't like it. (Levy calmly did and quit.) Bischoff wasn't any happier with Charles "Konnan" Ashenoff, who went overboard in Reno by grabbing a microphone and bellowing: "You guys look like you haven't had any pussy since pussy had you." They were supposed to be the family values alternative to the WWF, for *chrissakes*. What was Rey Misterio Jr. thinking when he asked an effeminate opponent if he was "going down the Hershey Highway" on national TV? It had to stop. *It all had to stop*.

About the same time those words were leaving his lips, an accountant on his staff back in Atlanta was shaking his head, sure he'd made a mistake. He was closing out the books on August, expecting to see a $1 million profit. Instead, he discovered a $5 million loss. "We went through it four or five times," says Greg Prince, WCW's controller. "I remember thinking that we must have missed some revenue somewhere. But we didn't. I sent the file down to Harvey Schiller's right-hand man and labeled it the 'Holy Shit!' file."

As the higher-ups at Time Warner were warned that the chances of breaking even in 1999 were bleak, and that 2000 was going to be worse, some very serious people began asking some very serious questions. Why had Bischoff gone ahead with his *Road Wild* pay-per-view, which was a party but never made a dime, if he knew he was in so much trouble? Why had he spent $600,000 to launch a Kiss character called the Demon, and another million to bring the band to Las Vegas for a one-shot appearance on *Nitro*, where they lip-synched a single song after 11 P.M.—well past a time they could have done the show any good? And what about his idea of trying to imitate *Who Wants to Be a Millionaire?* by giving away another $1 million on *Nitro*? Thank God they scrapped that one before it was too late. The man was spending millions like there was no end to his bankroll. No wonder they called him ATM Eric. And it was getting worse: He'd just booked the seventy-thousand-seat home of the NFL's Arizona Cardinals for a millennial Kiss concert and wrestling show on New Year's Eve. Not only was it wildly expensive, it had come close to causing a revolt. The wrestlers' wives were petrified to have their husbands flying while the nation's air traffic control system grappled with the prospect of a Y2K glitch.

Reporters who covered the industry were starting to publicly urge Bischoff to step aside before the damage got worse. In late August,

Mike Mooneyham used his long-running column in the *Charleston Post and Courier* newspaper to ask whether anyone was noticing "the growing similarities between Eric Bischoff and the Roman Emperor Nero" who famously fiddled while his empire burned? Accountants for WCW surely did. When they looked at the revenue side, they were aghast to see its arena business in a state of total collapse. Only thirty-eight hundred paying customers came to the sixteen-thousand-seat Miami Arena for a show to celebrate the fourth anniversary of *Nitro* on September 6; another five thousand tickets were given away just so they wouldn't have to be embarrassed about holding their anniversary in an empty building. Bischoff had lost $8 million in two months. As one Turner executive put it, "We've got a bleeder on our hands."

When Nick Lambross, who worked as Bischoff's business manager before leaving the company late in 1998, learned that his ex-boss had been fired four days after the Miami Arena embarrassment, he thought about the opening scene of the movie *Casino*. The camera pans a gaming room in Las Vegas while actor Joe Pesci laments: "It should have been perfect. But in the end we fucked it up. It should have been so sweet. But it turned out to be the last time that street guys like us were ever given anything that fuckin' valuable again." Lambross thought it was a perfect epitaph.

SEVENTEEN

Mark Kaline
Manager, Media Services
Ford Central Media

Mr. Brent Bozell:
   I am writing you in response to the letter you sent to Mr. Jacques Nasser regarding Ford Motor Company's participation in the UPN program "WWF SmackDown!" We share your concern regarding such programming and as such, Ford Motor Company does not participate in this program on a national basis. In fact, we steer clear of network wrestling programs overall.

John G. Clark
Chief Advertising Officer
Dr. Pepper/Seven-Up

Dear Mr. Bozell,
   It is our belief that the placement of any of our advertising on any television program should not be equated with our support of any theme, storyline or content. However, your comments do greatly concern us. Since the beginning of the year we have discussed both sides of the issue at length. The programming is extremely targeted to reach the teen audience. On the other hand, the content of the show has steadily deteriorated in both its quality and entertainment value. As a result Dr. Pepper/Seven-Up made a corporate decision not to advertise its brands in any type of wrestling programming.

Carol A. Sanger
Vice President, Corporate Communications
Federated Department Stores

Dear Mr. Bozell,
  Let me assure you that the day any of our stores sign on to sponsor world wrestling is a day to expect blizzard conditions in hell.

On October 19, 1999, some of the best bankers in Manhattan clinked champagne glasses to celebrate a yearlong effort to take the World Wrestling Federation public. When the closing bell clanged on Wall Street, Vince and Linda assumed a paper worth of more than $1 billion while raising $170 million more to finance an expansion. Now that the McMahons were moving out of cable and into the world of network television and quarterly reports to the Securities and Exchange Commission, the question was how much further would corporate America let them keep pushing? Where was the line? Was there even one anymore?

In a small office building in Arlington, Virginia, fifty researchers spend their days videotaping every show in prime time for a weekly report published by the nonprofit Media Research Center, a creation of Brent Bozell III, a conservative commentator whose father was an adviser to both Joseph McCarthy and Barry Goldwater. Before he syndicated a newspaper column, Bozell had dabbled in politics as finance director of Pat Buchanan's 1992 campaign for president. After that he founded the MRC and its fax-happy cousin, the Hollywood-based Parents Television Council. Though tiny, the PTC made a minor splash targeting a syndicated show with Howard Stern. When UPN allotted 40 percent of its advertising budget for promoting *SmackDown!* in the fall of 1999, Bozell decided to go after the WWF, too.

An indication that Bozell would be more than a nuisance came when he sent out a mass mailing and received a reply from Coca-Cola, where there was already high-level concern about the WWF. The bottler, which had pulled its ad dollars out of *Raw* earlier in the summer, had been promised that *SmackDown!* would be a toned-down version of its cable counterpart. But the first few episodes left Coke's executives feeling hoodwinked. There was the episode in which Mark Henry's sexual travails took an inexplicably dark turn with the story-line admission that he'd been having incestuous sex with his sister since they were eight. And the match where Terri Runnels and recent arrival Ivory wrestled a "hard-core" match in a shower stall dressed in thong panties. (It ended with Ivory burning an iron into Terri's back.) The reply to Bozell, from a lieutenant of chairman M. Douglas Ivester, expressed Coke's dismay. It was severing its two-year relationship with McMahon's company.

At UPN, Dean Valentine barely paid any attention to the flap because he'd been down this road before. While serving as the president of network television for Disney, he'd green-lighted the episode of *Ellen* in which Ellen DeGeneres kissed another woman on-screen. Between the Baptists that already hated Disney, the talk show demagogues who harped on the decline of American values, and the ideologues in Congress who loved bashing Hollywood because it helped them raise money, that show had become his gold standard for heartburn. Bozell was a hiccup by comparison. Valentine also didn't have much of a financial stake in the PTC's call for a boycott. In an unusual arrangement, he'd allowed the WWF to sell its own ads in exchange for giving UPN a guaranteed cut of the proceeds. UPN got the same money whether Coke came or left.

McMahon, on the other hand, had an enormous stake. Coke represented 3 percent of his advertising revenue; if other advertisers followed suit, he'd be left having to scramble to cover his UPN guarantees. At first he behaved badly, calling Coke's move "discriminatory, hypocritical and an affront to free speech" and "its worst decision since New Coke." But the publicity from his shoot-from-the-hip remarks only helped Bozell as he continued lobbying advertisers—from the U.S. Army to MCI. Not surprisingly, McMahon was more contrite by the time he spoke to the *Wall Street Journal* on November 29. He had heard the verdict of the advertising community, he said. "From now on you'll see less aggression, less colorful language, less sexuality." The concession wasn't only designed to stem the flight of money out of the show. It was also timed to impact the talks that he was having about his long-term future in television.

WHEN THE McMahons last re-upped with USA in early 1998, they were on the losing end of the battle with *Nitro* and the ground was shifting underfoot. Barry Diller was in the midst of taking over the USA Network and was sufficiently concerned about the ratings that he told his programmers he only wanted to renew the WWF for a year. Vince and Linda wanted three years. So a deal was worked out in which they agreed to a three-year contract with a caveat: either side could opt out a year early so long as they gave notice by November 30, 1999.

Diller naturally assumed that USA would be the one to pull the trigger. But thanks to *Raw*'s revival, it didn't turn out that way. While Vince was drafting his statement about Coke, Linda was drafting a letter to USA saying that they'd decided to invoke the opt-out clause. It didn't necessarily mean the end of the relationship. The McMahons would be happy to do a new deal with USA. But they wanted a bigger role, perhaps even an ownership stake.

The highest-ranking executive under Barry Diller at USA was a former St. Louis television mogul named Barry Baker. When he heard about Linda's intentions, he was adamant that she not send the letter. USA's stock was treading water, and he didn't want it to take another hit on bad news about its top-rated show. So he relayed an urgent message to her, saying that they needed to talk.

The two connected by cell phone while Baker was on a train to Baltimore, where his wife was going into labor. Trying to sound engaged yet casual, he said, "Go out into the marketplace and come back to me with the offer you get." He even said he'd give her more time to shop for the best deal and extended the deadline for terminating their contract to March 31, 2000. Between now and then, he'd try to work up a new offer. If she found something better, they'd certainly try to match it.

But to dampen her expectations, Baker added this: "I can tell you right now, nobody is going to give you a network." As Linda hung up the phone, she thought he was one of the most arrogant-sounding men she'd ever done business with.

At the Paramount lot in Hollywood, Kerry McCluggage was only too happy to hear that the McMahons might be shopping for a new home. The forty-five-year-old head of Paramount's television production group knew all about the relationship they had with USA. In the incestuous world of Hollywood, Paramount had briefly held a stake in USA, and he'd been selected to sit on its board of directors in the early nineties.

In the eight years he'd been at the helm of Paramount, McCluggage had developed a not altogether flattering reputation as one of the industry's more cautious programming executives. Though he could claim successes such as *Frasier, Entertainment Tonight,* and *Star Trek Voyager,* Paramount's rivals had gone into the 1999 season with better winning streaks. Warner Brothers, for instance, was producing *ER* and *Friends* for NBC. Twentieth Century Fox produced *The X-Files* and *Ally McBeal* for Fox. And Sony was a rising power with shows like *Party of Five* and *Dawson's Creek,* both hits on the WB.

McCluggage tried to shake his reputation by launching UPN and putting Valentine in control. But the internal turmoil there had only served to make both of them laughingstocks. The only thing that was keeping the 1999 season from being a complete disaster at UPN was *SmackDown!*

All of this left McCluggage in need of a bold, profile-raising move, and when he heard about the McMahons' restlessness, he thought he'd found it. The WWF's stable of shows represented what studio chiefs like to call beachfront property, and McCluggage knew exactly how he wanted to use it. The corporate sands were shifting again in Hollywood. His studio's parent, Viacom, had just paid $37.3 billion to merge with CBS. Given the enormity of the megadeal, few took much notice of the low-rated cable station that CBS threw into the pot as part of it: the Nashville Network.

Mel Karmazin, the powerful new president of the merged behemoth, cared deeply about TNN, however. Though critics snickered at its lineup of country videos and *Dukes of Hazzard* reruns, TNN had 70 million subscribers. In the war over the fracturing cable universe—one in which tiny networks would do anything to get picked up by big-system operators—that was enormously valuable. Karmazin's idea was to relaunch TNN as the National Network, filling it with enough broad-based entertainment to make it a "mini-CBS."

Unfortunately, TNN was at a crossroads. It had just lost its rights to NASCAR and needed something that had a high profile to keep those 70 million subscribers tuning in while Karmizin put his plan into effect. As an executive there put it, "If we didn't get something big fast, we were going to die faster than any cable network in history."

The politics of the situation were obvious to McCluggage: If he could wrest the WWF's shows away from USA and bring them to TNN, he could knock USA down a notch while giving TNN a lift. It was just the kind of power play he'd been looking for.

ON DECEMBER 2, McCluggage invited the McMahons to his office on the Paramount lot to talk about their future. Because he wanted them to see instantly that this was going to be a different atmosphere, he welcomed them warmly, almost theatrically. Then he proceeded to spell out his vision for weaving them through every fiber of Viacom—from MTV to UPN to CBS. He watched as a broad smile crept across Vince's face and was pleased to hear the wrestling promoter keep saying, "This is fantastic. Just fantastic." Indeed, Vince and Linda were still giddy the next day when they wrote McCluggage to say that they thought they could make "a dynamic tag-team combination."

Still, Vince wasn't ready to leave his television home of seventeen years on the basis of that one meeting. So a few days later, he went to his biggest ally at USA, a Harvard M.B.A. named Steven Chao.

Barry Diller made no bones about the fact that he didn't understand wrestling. He summered in East Hampton and hung out with Calvin Klein. But Chao was something else altogether, a man who loved to talk about how he sat on his grandmother's lap while she watched her favorite wrestler, Gorilla Monsoon. He made his reputation creating the first wave of reality-based shows at Fox in the early eighties, including *Cops* and *America's Most Wanted*. (He also cut a legendary figure on the L.A. party scene, once throwing a dog belonging to Fox owner Rupert Murdoch into a pool because he'd heard it had webbed feet. When the dog started to sink, Chao jumped in fully clothed to save it.)

The years since hadn't mellowed Chao much. He was the last one at USA who would be inclined to complain about the episode of *Raw* that had just aired, featuring Mark Henry lying in bed beside the seventy-six-year-old Mae Young, acting as if they'd just had sex. Nor would he moralize about the pay-per-view in which a Sable wanna-be named Stacy Carter flashed her breasts at a crowd of kids in Fort Lauderdale. (McMahon would try to top that the next month by having Mae Young flash her septuagenarian breasts to a packed crowd at Madison Square Garden. Only later would he admit that she had been fitted with a prosthesis, as if that somehow made it better.)

Chao understood that the WWF was an important part of USA's future, which was why he listened carefully as Vince explained that he wasn't just going to talk about wrestling in this negotiation. The WWF was serious about wanting part ownership of a cable channel. Even more immediate, Vince had a project that would make him a player in the legitimate sports world. He wanted to start his own football league.

If USA wanted to do a long-term renewal, Vince told Chao, the network had to step up. It had to take an ownership stake in his new league. It was going to be a wedge issue. Chao dutifully passed that message up his chain of command. But to his irritation, Baker and his chief negotiator, the network's president, Stephen Brenner, still seemed to be taking a relaxed, wait-and-see approach.

Brenner was the only one in the USA negotiating group who had been at the network under its old president, Kay Koplovitz. And to some extent, he shared her disdain for wrestling. Certainly, he'd been through enough talks with the McMahons to feel no particular pressure to jump through hoops for them. His first volley had been a two-page offer sheet that significantly increased the fees they got for their shows—*Raw*, for instance, would see its $12,000-a-week fee doubled in the third year of the deal—but didn't mention much else. The McMahons reacted angrily when they got the initial offer. The accumulated slights of seventeen years came spilling out all at once. They wanted to be wooed. Instead, they felt as though they were getting worked. And they let Diller know it when they convened in his West Fifty-seventh Street office two days before Christmas. The network's owner was just as surprised as Chao at how little progress had been made. Scolding his lieutenants, he told them to get together a better deal. And to get it done fast.

By then, though, McCluggage's woo-at-all-costs strategy was starting to pay off. Two days into the new year, he traveled to Stamford to continue fleshing out what the McMahons wanted, including a prime-time series for Steve Austin and a stake in what they were now calling *Raw Football*. Things were starting to happen fast and furiously. They agreed to meet again at the national cable convention, which was being held in New Orleans during the week of January 24, 2000.

At the Paramount booth there, McCluggage was pleased to see Linda, but he was also taken aback when, for the first time, she mentioned that USA had a matching rights clause. McCluggage had repeatedly asked their agents whether such a clause existed and was assured that it didn't. It wasn't the first time an agent had played fast and loose with the truth. But as he scanned it, McCluggage realized that this added a whole new dimension to what he'd hoped would be clean negotiations. Suddenly he had a deadline: the March 31, 2000, date that USA's Baker had set for Linda to return with a rival offer. More than likely, there was also the possibility of litigation.

As McCluggage was scanning the document, Steve Chao was walking the convention floor nervously. He'd picked up signals that Viacom was becoming a serious rival in the talks, perhaps even starting to pull ahead of USA. Writing an urgent e-mail to Diller from New Orleans, Chao said he was "at Def-Con 3" and urged that

> we should go halfsies on football (50% up to $50 million). We should commit to a man-cable channel using our respective libraries as payment into this USA-WWFE [World Wrestling Federation Entertainment] partnership. And we should renew WWFE for USA on same terms as before (since we will plow investment into cable channel and football). Our clumsy USA process is getting in the way of a speedy conclusion to this. Because Vince is Vince and we do not want to lose this, you should call Vince with as much detail as possible and shake hands.

But Chao's influence on the negotiations was limited. His higher-ups at USA continued to believe that they were safe because their contract gave them the right to match rival offers. Their first real sense that they were in trouble came on February 2, when *Variety*'s website reported that Viacom "was convinced it had locked up a deal with the WWF." That might have been a bit premature, but Baker didn't help himself much when he trucked up to Stamford on February 17 to deliver the presentation that Diller had promised would be better. Vince and Linda watched the slide show that had been prepared for them, straining to figure out what was new in it. There was a mention of a prime-time show, a WWF version of *Baywatch*. And there were a few words about cross-promotion on the Home Shopping Network and Ticketmaster, which USA also owned. But there was none of the sweep or the dollars of the Viacom blueprint.

Vince was grossly disappointed. He'd hoped that he'd proven his seriousness about wanting to launch his new league when he'd held a press conference at a theme restaurant he'd recently opened in Times Square. One reporter had asked if this thing he was now calling the XFL was his chance to go legit. "Oh, I love that question," he sneered. "May I never be thought of as fuckin' legit." Had he learned anything from his failed World Bodybuilding Federation? "Yeah," he replied curtly, "don't make mistakes." But what about the fact that his stock price lost 20 percent of its value on the news that he wanted to take the WWF into football? "Wall Street can kiss my ass," he said.

It was a vintage performance. Afterward, when he'd climbed into his limousine for the ride back to Stamford, he got a surprising cell phone call from his friend Dick Ebersol. The president of NBC Sports had tried and failed to get his own idea for a spring football league off the ground some years earlier, but the notion of placing one in the lead-in spot before *Saturday Night Live* still had enormous appeal to him. "Don't do anything until you've spoken to me," he'd told Vince.

Now, as McMahon finished listening to the presentation being given by Baker, he found himself becoming incensed. There was nothing even remotely resembling what Chao had suggested in his e-mail to Diller about the XFL, just vague allusions to future talks. It was meet the new boss, same as the old boss. Nothing had changed. USA was still taking him lightly.

But not McCluggage. In fact, while Diller's aides were dithering, McCluggage was having his own lawyers look at the contract that gave USA the right to match rival offers. If he was going to make a play for the WWF, he wanted to make this a clean sweep and not leave USA any room to counteroffer.

So on February 24—five days after Baker's visit—the studio chief led his own contingent to Stamford. He'd gotten together an all-star cast from the various divisions of Viacom. It included John Dolgen, McCluggage's boss as the head of Viacom entertainment; Tom Freston, head of MTV, who controlled the music channel's offerings as well as the Nickelodeon family of kids' stations; and David Hall, the head of TNN. Vince and Linda were impressed. These were busy people.

McCluggage started by saying the package he was about to unveil had been approved at his company's highest level—by Viacom's president, Mel Karmazin, and its CEO, Sumner Redstone. It started with their desire to move all four of the WWF's shows currently on USA to TNN. In addition, he was prepared to link that with a thirteen-week pilot for a Steve Austin drama, a book deal with Simon & Schuster, five annual events at their theme parks, seven specials a year, and a boatload of cross-promotion on radio stations and billboards. UPN was also serious about wanting a piece of the XFL.

With slightly more than a month to go before the McMahons had to give USA their final answer, they were on the verge of getting everything they had ever wanted, including respect from some very heavy hitters.

SATURDAY, APRIL 1, was cool in Anaheim, the perfect kind of day to prepare for the biggest show of the year and bank $60 million at the same time. Ebersol had been right. NBC had been willing to go along with McMahon's idea for a new football league. In fact, it was in the midst of acquiring $30 million in stock in the recently renamed World Wrestling Federation Entertainment—which equalled 3 percent of its outstanding shares—in order to become a part owner in the XFL. "In Vince McMahon, we're getting the best marketer in America," Ebersol enthused.

Now, as Vince was going over the final preparations for the next day's *Wrestlemania 2000*, McCluggage thought he'd put the finishing touches on his own wet kiss. The evening before, he'd broken open a bottle of Kettle One vodka and toasted the lawyers arrayed around his conference room table for sealing the deal that he hoped would trump USA and bring the WWF to Viacom. All that remained was for the McMahons to sign the short-form agreement he'd faxed over that morning to the Arrowhead Pond auditorium. McCluggage assumed this was a formality. But he learned otherwise when his office phone rang shortly after noon.

"Kerry," Vince said. "We have a problem."

McCluggage winced, then sank into his seat, preparing himself for what would come next. "It's this exclusivity thing. I can't do it." The studio chief told himself to be patient. He had a deal worth more than $100 million on the table. Surely he had the right to demand that the

WWF produce its programming exclusively for Viacom. But McMahon, the Hollywood outsider, didn't see it that way. No matter how much he was getting, he still bristled at the idea of being tied down. McCluggage tried to read into what was happening. Had he mis-judged Vince's willingness to follow these talks all the way through? No, he couldn't have. They'd be fools to walk away from this; it was what their whole lives had been building toward. Surely all Vince needed was a little hand-holding before. So that's what he did. He told Vince that this was going to be the best thing he'd ever done, but he had to trust his new partners. And as far as they were concerned, exclusivity was a deal breaker. After a flurry of phone calls, Vince finally agreed. The McMahons of Havelock, North Carolina, would be Holly-wood outsiders no longer.

The pay-per-view that Vince aired the next day was a perfect example of the kind of product that they'd sold to one of the largest entertain-ment companies in the world. Because this was pay-per-view, Vince could be unfiltered, not having to worry about talk show moralists like Bozell. So right from the opening, the Godfather and his ho train were led out by Ice T, dressed in a feathery red pimp coat and hat, rapping the lyrics, "Pimpin' ain't easy, pimp or die. Yeah bitches, God-fatha's in the house." Not long after that, the newest staple of Vince's harem, a curvy blonde named Trish Stratus, sauntered to the ring in skintight hot pants as the manager of a tag team called T&A. This gave one pimply boy a chance to unfold a sign that read, "Trish, show us your T&A."

Backstage, the even more uninhibited Stacy Carter filmed a seg-ment where the grandmotherly Mae Young helped her get dressed. At one point, Young spied a shirt with a furry cat face on it and held it up. "Oh, I love that one," Carter said, moving her nude body into the cam-era frame in such a way that the only thing covering her thatch was the furry cat face on the shirt being held by Young. Carter would come out a short time later to wrestle Terri Runnels in a match where they pummeled one another until Carter used her long nails to tear the spandex covering off Runnels's rear end. If one squinted, it became clear that Runnels was wearing a flesh-colored thong. If one didn't, it looked convincingly like she was wrestling bare-assed.

The main event was a four-way elimination match, with each member of the McMahon family standing in the corner of a different contender. Paul "Big Show" Wight was thrown first from the ring, followed by Mick Foley, who endured a last crowd-pleasing torture before his retirement—a leap off the top rope onto the announcer's table where Hunter Hearst Helmsley lay. Because he'd hurt his shoulder when the 450-pound Wight fell on him earlier, he landed short—caroming off the table and onto the floor. With a rib possibly broken, he dragged himself into the ring one final time, waving a two-by-four wrapped in barbed wire before he let himself get pinned. The Rock and Helmsley brawled after that, though not to the match's conclusion. This, after all, was a night for the family McMahon.

Shane had already proven to be a provocative, risk-taking amateur. The more pleasant surprise was Stephanie. The twenty-three-year-old product of Greenwich private schools was a firebrand. She'd been introduced to her father's viewers as an ingenue but now, in a turn-around only he could engineer, she'd traded sweater sets for leather miniskirts and an on-camera marriage to Helmsley. (In real life, Helmsley would leave his live-in lover, Chyna, to begin an affair with Stephanie.)

If hearing his daughter called a slut every time she entered the ring mattered to Vince at all, it was only because it proved she could carry herself before a frothing arena. Now, fulfilling the promise of ads that boasted "the most dysfunctional family in America," he had his son run in to ambush him at ringside as his daughter looked on in apparent delight.

As Vince staggered to his feet from a vicious head shot with a television monitor, he kicked his son in the groin with his Italian leather shoes, then turned his back, giving the thirty-year-old heir a moment to heave a folding chair over his old man's head. It connected so loudly that even Shane seemed surprised. To make it look worse, Vince took a razor from his pocket to cut his forehead; he cursed when it didn't bleed very much. The denouement of the match required him to influence the outcome by turning against one of the two survivors. Helmsley was the heel husband of his estranged daughter. The Rock was his million-dollar champion. The fans would expect him to turn on his heel. Instead, he climbed into the ring and brought a chair down over his babyface. As Helmsley rolled over on his side to pin the surprised-looking Rock, Stephanie joined her father in the ring, signaling a new father-daughter alliance and a new booking year of twists and turns.

The next day, Linda would call USA and say they were accepting Viacom's offer, ending a relationship that started when Kay Koplovitz allowed Vince to replace a wrestling show in which two Texans jousted in pig shit. That was seventeen years before. Now, as Vince scanned the fresh faces of the sold-out Arrowhead Pond auditorium, he had to wonder what his father would think. He'd gotten America's mall majority to scream at him, to hurl cups on his thousand-dollar suit. He'd twisted their well-scrubbed young faces into a rage. He'd gotten them to believe in what he was selling.

Most of the kids in that crowd in Anaheim weren't even alive when Vinnie walked into the Warwick Hotel with two bags full of contracts and the smoke-and-mirror financing to take over the World Wide Wrestling Federation. That was two wrestling lifetimes and a bloody war with Ted Turner ago. That was before the feds tried to convict him as a drug pusher, before he'd watched Brian Pillman and others die. Now anyone who attacked him—a conservative activist, a publicity-seeking U.S. attorney, even a billionaire—could expect to be met with the full force of his rebuilt machine. Wrestling wasn't nearly as innocent, funny, or well mannered as it once was.

But neither was Vince McMahon.

OUR STORY SINCE THEN...

LINDA MCMAHON WAS ON the French Riviera, in Nice, for an international television convention when she received a fax copy of USA's response to Viacom's offer.

Had she known what kinds of discussions had been going on at USA, all the red lines through the paragraphs would have made more sense. Over the prior week, the company's executives and lawyers huddled, trying to figure out what to do with the mess they'd made. If the network matched the deal, USA stood to lose $6.79 million the first year, $6.60 million the second year, and $4.96 million during the third year of the contract.

Viacom's lawyers had played dirty, they decided, by dissecting USA's matching agreement word for word and then creating a deal designed to thwart it. Why else would a studio chief like McCluggage throw theme park events into the mix? In the end, they concluded that they were only obliged to match the part of the offer that dealt with the WWF's five programs. Everything else was irrelevant. That was why Barry Baker faxed a copy of the Viacom offer sheet with cross-out markings everywhere.

Irritated, Linda called her office in New York, where it was morning, and had her assistant get Baker on the line. Baker tried to sound cheerful, saying he hoped that there might still be fruitful negotiations ahead. But then he added, "We also believe that this is ultimately going to be an issue for the courts to decide, so we've asked their opinion."

"How have you done that?" Linda asked warily.

"Well, we've sued you."

At a four-day trial in June 2000, USA's lawyers offered their narrow interpretation of what their matching rights required. To the McMahons, it was nothing more than the last desperate gasps of a network trying to keep them on the cheap. "There was very little dialogue on the part of USA," Vince testified. It came "only from the standpoint of Stephen

Brenner, who I consider to be intellectually challenged. He presented a proposal to us in its initial state which was, I think, embarrassing."

In ruling on the case, a Delaware judge agreed that Viacom indeed had put together a package that it knew USA didn't have the assets to match. But that didn't mean USA was out of the woods, the judge said. Even if USA's strict interpretation of the contract was used, Viacom still presented the better offer. For instance, while USA belatedly agreed to pony up $500,000 per week for its WWF shows, it continued to balk at giving the McMahons a guarantee that they wouldn't be preempted for special events like the U.S. Open or the Westminster dog show.

When the ruling was made public, Steven Chao tried to put the best face on things for USA. Since the WWF kept most of *Raw*'s advertising inventory, he said the network would actually do *better* because it would have more ad time to sell. "It will have a negligible effect on our ratings and a positive effect on our cash flow," he insisted.

Brenner was the first to be called to account; he was summoned to Baker's office and told he was being reorganized out of a job. Shortly thereafter Baker also resigned. Ultimately, Chao would be fired, too, as USA's ratings nose-dived by 15 percent and the loss of the WWF caused it to lose its claim to being the highest-rated network in cable.

As for Linda McMahon, she went on CNBC the day after the Delaware ruling to boast that the WWF was expecting to post a 15 percent increase in revenues in fiscal 2001, helped by the $85 million that the WWF expected to earn in the first season of the XFL.

VINCE'S AIDES had begged him to wait a year before launching the new football league. The coaches needed the extra time. The production staff needed the extra time. But most of all, the people positioning the upstart league needed more time.

The early strategy was to sell more flesh than football. "We want our viewers to be on a first name basis with the cheerleaders," Vince told *ESPN The Magazine*. "That way, when the quarterback fumbles or the receiver drops the ball, we'll know who he's dating and our reporters will be right in her face on the sidelines demanding to know whether the two of them did the wild thing last night." When told about the remark, an XFL general manager by the name of J. K. McKay bristled. "Yes, we have cheerleaders," he snapped. "But so do the Raiders. What are people expecting? That our cheerleaders are going to take their clothes off on the sideline?" *Uh, yeah.* And who could blame them, considering that the first ad that NBC aired featured an army of next-to-naked women in a steamy locker room?

At points, it seemed that the only thing that kept the mainstream sports press from completely pillorying the raunch launch was the supreme confidence of Dick Ebersol, who kept insisting that he'd heard similar doubts when he helped start *Saturday Night Live*. After the XFL's first Saturday game on February 3, 2001, his calm seemed well-placed. Ten million households tuned in to see the maiden game between the New Jersey Hitmen and the Las Vegas Outlaws, outrating everything else on television.

But the excitement was short-lived. When eight o'clock arrived the next Saturday night, viewers didn't see a moonlighting Governor Jesse Ventura sitting beside Jim Ross in the NBC announcer's booth. Instead, they saw dead air; a power failure stalled the start by ninety seconds. It's hard to know how many fans tuned out because of that, but only half as many viewers as the week before soldiered on to watch a double-overtime game between Los Angeles and Memphis.

One of them was Lorne Michaels. When NBC committed $100 million to starting up the new league, the producer of *Saturday Night Live* had been promised that his 11:30 P.M. starting time would be protected. But there he was, with Jennifer Lopez—a star with the number one movie *and* number one album in the nation—ready to go on for what was expected to be his biggest show of the year...and the XFL game was still lumbering on. Michaels was mad enough that he considered canceling the show and having NBC run a repeat. Instead, he sent his cast onstage, most not knowing that they weren't airing live. The next day, when the overnights showed that his delayed broadcast didn't even reach the 7.4 rating he'd done the week before, Michaels made sure that his old partner heard about it. "It was one of the most bizarre nights I've ever been a part of," Ebersol told the *New York Times*.

If Ebersol was having doubts, he kept them to himself, as did everyone else at NBC. After the XFL's fourth game drew four million viewers—ten million fewer than three weeks earlier—network president Bob Wright insisted that they were all in it for the long haul. "This season's start-up costs represent less money than we would have lost airing three NFL games under the current contract," he said, trying to sound casual. But while that was true, only the opening week's rating was saving NBC from taking a bath. The average four-week rating of 5.1 was just a hair above the 4.5 level that NBC guaranteed advertisers who paid an average of $130,000 for thirty-second spots.

By the fifth week, when the NBC game drew only a 2.4 rating, advertisers weren't the only one complaining. The network's West Coast stations begged to be allowed to broadcast the games on tape-delay because the live East Coast feeds were leaving them nothing to show in West Coast prime time. By the seventh week, when NBC's broadcast drew the lowest recorded rating since Nielsen began tracking them, the deathwatch was on. No one was surprised, then, when Ebersol confirmed that his network wouldn't be sticking around to make the second year work.

For NBC, it was a bigger public relations disaster than a financial one. But the same wasn't true of the UPN affiliates that had broadcast XFL games on Sunday night. "Their sales forces were trying to build up the XFL and get people excited about it," says Adam Ware, UPN's chief financial officer. "But they got undercut by the NBC sales guys who were used to selling the Olympics. When our affiliates went into the local Cadillac dealership, the owner had just finished getting an earful from the local NBC guy, who was selling his ads at a 20 percent discount because they were so embarrassed by the whole thing. When our guys came in trying to sell ads at full price, his reaction was, 'One of you is lying.'"

Despite this, McMahon remained hopeful that UPN would stay in for the long haul. In fact, he'd gathered the league's general managers around him at Titan Tower on May 7 to tell them that they should all get ready for play the next spring. But his optimism belied the warnings that Adam Ware and Dean Valentine were giving him. For weeks, they'd been saying that UPN would need a concession before it invested in a second XFL season. The central one they now wanted was a reduction of the length of *SmackDown!* by a half hour so they could tack a new show at the end of it.

McMahon stalled. He'd already allowed the ratings for *SmackDown!* to decline while he focused on the XFL. The last thing his listing company needed was to lose thirty minutes of network advertising revenue. But the morning after he'd promised his GMs that they'd have another season, Ware told him that UPN couldn't wait any longer. It needed an answer. Would he go along with shortening *SmackDown!* or not?

And it was then, after all the bravado and public posturing, that Vince was finally forced to acknowledge that his beloved XFL had done enough damage. "All the stars had to line up for us to go forward and the broadcast component was the most important one," he sullenly told reporters a few hours after telling Ware that he'd fold his league before shortening *SmackDown!* "It just didn't happen."

WWF stock briefly shot up on the news that the country's most famous wrestling promoter was returning his attention to where it belonged.

AS LONG as Ted Turner was in control of the network that bore his name, wrestling served as a kind of Rosebud, a reminder of what had been set in motion on the day that Ray Gunkel agreed to move *Georgia Championship Wrestling* to Channel 17. Turner's paternalism spanned the next thirty years, surviving even his merger with Time Warner.

But in January 2000, Turner made a rare miscalculation, or at least a misjudgment about the reverence with which a new generation of Internet moguls regarded him. As the largest single stockholder in Time Warner, he gave his approval to a merger with AOL, only to find out in April that the new owners wanted him gone. Gerald Levin, the chairman of Time Warner, told Turner that the networks that bore his name would now be reporting to the chief operating officer of AOL.

The news sent appropriate tremors through WCW, which was on pace to lose $80 million that year. After Eric Bischoff's firing, the company hired Vince Russo away from the WWF, hoping the chief writer could lend *Nitro* some sizzle. His first show as booker featured a stripper match and the debut of a group called the Filthy Animals. But after four months, all he managed to accomplish was to elevate the show's mean-spirited violence while keeping its ratings flat. By March, there was such desperation in CNN Center that Bischoff was brought back from his six-month exile by the president of both TNT and TBS, Brad Siegel. (Mindful of Bischoff's spendthrift habits, the accountant who'd Siegel hired to run things, Bill Busch, promptly resigned.)

Even before he agreed to come back, Bischoff knew the odds were good that WCW would be put up for sale. America Online was a bottom-line company, and with Turner's influence diminished, WCW no longer had a high-profile defender within it. At first, Siegel denied an interest in selling. Then, in June 2000, he called Bischoff to ask if he thought he could put together a buyout. Bischoff said he did, and over the next six months lined up a package of financing that was worth $50 million. Three days before the Federal Trade Commission gave its final regulatory approval for the AOL merger in January 2001, the *New York Post* reported his group's purchase as a certainty.

But the report was premature. In March 2001, AOL named Jamie Kellner, the fifty-three-year-old programming whiz who helped start the WB Television Network, to be the new head of Turner Networks. In his first move, Kellner concluded that wrestling didn't fit the upscale image he wanted for the vestigially named company. Bischoff was on a beach in Hawaii with his wife and two teenage kids when he got word of the decision. The final WCW show would be March 26; Bischoff's last-ditch effort to keep the Monday night wars alive was dead.

Without a television outlet, who would want the motley collection of assets that was left of WCW? The 3 million viewers who tuned in to see the final episode of *Nitro* got the answer when the nine o'clock hour began. What they saw was the same thing that viewers of *Raw* were seeing, which was Vince sauntering into the Gund Arena in

Cleveland with a wicked smile. "People ask me, how did you do it, Vince?" he began, speaking by simulcast to audiences of both shows. "You were up against this conglomerate, this millionaire. How did you do this?" He walked around the ring, giving the question time to settle. "Some would say I had help along the way with some WWF superstars, but the truth is I did it all on my own. It was my effort, my money. Okay, Vince, how can you possibly beat a billionaire? There's only one way—become one yourself."

Of course, he hadn't beaten Turner so much as outlasted him. But the plan that he put in motion on the day that he told Verne Gagne, "I don't negotiate" had finally been realized, and without much negotiation. He paid $4.3 million in cash for little more than the WCW name and a tape library. When Extreme Championship Wrestling filed for bankruptcy the next week, McMahon hired its founder, Paul Heyman, and started using the ECW name, too. The consolidation allowed him to create a three-way war for his cameras, a perfectly designed faux rendition of the real Monday night war he'd just won.

BARELY A year into his new relationship with Viacom, Vince was already demonstrating that he was ill-suited for corporate monogamy. When MTV programming executives presented him with an idea for a reality-based show, he went behind their backs and offered it to his friends at NBC, infuriating Tom Freston, the head of MTV networks. He also irked Kerry McCluggage when, during the course of his negotiations to purchase WCW, he argued that he should be allowed to produce a version of *Nitro* for TBS. McCluggage scratched his head in disbelief, wondering what Vince thought he'd signed when he agreed to the exclusivity clause with Viacom. Ultimately, McMahon gave up on the effort, contenting himself with buying the WCW name and using it to further his storylines on *Raw* and *SmackDown!*

By late 2001, McCluggage's reign as a player at Viacom would be over. Once CBS boss Les Moonves got tired of waiting for UPN to turn around, he assumed control of the struggling network, cutting the legs out from under McCluggage, who resigned shortly thereafter, and laying the groundwork for Dean Valentine to be fired.

By then, Wall Street had become skeptical about whether Viacom would ever earn back its investment in the WWF, and whether Vince would regain the momentum he had in the late nineties.

In April 2001, the WWF reported that its wrestling-related revenues had grown by 20 percent, less than half of what it grew the preceding year. While the growth was respectable, the company's ballooning expenses troubled analysts. Thanks to a new layer of upper management that the McMahons added in the belief that they could model themselves after Disney, operating income grew in fiscal 2001 by a measly 5.5 percent. When the cost of shutting down the XFL was factored in, the couple had barely eked out $16 million of profit on $456 million in revenues. The news got worse when the slumping economy finally hit the media sector in the summer of 2001. That July, the WWF announced that its television advertising plummeted by 17 percent, and its stock hit an all time low of $10.31—60 percent off the price it closed at when it went public in October 1999.

It didn't help that Vince was ceding many day-to-day chores to his kids. Shane had evolved into one of the show's largest daredevils, taking such risks as a fifty-foot fall from a scaffolding rig. Stephanie, meanwhile, embraced the post-Sable archetype of the heel slut, encouraging the chants of "bitch" that accompany her ring entrances. As one of the show's key writers, she even placed herself in situations to provoke them. On the same day that the *New York Times* carried a story about teen magazine editors declining ads for breast enlargement surgery, the twenty-four-year-old paraded her newly (re-) enlarged breasts on *Raw*. When asked why she did it, she replied that she had seen a sign in the audience that read, "Steph's puppies sag."

But audiences tired of the self-involved stories that centered on the family, sending *Raw*'s ratings to their lowest points in years. The McMahons reacted by cleaning house, firing thirty-nine employees, or nearly a tenth of their workforce. Vince also made a much-discussed appearance at a meeting of his department heads, many of whom were wondering if he still had the energy to produce ten hours of weekly television. He acknowledged that he'd allowed himself to get out of touch but assured the gathering that he was going to be hands-on once more. "It's time to have fun again," he said. "If Wall Street doesn't like it, fuck 'em."

Linda carried a less combative message to a conference of analysts in November 2001. Conceding that the XFL had taken its toll, she said matter-of-factly: "Sometimes you're sharper creatively than at others. It happened before and it will happen again."

The rest of the year found McMahon searching for a way to revive his TV persona. He spent one show humiliating his latest Sable knock-off, Trish Stratus, by having her get on her hands and knees and bark like a dog before ordering her to strip down to her bra and panties. On another, he whisked a breast-enhanced blonde named Torrie Wilson to a laundry room and moaned in delight as she unbuttoned his shirt, pulled his pants past his ankles, and disappeared beneath the eye of the camera. (When she told him to close his eyes for a "big surprise," he did as he was told, only to open them and see his wife standing before him.) In a show that aired at Christmastime, he made a series of wrestlers kiss his bare ass. Recognizing the need for a new foil, Vince next brought Ric Flair aboard, creating a role for the white-haired legend as the WWF's "co-owner." Their scripted struggles led to McMahon's most violent ring work since the Austin era, including a graphic end to the January 2002 *Royal Rumble* in which Flair sank his teeth into Vince's bloodied forehead after belting him with a lead pipe. Finally, McMahon did something few would have thought possible in burying the hatchet with Hogan, who hadn't worked for him since 1993. Revisiting a contentious piece of his past, he used Hogan to reprise the nWo with Scott Hall and Kevin Nash.

The length of the road they'd all traveled was demonstrated on a February 2002 night in Chicago. Hogan challenged The Rock to meet him in the main event of the forthcoming *Wrestlemania*, and after the typical stare-downs and boasts, things took a dark turn. Nash and Hall ambushed The Rock, leaving him prone on the mat, whereupon Hogan grabbed a hammer and brought it down "hard" over the movie star's head. As the scene unfolded, paramedics rushed The Rock into an ambulance, only to be ambushed again, this time when the old (and old-looking) Outsiders blocked its departure with their limousine. As the segment built to its climax, Hogan commandeered the cab of a 16-wheeler and used it to ram the side of the ambulance. To approximately five million people watching in the ten o'clock hour, announcers Jim Ross and Jerry Lawler left the impression that The Rock lay inside, dying. "Some things happen in real life and some things happen in wrestling, but this isn't good. . . . Tragedy has struck a WWF superstar," Ross exclaimed in a voice much like the one he used three years earlier as he watched Owen Hart fall to his death in Kansas City.

Anyone who has watched Vincent Kennedy McMahon battle for ratings over the past twenty years instantly recognized the formula: the blending of unsettling fiction and frequently tragic fact. It may not be everyone's idea of entertainment, but it has made McMahon the consummate survivor on TV, where he continues to wrestle with his demons every week, live and in front of all America.

AFTERWORD

SHORTLY AFTER WE FINISHED this book in early 2002, Vince and Linda McMahon moved into a $14 million vacation home in Boca Raton's exclusive Excelsior resort, with polished granite floors and wraparound terraces overlooking the Atlantic. Despite losing $35 million on the XFL, they were unabashedly optimistic about their future. They even built a monument to their TV thrill machine—a roller-coaster ride beside a WWF theme store in Niagara Falls that they called The Pile Driver. On its first day of operation, state officials shut the ride down, citing safety issues. As we write this in September 2003, the renamed WWE (World Wrestling Entertainment) seems every bit as grounded by capricious management and creative gridlock. The $19 million loss it posted at the end of its 2003 fiscal year was the worst in its history.

In the summer of 2003, the McMahons made a move that many considered a prelude to taking the company private again. They decided to spend $20 million to buy back all the WWE's shares that had been bought by Viacom. If they use the $270 million they have on hand to buy the rest of the outstanding shares, that would end the incessant intrusions of analysts. But not the shift that led many of those analysts to warn that the wrestling industry is in for a prolonged downturn. A nation living under color-coded terrorist threats just doesn't consider its brand of violence fashionable or fun anymore.

McMahon, at fifty-eight, isn't conceding a thing. He bloodied himself to boost pay-per-view buys in a match with Hogan during Wrestlemania XIX. In interviews, he's been defiant and nearly violent, like when he seemed to lose control in an appearance on HBO and lunged at Bob Costas. (The two staged a subsequent interview that was so sickeningly sweet, it could have been seen on *The View*.) And he supervises every word that goes out over the air. Still, the man who could always fall back on wrestling when debacles like the XFL derailed his other ambitions is unquestionably having a hard time staying relevant in 2004.

As former scriptwriter Vince Russo said when he was briefly rehired as a consultant, "I was absolutely shocked and taken back, because this was not the same guy that I worked so closely with for three years. The fire wasn't there. The hunger wasn't there. . . . I just felt like I was dealing with a totally different individual."

A favorite pastime for "smart" fans is debating when McMahon seemed to lose his creative compass.

Was it on October 21, 2002, when *Raw* featured Triple H simulating sex with a corpse in a casket? (After slipping a bra and panties off the "corpse" and taking off his tights, he crawled into the casket, gyrated his hips, and threw a glob of goo intended to look like brain matter over the side, crowing that he'd "screwed her brains out.")

Was it when Vince duped the gay rights advocates at GLAAD into helping him promote the in-ring "wedding" of two supposedly gay wrestlers—an endorsement that helped get them on the *Today* show—only to pull out at the last minute and declare the whole thing a hoax?

Was it when the World Wrestling Federation lost the use of its trademark in a case brought by the World Wildlife Fund, prompting the *Wall Street Journal* to cluck that it "got beat by a panda"?

Or was it when the Rock decided to become a film star, taking away the WWE's most bankable act when it needed him most?

We'd argue the key moment was in September of 2002, when McMahon walked into his now-defunct Times Square restaurant for an annual meeting of shareholders. Two years earlier, when he'd announced the start of the XFL there, the room was packed with reporters. Now, there were maybe three dozen investors mixed in with WWE executives arrayed before him. The mood was glum, and as McMahon started to speak, he seemed to give in to the pessimism. Then he caught himself and shook it off. Demanding that the house lights be turned up, he barked, "Hey, this isn't a wake."

The remark was off-the-cuff. But it reminds us of another sobering reality that has to be weighing on him: Wrestlers have been dying left and right since this book was first published. The community has mourned the passing of Freddie Blassie, Lou Thesz, Ed "The Sheik" Farhat, and Tim "Mr. Wrestling" Woods—all of whom led full and relatively healthy lives. It has also buried stars who haven't.

On May 18, 2002, Davey Boy Smith died of a heart attack after spending two decades in constant pain. The last, and most fateful accident, happened to him when he broke his back wrestling for WCW. It pushed him over the edge and into a methadone addiction. His wife, Diana Hart, threw him out and he became romantically involved with his sister-in-law, Andrea Hart. He was in bed with her when he died, though just a day earlier he'd talked with Diana about coming home to her and his kids, Georgia and Harry.

The WWE argues that there is no evidence that steroids killed Smith. But they couldn't have helped his heart. Family members say he was taking heavy doses of steroids in a last-ditch bid to make a comeback with WWE. "Right up to the end, Davey was 'roided out," Bruce Hart says. Even Andrea concedes that "Davey was in pain because he'd put on fifteen or twenty pounds of muscle weight. Some days, he had a hard time walking."

It's not just has-beens who are succumbing to a decade of fully ratcheted violence. At Wrestlemania, in March of 2003, Kurt Angle and Steve Austin performed with degenerative neck conditions that were so serious, both had been advised by their doctors that they risked crippling themselves. They decided to go on, anyway. Angle has opted for surgery to extend his career, while the thirty-eight-year-old Austin, who spent the night before the match in the hospital, has decided to retire from in-ring competition. At the time of the match, Austin was on probation for an assault on his wife in June 2002. He's since blamed the incident on the constant pain that he's been forced to accept.

McMahon's empire never seemed as fragile as it did on April 27, 2003, when he addressed his touring company prior to the Backlash pay-per-view at the Centrum in Worcester, Massachusetts. He told them that they needed to tone things down, work slower matches, and protect their bodies from the suicide stunts that drove the company to its heights in the late 1990s.

McMahon has been masterful at exploiting violence. But the speech he gave that day suggests that he sees another backlash coming—part of the inevitable cycle that causes fans to veer between excitement, boredom, blame, and rediscovery.

Right now, WWE is teetering in the space between boredom and blame. And the May 2003 death of one of the most beloved acts in the business, "Miss Elizabeth" Hulette, hasn't helped matters. Hulette's sweet looks were indelibly linked to the WWF's eat-your-vitamins-and-say-your-prayers era. But cops who found her passed out in an Atlanta condo on May 1 saw a different woman. She still bore the bruises from a domestic abuse call that had brought them to the same residence weeks before.

Her live-in lover, Lawrence "Lex Luger" Pfohl was charged in that abuse, though the charges were later dropped. He was not charged in her death, which was ruled accidental after the medical examiner found that she choked on Vodka and pain pills. Pfohl, however, didn't get away clean. Cops who searched the condo busted him for possessing massive amounts of steroids.

Pfohl's arrest was prominently covered in major newspapers, as well as on a program called *Confidential* that McMahon launched in 2002. As a wrestling version of a newsmagazine, the show is a useful tool for the WWE to spin events before its critics can. In this case, the coverage painted Pfohl as a fuck-up who's hurt everyone who's ever befriended him. But the truth is that Pfohl's relationship with Hulette is part of a calamitous continuum in wrestling. The business creates stars, watches them self-destruct, and then pedals their destruction as infotainment.

We'd like to believe that the tragedies of the last few years will push McMahon into a new direction. Maybe the speech he gave his wrestlers, encouraging them to take more care of themselves, is a start. Wrestling, at its best, is a vehicle for storytelling, and he's the last man standing from a generation that understands this. The trouble is, he's also the last man standing.

Increasingly, McMahon is reaching back into the past to rely on past glories. Even his choice of Madison Square Garden in 2004 to celebrate the twentieth anniversary of Wrestlemania, which began there, feels more derivative than bold. McMahon may be one of the four hundred richest people on *Forbes'* list of wealthy Americans, but as he runs out of glories to resurrect (and stars to help resurrect them), he seems more out-of-step than ever. No one is saying "no" to the king of the ring except the fans.

SHAUN ASSAEL
MIKE MOONEYHAM

ACKNOWLEDGMENTS

KIM WOOD, THE STRENGTH coach for the Cincinnati Bengals and one of Brian Pillman's mentors, insists that he's read more words by Dave Meltzer than any other single writer. Having backtracked through ten years' worth of Meltzer's weekly *Wrestling Observer*, I see what he means. Meltzer's *Observer* provides an indispensable chronicle of the years covered in this book. The chapters having to do with McMahon's drug trial and the death of Brian Pillman owe it a special debt.

When this project was launched in mid-1999, it had no better friend than Alan Sharp, then the publicist for WCW. He relentlessly helped to introduce me to wrestlers and others who would become invaluable over the next two years. One of them, James Barnett, is the Zelig of this book. Anyone who's befriended Rock Hudson and guitar god Bob Mould in the same lifetime has to be remarkable, and I learned more about wrestling from him than anyone else. Also, many thanks to Ole Anderson, Arn Anderson, Will Bird, Michael Braverman, Gary Considine, David and Jim Crockett, Jim Herd, Jack Petrik, Gary Juster, Nick Lambross, Bill Shaw, Mike Tenay, and Cowboy Bill Watts for helping me with the sections on WCW.

There was no official help from the WWF because Vince McMahon chose not to lend his cooperation to this book. Fortunately, that didn't stop people who've worked for him from offering a hand. I'd like to single out two for their patience and memories: Nelson Sweglar, who acted as the WWF's director of operations through the 1980s, and Mike Ortman, a razor-smart strategist who taught me about the economics of cable TV. Also thanks to Jim Troy, Bob Arum, the Brisco brothers, Tom Chiappetta, J. J. Dillon, Verne Gagne, Les Garland, Kevin Nash, Bob Ryder, Ted Smith, David Wolff, and Grant Zwarych.

Select thanks go to an even smaller group who let me hound them on a regular basis. That group includes Jim Bell of Jim Bell Consulting,

Stu Saks of London Publishing, Dave Schwarz of Viacom, and Craig Smith of wrestlinggod.com. But the most mercilessly hounded one of all is Mike Mooneyham, who started out as a friend and—midway through this book's life—signed on to help me finish it. Without Mike, these pages would lack much of their savvy or detail.

Thanks to Peter Gethers for his direction, and to Dominick Abel for his management. And thanks to Ellen and Jake for not body slamming me on all those days when I was a monster heel.

SHAUN ASSAEL

February 2002

INDEX